PARIS ARTISTIQUE

INDICATEUR OFFICIEL

DES AMATEURS ÉTRANGERS

BELGES ET AMÉRICAINS

EN FRANCE

ANNÉE 1896-1897

Paris Artistic

INDICATEUR DES SALONS RUSSES, ETC.

Paris Artistic

INDICATEUR

DES

SALONS RUSSES

Anglais et Américains

EN FRANCE

1896

C.W. Jarrett-Knott.

2, rue de l'Échelle and 182, rue de Rivoli.

PARIS

JARRETT-KNOTT'S

PARIS ARTISTIC

ХУДОЖЕСТВЕННЫЙ

РУКОВОДИТЕЛЬ

ПАРИЖА И ЕГО ОКРЕСТНОСТЕЙ

Этотъ руководитель содержитъ адресы всѣхъ русскихъ живущихъ во Франціи.

A short, clear, concise and complete Guide to Paris and neighbourhood. For all strangers visiting Paris, there are three things of paramount importance, viz. : Time, Money and a good and reliable Guide. Presuming my readers are possessed of sufficient of the two former necessaries, will endeavour in the following pages to supply the latter.

C. W. JARRETT-KNOTT, Editor

LONDON, NEW-YORK AND St-PETERSBOURG

FOR THE PUBLISHER AND SOLE PROPRIETOR

R. H. JARRETT-KNOTT

Paris, 2, rue de l'Echelle, 2, Paris

INAUGURATION OF THE PARIS OPERA. — ОСВЯЩЕНІЕ ПАРИЖСКОЙ ОПЕРЫ

PREFACE

The Editor of " PARIS ARTISTIC *" issued a small Paris Directory last year, which was favourably received and circulated largely in the English and American Circles of Paris.*

This Directory has been revised and under the title " PARIS ARTISTIC *" will be published half-yearly in Paris and will contain the names and addresses of prominent persons where mail matter can be addressed either on the Continent, in America or in England.*

To the Directory has also been added an Artistic Description of Paris. This will speak for itself. The Editor only hopes that it will be of use and interest to his readers and that it will meet with the same unanimous approval as have done his " Universal Graphic Railway Guide " and " Paris Directory ".

The Publisher begs that the subscribers of " PARIS ARTISTIC *", will kindly send any information of change of address or correct any errors which this, the first number, may contain.*

*The Business Directory and the selected class of adverti-
sements will be found very useful to visitors or residents
both in Paris and on the Continent. Any information will
be gladly received addressed to :*

Mr JARRETT-KNOTT,
Publisher " PARIS ARTISTIC "
2, rue de l'Echelle (Avenue de l'Opéra)
PARIS.

INTRODUCTION

The aim of the Editor of this book is to present to the public something having claims to real artistic merit and value, and not a Guide issued as an advertising medium, but as a good guide, that is to say a friend, a confident, who being broken in to Parisian manners and habits says to you on arriving: Go to such an hotel, take such a cab and pay so much, apportion your time in this manner, follow this or that itinerary.

Such is the object of this work, which takes the traveller at his departure and does not leave him till he returns. As a devoted friend it will be your companion and nothing more.

THE GREAT QUESTIONS

The stranger who makes up his mind to come to Paris without friends or relations asks himself generally these five questions :

1º Where shall I lodge ?

2º How shall I live ?

3º How shall I find my way in the Parisian labyrinth ?

4º How shall I portion out my time ?

5º How much shall I spend ?

Where shall I lodge ?

The question of accomodation is for the stranger an important consideration, for a good bed, a comfortable apartment and good service are items not to be despised.

Thus I have chosen, after having classed them by quarter, the hotels and pensions that may be recommended, both for situation and comfort, to all classes of travellers.

Much has been said of the exaggerated prices of Paris hotels ; but I am not at all of that opinion if I compare them with the prices of the hotels of Holland, Germany or other countries.

In Paris for ten, six or even five francs a day a good room may be had near the avenue de l'Opéra or the Bourse.

Besides, the traveller may be reminded that in Paris he enjoys the most complete liberty, that is to say that he can, in certain hotels, take his meals outside without having the price of his room augmented. In order to be really comfortable it is best to write in advance to some known establishment or to present yourself *on our part,* our Guide in hand, to one of the hotels that we recommend.

THE JULY COLUMN (Place de la Bastille)

ЮЛЬСКАЯ КОЛОННА (БАСТИЛЬЕВСКАЯ ПЛОЩАДЬ)

GENERAL INFORMATION
LETTERS OF CREDIT

The best thing for travellers coming to Europe are Letters of Credit issued in Sterling or Francs which are available through-out Europe and the East.

American mails are generally received in Paris on Monday, Thursday and Friday of each week, occasionally Sunday.

PASSPORTS

Travellers are recommended always to carry a passport in Europe, as they will be found very useful when clearing registered letters and for proof of identity. They are absolutely necessary when travelling in Russia, Germany, Austria, Greece, Portugal, and Turkey ; they should on no account be omitted in France, Spain, or other countries where the rigour is not seemingly so intense. If you receive a registered letter addressed to any *Poste restante* Office in France, where you happen not to be well known, and cannot produce your passport, no entreaties will enable you to obtain possession of that letter. Students who wish to enter the *Ecole des Beaux-Arts,* to read at the *Bibliothèque nationale,* or to copy in the public art galleries, for instance, must be provided with a passport. If you have not brought one with you, and are English, apply to the Passport Office at H. B. M. 's Embassy, 39, rue

THE TROCADERO PALACE   —   ДВОРЕЦЪ ТРОКАДЕРО

du Faubourg St-Honoré; or, if a citizen of the United States, to the Office of the U. S. Legation, 59, rue Galilée, Paris. If you live in the Provinces apply to the Consulate of the country to which you belong, and on proof of your identity, all necessary questions being answered and the fees paid, the passport will in due course be delivered to you.

FOREIGN COINS	AND THEIR U. S. NOMINAL VALUE		S. C.
France	1 franc		20
Belgium	1 »		20
Greece	1 drachma		20
Italy	1 lira		20
Switzerland	1 franc		25
United Kingdom	1 shilling		20
» »	1 pound stg	5	»
Germany	1 mark		20
Austria and Hungary	1 florin		52
Russia	1 rouble		80
Spain	1 peseta		20
Portugal	4 milreis	1	16
Holland	1 gulden		48
Denmark, Norway and Sweden	1 khrouor		20

(France, Belgium, Greece, Italy, Switzerland bracketed as "Monetary Union")

THE ATTRACTIONS OF PARIS

Almost anything can be said of Paris except that it is wearisome. Paris is really the city of pleasure, and of pleasure *par excellence*; nowhere else can one amuse oneself so much or in so many ways, and he who does not find any distractions to his taste is a man who does not know how to amuse himself.

In this graceful edifice, situated in the rue Daru, on Church fête days, the
gorgeous ceremonial of the Greek Church may be observed in its entirety.

A FEW WORDS ABOUT PARIS

Paris in spite of its agitations and its political commotions will always be the capital of the world.

One comes, and one will always come, to Paris, for there is only one Paris in the world. To see Paris is the desire of all foreigners, of everyone from the provinces, and the newly married couples wish to spend their honeymoons there. Where can we find a town more seductive, with more attractions and pleasures? Every thing in Paris enchants you : the museums, theatres, shops, etc. I would add that it is *sometimes wise to resist the etc's* Come, then to Paris, stran-

CRUSH ROOM OF THE OPERA HOUSE — БОКОВАЯ ЗАЛА ОПЕРЫ

gers of all nations, and be completely reassured, for according to its ancient decree, the Parisian skiff has often been tossed by the tempest but it has never been submerged ; *"Fluctuat nec mergitur"*. The town, divided into two parts by the Seine, contains twenty arrondissements, which are subdivided in their turn into eighty quarters. At the head of the twenty arrondissements is the Prefect of the Seine, who fulfils in addition the function of Central Mayor. Each arrondissement is directed by a Mayor and three deputy Mayors.

Paris counts 2,422,696 inhabitants. The town as enclosed by the fortifications covers 8,000 hectares and its circumference is more than twenty-one miles.

RESTAURANTS

Paris, the town of all resources, and for all purses, contains different restaurants whose prices vary according to the quarter and the reputation of the house. You have only to make your choice. I permit myself to offer you in this matter a few suggestions which may enable you to live in a manner suitable to your taste and means.

The restaurants of Paris may be divided into four categories :

1º Restaurants *à la carte*;
2º Restaurants at fixed prices;
3º Bouillons and cremeries;
4º Tables d'hote.

If you listen to an epicure he will tell you that the restaurants *à la carte* are the only ones to be recommended. I am not of that opinion.

The prices of these restaurants are usually very high, but the service is better, the cooking more appetizing, the wine better, the menu more varied and the portions larger.

GRAND STAIRCASE OF THE OPERA HOUSE
БОЛЬШАЯ ЛѢСТНИЦА ОПЕРЫ

Would you be served at express speed? Consult the menu on entering and tell the waiter what you desire for your dinner. The waiter will bring, meanwhile, especially if you are with a lady, a hors-d'œuvre of some sort, such as radishes and butter, shrimps, or anchovies, temptations which sometimes come very expensive. When you have finished, the bill will be brought to you; always verify it, for cashiers, even in Paris, are not infallible.

Restaurants *à prix fixe* or at so much per head have an incontestable advantage over all the others. They offer for a stipulated price: two, three, four or five francs, a certain number of courses which vary every day according to the menu. We recommend these restaurants to people of limited means and who like to know in advance how much they will have to pay.

Many of these restaurants *à prix fixe* are to be found in the Palais-Royal, in the *passages* and in the great centres. The prices vary from 1 fr. 25 to 4 fr. per head and per meal.

TABLES D'HOTE. — If you are afraid of being poisoned by uncertain and unknown dishes, choose by preference the table d'hôte. You may for 8 fr. at the Grand Hôtel, 7 fr. at the Hôtel Continental and the Hôtel Terminus, or even for 3 or 4 fr. at the ordinary table d'hôte live as at home.

CABINET PARTICULIER. — These " cabinets particuliers " are private rooms where one may dine either in society or *en bonne fortune*. Outside the reach of the indiscretions of the public, these " cabinets particuliers " are to be found in all large restaurants. They usually have a separate entrance, separate staircase, separate bell and special furniture. Naturally the prices are high and sometimes even exaggerated. It is wise to have an understanding in advance and *always to verify the bill*.

RESTAURANTS OPEN ALL NIGHT. — Certain restaurants have the privilege of remaining open all night and the permission to open their rooms to private parties. It is said that great amusement is to be had in this way, but remember that *prudence is the mother of safety*.

PURCHASING GOODS

Few people come to Paris without profiting by their visit by making certain purchases. We have thought of being useful to our readers by giving, at the end of this book, a list of commercial houses, arranged according to trade, in alphabetical order, which we can personnally recommend as being good, first-class houses of business, where one may be sure of fair treatment, even though a foreigner. Avoid especially sales, sales after bankruptcy and liquidations etc., and always go to a known and honourable house, where the prices are marked and invariable. It is unquestionably the cheapest in the end, by a great deal.

The best and most elegant business houses are to be found on the grand boulevards and on the principal arteries leading to them, such as the avenue de l'Opéra, rue de la Paix, etc. Don't leave Paris without making a promenade of the grand boulevards, from the Madeleine to the site of the Bastille, which form a splendid and incomparable exhibition.

IMPOSITIONS AND OBLIGATIONS

Paris, like all great centres, has its annoyances and its abuses. It is usual, for instance, if you take a cab either by the hour or by course, to give 25 centimes at least to the cabman, or if you go to a restaurant or a café to leave some change for the waiter. If you go to a theatre with a lady, she will be forced to accept a footstool for which the box-opener will ask you politely for 50 centimes. The coiffeur (hair dresser) also always expects a gratuity.

CORRESPONDENCE

It is the custom in Paris to write one's mail in the cafés. The necessary paper, pen and ink are brought gratuitously by the waiter.

THE LETTER POSTING

Do not forget, if you wish your letter to go the same evening, to post it : before five o'clock in the street boxes, before 5.30 in the ordinary post offices, and before 6 o'clock at the general post office, and at the offices at the rue de Clery, place de la Bourse, rue Marsollier, 13 rue des Capucines, and place du Théâtre-Français. Letters are registered at the ordinary offices, at the general post office and at the offices above named untill 4.45 p. m.

TOO LATE !!!

If you are too late with your letter it may go all the same either by taking it to one of the stations or by affixing an additional stamp of 15 centimes. We must mention certain agencies: notably that at the office of the *Petit Parisian*, 20, boulevard Montmartre, where for 5 centimes one can leave one's letters up to the last minute.

INFORMATION

Do you want information? Have you lost your way? Are you looking for a street? With all confidence you may ask the " sergents de ville " (policemen) to be found in every quarter.

Are you looking for an address? Consult the *Bottin*, *Tout Paris*, or if for English, Americans or Russians the *Paris Artistic*. These first-class directories are to be found in all hotels, cafés and public buildings.

THE BATHS

The baths of Paris are a great convenience to the traveller, who has often but little time at his disposal. The price varies from 60 centimes to 1 franc, and they are to be found in every quarter. All the large Hotels have bath rooms installed with all the latest improvements.

TOO LATE

CABS

There are naturally in Paris cabs of all sorts, omnibuses, tramways and boats. You have only to make your price. The cabs can be taken by the hour or by drive. The tariff varies according to the case : if it is a cab for two or four people, if the drive is taken in Paris or outside of the fortifications, if the cab is taken by day or by night. If you take a cab by the hour compare the time of your watch with that of the cabman. That will avoid discussions.

Stands of public vehicles may be seen all over Paris. The following are the fares:

INSIDE PARIS					BEYOND THE FORTIFICATIONS	
From 6 o'clock a. m. in summer (1st April to 1st October), and from 7 a. m. in winter (1st October to 31st March) to half-an-hour after midnight.			From half-an-hour after midnight to 6 a. m. in summer and to 7 a. m. in winter.		Bois de Boulogne, Bois de Vincennes, and the *communes* outside the fortifications. From 6 a. m. to midnight in summer or 10 p. m. in winter.	
Hackney cabs or "*voitures de place*" taken on the *public* stands.	Drive. f. c.	Hour. f. c.	Drive. f. c.	Hour. f. c.	When returning with the cab to Paris. The drive or hour. f. c.	When quitting the cab beyond the fortifications Return indemnity.
Holding two or three persons	1 50	2 —	2 25	2 50	2 50	
Holding four or five	2 —	2 50	2 25	2 75	2 75	1 franc
Do., with railing on top	2 —	2 50	2 50	3 —		
LUGGAGE : One package, 25 c.; two 50 c.; three or more, 75 c.						

NOTE : The Cabman is entitled to an indemnity of 1 fr. when the cab is discharged outside the fortifications. Fee (pourboire) to cabman : **25 ctmes.** per course or per hour.

There are no police regulations concerning fares for drives beyond the fortifications after 10 p. m. in winter and 12 in summer ; but a bargain may be made. A printed list of the fares is affixed inside the vehicle.

Coachmen load and unload all trunks, etc. Whatever article can be carried in the hand, or taken inside without injuring the vehicle, cannot be charged as luggage.

When the carriage is taken by the hour, the driver must be told so beforehand, or he can demand the price of a *course* or journey, for each stoppage. The traveller should show the driver the time by his watch. After the first hour, the time above the full hour is paid in proportion. The driver is bound to give a printed slip (*bulletin*) with his number, which it is as well to preserve for the recovery of any articles that may have been forgotten in the cab.

Articles left in cabs or omnibuses are claimed by application to the Préfecture of Police, 7, boulevard du Palais.

Promenades in the Bois de Boulogne. — Cabs hired for drives in the Bois de Boulogne can only be taken by the hour (see tariff for outside Paris). If you dismiss the cab outside the fortifications, you owe an indemnity to the *cocher* of 1 fr. if it is an ordinary cab, or 2 fr. if you have hired it at a livery stable.

LOST OR MISLAID OBJECTS

If, during a walk, or in a cab, you happen to lose anything, you should immediately direct your steps towards the office of the commissaire de police of the quarter, make your declaration, note will then be taken and in case the object is found information will be sent you in the course of a few days. In case you should find anything ; unnecessary for me to say that the article found should be immediately handed over to a police agent, who will do the necessary.

HEALTH! ILLNESS!

Life in Paris is full of agitation, the temperature is variable and it is always possible for one to feel a little indisposed. Every Hotel has its Doctor, and we give, page 300 a list of English and American Doctors practicing in Paris and neighbourhood. In case of sudden serious illness one cannot do better than go to the Hertford British Hospital, rue de Villiers, Levallois-Perret, Paris, where you will be sure of having the best medical attention.

THE LOUVRE (Sully Pavillon)

ATTRACTIONS

The attractions of Paris, so numerous, and above all, so inviting to the visitor, have their special days, varying according to the season. We cannot therefore indicate them in any absolute manner.

PERMANENT ATTRACTIONS

The Folies-Bergère, rue Richer, near the fbg. Montmartre. — By reason of its excellent programme, is one of those privileged establishments which boasts of a good audience every night of the week. Representations every evening. Sundays and fête-days, matinées. Entrance from 2 francs.

Olympia. 28, bd. des Capucines. Summer : 1 fr. Winter : 2 francs. The nearest thing in Paris to an English music-hall, and is to be specially recommended, by reason of its spectacular attractions to all who are but superficially conversant with French. Every evening Sundays and fête-days, matinées.

The Casino de Paris, 15, rue Blanche and 16, rue de Clichy. Every evening. Entrance 2 francs.

Nouveau Cirque, 25, rue St-Honoré. This circus is one of the favourite resorts of English and Americans in Paris. It possesses a moveable arena, which by means of powerful machinery may

CENTRAL DOME OF 1889 EXHIBITION

be made to descend, disclosing a large sheet of water which serves admirably for the frequent nautical pantomimes. Every evening. Thursdays, Sundays and fête-days, 2.30 p. m.

Cirque Fernando, 63, boulevard Rochechouart. Equestrian representations every evening. Entrance from 50 c. to 3 frs.

Salle Robert-Houdin, 8, bd. des Italiens, conjuring etc. every evening. Sundays, and fête-days matinées.

WINTER ATTRACTIONS

Cirque d'Hiver, Bd. des Filles-du-Calvaire. Every evening at 8 p. m. Equestrian exercises. Performing dogs, trapese, etc. Thursdays, Sundays and fête-days 2.30 p. m.

SUMMER ATTRACTIONS

Cirque d'Eté, Champs-Elysées. Is to the right of the Avenue. Equestrian exercises, etc. every evening at 8 p. m. Do not forget, if you pass an evening at this circus, to visit the stables, which are a marvel of care and neatness.

CONCERTS OF THE JARDIN D'ACCLIMATATION

Grand concerts in the open air, Thursdays and Sundays at three. Thursdays, 1 fr., Sundays, 50 c.

SUMMER CAFÉ-CONCERTS

The **Ambassadeurs** (Champs-Elysées). — Is the first to the right of the avenue, and quite close to the place de la Concorde. This establishment is a type of the kind. There are open air concerts every evening in summer.The entrance is nominally free, but refreshments, which must be ordered at once, cost from 1 fr. to 3 fr., according to place occupied. *Matinées, Sundays and fête days.*

The **Alcazar**, the second to the right of the avenue, is conducted on much the same lines as the Ambassadeurs. *Matinées, Sundays and fêtes.*

The **Horloge** is similar to the above but possesses the additional advantage of being provided with a moveable roof, a convenience by no means to be despised in the event of a thunder-storm.

The **Eldorado**, on the boulevard du Strasbourg, is one of the best of the café-concerts of Paris. It may also e classed among the

WINTER CAFÉ-CONCERTS

The **Scala**, boulevard de Strasbourg, in front of the Eldorado.

The **Cigale**, boulevard Rochechouart.

Bataclan, 50, boulevard Voltaire, near the place de la République, is an excellent café-concert, but, like all the others of the quarter, it is too far from the centre of tho city.

The other popular concerts are :

The **Moulin-Rouge** (place Blanche). — Which is too well known to require any notice here.

The **Jardin de Paris** (Champs-Elysées). — Behind the Palais de l'Industrie. Concert and ball every evening at 8 o'clock from the 1st of May to the 1st of October.

Bullier, at the extremity of the boulevard Saint-Michel and near the observatory. Situated in the centre of the Latin Quarter, it is the favorite rendez-vous of the students and their lady friends. There are *Bals* every Thursday, Saturday and Sunday evening and *Bal masqués* during the Carnaval.

IMPORTANT NOTICE

There are three concerts which no lover of good music should fail to visit. They are :

The **Concerts Lamoureux**, founded in 1882 and directed by M. Lamoureux. These concerts take place on Sunday at 2 o'clock at the *Cirque* of Champs-Elysées.

The **Concerts of the Conservatoire** (faubourg Poissonnière). — These concerts, so justly celebrated for their marvellous execution, are given every other Sunday from January to April. Religious music is performed during Passion and Easter Weeks.

The **Concerts Colonne**, directed by M. Colonne, which are given Sunday afternoons at 2 o'clock. The orchestra is composed of 250 executants.

POSTAL SERVICE

Nouvel Hôtel des Postes. — The new General Post Office, constructed on the site of the old one, which, by reason of the thickly-built state of the quarter, was extremely difficult of access. The present building, at the junction of the rues du Louvre, Etienne-Marcel and Jean-Jacques-Rousseau, can boast of no architectural beauties, but is remarkable for its well-regulated departments. The public enter by the Rue du Louvre, into a hall fifty metres long where are installed the various bureaux. The first and second floors are used for sorting and the van-service; the third story is reserved for storage, etc. and for the preservation of the Archives.

AT THE POSTE-RESTANTE

Poste-Restante. — Many visitors not knowing at what hotel they will stay, have their letters addressed at the poste-restante either at the G. P. O. or to one of the district offices. These latter have often the same hours as the chief office. As a proof of identity there is nothing better than a passport.

Parcel-Post. — The parcel-post service for Paris only, is undertaken by the Company of the Messageries Nationales.

Tariff. — From any part of Paris to another ; per parcel 25 c.

There are three distributions each day. From 7 a. m. to mid-day; from mid-day to 5.30 p. m. and from 5.30 p. m. to 9 p. m.

Letters. — French Postage Tariff. — Letters under 15 grammes for France, Corsica, Algeria and Tunis, 15 c. From 15 to 30 grs 30 c. For every additional 15 grs 15 c.

Registered Letters (in addition to postage) 25 c. Letters may be insured at the rate of 10 c. for every 100 frs. Maximum of insurance 10,000 frs.

Post-cards cost 10 c. Letter-Cards 15 c. If used for the Postal-Union 10 c. extra.

Foreign Postage Rates. — For any country in the Postal-Union 25 c. per 15 grs. Post-cards 18 c. Registration 25 c. Letter-Cards 25 c.

TELEGRAPH SERVICE

The Offices are open in summer from 7 a. m. to 9 p. m. In winter from 8 a. m. to 9 p. m. Sundays and fête days the offices are closed at 6 p. m. The following offices are open until 11 p. m. :

Champs-Elysées, Gare de Lyon, Place de la République, Gare du Nord, Gare d'Orleans, avenue de l'Opera, rue de Vaugirard, rue Saint-Lazare, rue des Halles and boulevard des Capucines.

Until midnight : bureaux of the Grand-Hotel, rue Boissy-d'Anglas, Theatre-Français, boulevard Saint-Denis, Gare Saint-Lazare. Open all night : rue de Grenelle, place de la Bourse.

General Information. — Despatches must be written legibly in Roman characters or Arabic figures. The letters R. P. (Reply Paid) count as one word. For each sentence or phrase under-lined count one word. Telegrams written in figures are counted at the rate of one word per 5 figures. In the International service 15 letters are counted as one word. The Paris Telegraphic service is carried out by the pneumatic tube system. Special cards are provided which cost 30 c. if open and 50 c. if closed. These

WHY THAT TELEGRAM WAS LATE !!!

should be posted in the boxes marked " Cartes Télégrammes ".

Between France, Corsica and Monaco (minimum 50 c.) per word 5 centimes. Between France and Algeria (minimum 10 words) per word 10 c.

INTERNATIONAL SERVICE (TARIFF PER WORD)

Between France and Great Britain, Ireland and the Channel Islands	20 c.	Germany	20 c.	Norway	40 c.
		Greece (continental)	55	Portugal	20
Austria-Hungary	25	Spain	20	Russia in Europe	50
		Italy	20	Sweden	15
Belgium	15	Luxemburg	12 1/2	Switzerland	15
Denmark	30	Netherlands	20	Turkey (Europe and Asia)	55

TELEPHONES

The telephone service is placed under the direction of the Directeur Général des Postes et des Télégraphes.

The subscription to a Telephonic district confers on the subscriber or his successor the right of correspondence with all the other subscribers of the same district.

Subscriptions are classed under two heads : principal and supplementary. Persons frequenting a club or other public building have the right to use the telephone, but it is formally forbidden to the subscriber to receive therefor any remuneration whatever for such use. For five minutes communication between any public call-offices the charge is 25 c., and twenty-five c. in all the other towns in France where telephonic communication is established.

For communication with towns the cost is 50 c. for every 100 kilometres, or fraction of 100 kilometres. The normal duration of communication is fixed at five minutes : at the tariff above mentioned.

Night Service. — Between 9 p. m. and 7 a. m. in summer and 8 a. m. in winter the tariff is reduced for the service of telephonic communication between Paris and Lyons, Marseilles, Lille, Havre and Rouen. The call-office for communication between Paris, Brussels and London, is installed at Paris at the telegraph office of the Bourse.

SUBSCRIBER — TELEPHONE CLERK

DIFFERENCE IN TIME

BETWEEN PARIS AND THE FOLLOWING CITIES — Paris, Noon (12 h. 0 m. 0 s.) equals :

Berlin	12.44 p. m.	New-York	6.55 a. m.
Boston	7.08 a. m.	Philadelphia	6.50 a. m.
Chicago	6.— a. m.	Rio Janeiro	8.58 a. m.
Dublin	11.25 a. m.	San Francisco	3.41 a. m.
London	11.50 a. m.	St-Petersbourg	1.31 p. m.

Before.

After.

LAWS
AFFECTING FOREIGNERS
NATIONALITY

1. — Persons born in France of English or other foreign parents, both of whom were also born in France, are irrevocably French, enjoying all the rights, and liable to all the obligations of French citizens.

2. — Persons born in France of an English or American father who was born in France, but of a mother born abroad, are also irrevocably French.

3. — Persons born in France, and whose mother was born in England or any other foreign country than France, have a right to claim their father's nationality by certain formalities, within one year from the date of their majority.

4. — Persons born in France, both of whose parents were born in England or any other foreign country, and who are themselves domiciled in France at their majority, may also claim their parents' nationality by the same formalities during the year following their majority.

5. — Persons born in France of foreign parents who have become naturalized French, may also recover their parents' original nationality in the manner described in pars. 3 and 4.

The formalities to be observed for the retention or recovery of foreign nationality where permitted are : An attestation made in due form before the British or American Consul, and followed by a declaration before the Juge de Paix of the place of residence. This declaration must be accompanied by the following papers, which are retained by the French authorities :

1. — The attestation signed and sealed by the Minister for Foreign Affairs in London, or in America.
2. — A certificate of birth of the applicant.
3. — Birth certificates of the applicant's father and mother.
4. — Marriage certificates of the applicant's parents.
5. — A certificate of the applicant's residence in France at the date of his or her majority.

The attestation as returned by the Foreign Office is drawn up in English, and French, and the translation is accepted by the French authorities, but the Consular signature requires to be legalized at the Ministry of Foreign Affairs; all the other documents, if in English, must be accompanied by a legalized translation by a French sworn translator. The documents, including the attestation from the Foreign Office, must be stamped in France.

As the papers deposited with the Juge de Paix when the declaration is made have to be afterwards submitted to the French Ministers of Foreign Affairs and War, the formalities occupy a considerable time, and should be commenced without delay after persons have attained their majority.

The new law does not affect foreigners who had attained their majority before the passing of the law of the 26th June, 1889. The nationality of the parents was definitely acquired to them, but children of foreign parents, who became or shall become of age since that law, must make the declaration within a year from their majority.

ARC DE TRIOMPHE DE L'ÉTOILE

REGISTRATION
Law of 8th.
August, 1893

Art. 1. — Every foreigner not legally domiciled in France (since extended to Algeria) must, on arriving in a locality to exercise a profession, trade or industry, within one week, make at the Mairie a declaration of his residence with proofs of his identity. For that purpose a register will be kept in a form determined by a Ministerial decree.

A copy of the entry will be delivered to the person making the declaration, in the same form as certificates of births, deaths and marriages, and on payment of the same fees.

In case of removal from one locality to another the foreigner must have his certificate visa'd at the Mairie of his new residence within two days of his arrival.

Art. 2. — Any person knowingly employing a foreigner not provided with a certificate will be liable to the penalties of the Courts of simple police.

Art. 3. — The foreigner who has not made the declaration required by the law within the specified time, or who refuses to produce his certificate on the first demand, will be liable to a fine of from 50 fr. to 200 fr.

If he has knowingly made a false or incorrect declaration he will be liable to a fine of from 100 fr. to 300 fr. and may be temporarily or permanently excluded from French territory.

The foreigner expelled from French territory and who shall have returned without authorization from the Government, will be punished by imprisonment for one to six months and be sent out of France on the expiration of his sentence.

Art. 463 of the Penal Code is applicable to the cases provided against in the present law.

Art. 4. — The amount of the fines levied under the present law shall be paid into the municipal funds of the locality in which the delinquent resided.

Art. 5. — Foreigners to whom Article 1 applies, and already in France, will be allowed one month to conform to the prescriptions of the law.

THE MONUMENTAL FOUNTAIN AND CENTRAL DOME
OF THE 1889 EXHIBITION

This Dome is above the principal entrance to the exhibition of 1889. On the left is the Palais des Beaux-Arts, and on the right the Palais des Arts Libéraux. It is an interesting specimen of modern construction in iron, decorated with terra-cotta mouldings and ornaments in lead, zinc, brass, masonry, glass, coloured tiles and painting. Exterior diameter, 130 ft., height 212 ft. On the summit is a statue in copper representing France distributing palms and crowns. The immense portal is flanked by colossal statues of Commerce and Industry, executed by Bouvard aided by 39 assistants.

TABLE showing the days and hours of admission to the principal Museums, etc. of Paris

MUSEUMS AND MONUMENTS	SUNDAY HOURS	MONDAY HOURS	TUESDAY HOURS	WEDNESDAY HOURS	THURSDAY HOURS	FRIDAY HOURS	SATURDAY HOURS
Bibliothèque nationale			10-4			10-4	
Gobelins (Manufactury of)				1-3			1-3
Hospitals	1-3				1-3		
Jardin des Plantes — Menagery	1-4	1-4	1-4	1-4	1-4	1-4	1-4
Jardin des Plantes — Galleries	11-3		11-3		11-3	11-3	11-3
Jardin des Plantes — Paleontological section			1-4				
Jardin des Plantes — Hot-house			1-4			1-4	1-4
Art Gallery of the City of Paris	12-4						
The Carnavalet museum	11-4						
The Artillery —	12-3 or 4		12-3 or 4		12-3 or 4		
The Cluny —	11-4 or 5		11-4 or 5	11-4 or 5	11-4 or 5	11-4 or 5	11-4 or 5
The Opera —		11-4	11-4	11-4	11-4	11-4	11-4
The Mineralogical —			12-4		12-4		12-4
The Ethnographical museum	12-4				12-4		
The Sculpture Gallery	11-4 or 5		11-4 or 5	11-4 or 5	11-4 or 5	11-4 or 5	11-4 or 5
The Archives nationales	12-3		10-5		12-4		
The Decorative Arts	10-5	10-5		10-5	10-5	10-5	10-5
The Arts et Metiers	10-4		10-4		10-4		
The Mint			12-3			12-3	
The museum of musical instruments at the Conservatoire		12-1			12-4		
The musée du Garde-Meuble	10-4				10-4		
The Louvre museum	9-5 or 10-4		9-5 or 10-4	9-5 or 10-4	9-5 or 10-4	9-5 or 10-4	9-5 or 10-4
The Luxembourg museum	9-5 or 10-4		9-5 or 10-4	9-5 or 10-4	9-5 or 10-4	9-5 or 10-4	9-5 or 10-4
The Guimet —	12-4 or 5		12-4 or 5	12-4 or 5	12-4 or 5	12-4 or 5	12-4 or 5
The Typographic —							
The Pedagogic —		10-5	10-5	10-5	10-5	10-5	10-5
The Palais-Bourbon	9-5 or 6	9-5 or 6	9-5 or 6	9-5 or 6	9-5 or 6	9-5 or 6	9-5 or 6
The Bourse (Stock Exchange)		12-5	12-5	12-5	12-5	12-5	12-5
The Palais des Invalides	12-3 or 4	12-3 or 4	12-3 or 4	12-3 or 4	12-3 or 4	12-3 or 4	12-3 or 4
Tomb of Napoleon I (Invalides)		12-3 or 4	12-3 or 4		12-3 or 4	12-3 or 4	
The Palais de Justice		11-4	11-4	11-4	11-4	11-4	11-4
The Palais du Luxembourg		9-5 or 6	9-5 or 6	9-5 or 6	9-5 or 6	9-5 or 6	9-5 or 6
The Hôtel de Ville		1-3	1-3	1-3	1-3	1-3	1-3
The Panthéon (dome,	10-4		10-4	10-4	10-4	10-4	10-4
— — (vaults,	1-4		1-4	1-4	1-4	1-4	1-4
The Sainte-Chapelle			11-4 or 5	11-4 or 5	11-4 or 5	11-4 or 5	11-4 or 5
The Tobacco Manufactory				11-12 and 1-4			
Notre-Dâme (treasury)		10-4	10-4	10-4	10-4	10-4	10-4

IMPORTANT AND FASHIONABLE HEALTH RESORTS

In issuing the following short list of important and fashionable watering-places and health resorts, we wish to inform our readers that we intend in our next Edition to publish a concise Epitome of the health resorts and baths of Europe and North Africa

We shall try to make our Epitome in the next Edition of the Paris Artistic as complete as possible, and the mistakes so commonly made by people going to unsuitable places, may in the future be avoided by a little care and attention.   THE EDITOR.

NOTED BATHS AND WATERING-PLACES
ON THE CONTINENT
(Extract from Jarrett-Knott's Universal Graphic Railway Guide)

ACI-REALE (Sicily). — Winter station. recommended by all the Italian medical authorities, amongst whom are MM. Cantani, Moleschott. and Cordarelli. Grand bathing establishment, thermo-mineral and hydrotherapic.

AIX-LA-CHAPELLE. — (Prussia). — Hot sulphur springs and saline and chalybeate waters, for curing diseases of the skin, rheumatism, gout and digestive disorders.

AIX-LES-BAINS (Savoy). — Mineral springs, warm and sulphurous, good for the digestive organs rheumaloid arthrites.

AUSSEE (near Ischl).—Strong brine springs, saline vapour baths. Dr J. Linn, American physician there.

BADEN-BADEN (Duchy of Baden). — Hot saline chalybeate and arsenical waters, for digestive disorders. Most fashionable and delightful of German watering-places.

BADEN (near Vienna). — Warm sulphur springs; impregnated with carbonic acid gas; good for skin diseases, gout or rheumatism.

BADEN (Switzerland). — Warm sulphur waters, which cure rheumatism, gout, etc.

BADENWEILRE (Duchy of Baden). — Warm alkaline springs and baths.

BAGNÈRES-DE-BIGORRE (Pyrénées). — Warm springs, saline, sulphurous and chalybeate, aperient and tonic. They are very efficacious in rheumatism, gout, etc.

BAGNÈRES-DE-LUCHON (Pyrénées).—Sulphurous, saline and ferruginous, good for rheumatic complaints, paralysis and cutaneous diseases.

BELLTHAL (near Coblence, Prussia). — Mineral springs, acidulated, alkaline, rich in contents of bicarnate of soda and magnésia, good against general debility and lassitude, digestive disorders, etc. in a valley close to the village of Cobern, 15 minutes by rail from Coblence.

BIARRITZ (near Bayonne). — Sea-bathing. A very fashionable place.

BOURBON-LES-BAINS. — On the Eastern of France line. Very fashionable place. Summer season.

BOURBOULE (La) near Clermont-Ferrand. — Arsenical. Radical cures of scrofula, lymphatism, skin diseases, intermittent fevers, diseases of the joints, diabetes, etc.

BUSSANG. — Very renowned for its mineral waters. Baths. Table waters.

CANNSTADT (Wurtemberg). — Mineral springs, containing carbonic acid, sulphur, salts and iron, for curing digestive disorders.

CARLSBAD (Bohemia). — Springs containing sulphate of soda and carbonate of soda, etc.; for complaints of the liver and the kidneys. Aristocratic watering-place.

CAUTERETS (Pyrénées). — Sulphur springs, useful in the early stages of consumption, rheumatism, asthma. indigestion, diseases of the skin, etc.

CHAMPEL-LES-BAINS, near Geneva. — First-class hydrotherapic establishment. Room for inhalations, Galvano-caustic treatment for neuralgia, rheumatism, and cases of general debility.

CONTREXEVILLE. — Of great repute for the cure of gravel.

DAX (near Bordeaux, France). — Hot springs and mud baths, good for rheumatism, diseased joints, etc, and gout.

DIVONNE-LES-BAINS (near Geneva). — Hydropathic establishment, with abundant springs, constant temperature 5 Réaumur. Open all the year.

EAUX-BONNES (Pyrénées). — Hot sulphur springs beneficial in intermittent fevers, skin diseases, early consumption, throat affection.

EAUX-CHAUDES (Pyrénées). — Sulphur and other hot springs, good for rheumatism, paralysis and derangement of the viscera.

ELSTER BAD (near Eger). — Mineral springs, containing iron, soda, and carbonic acid.

EMS (near Coblentz). — Warm springs, containing carbonic acid, carbonate of lime, etc., beneficial in affections of the chest, and particularly efficacious in female complaints.

FRANZENSBAD (Bohemia). — Iron springs, mostly visited by ladies; baths reputed highly beneficial in quite a number of female complaints.

GASTEIN, also called Wildbad-Gastein (in Austrian-Tyrol). — Saline and alkaline springs, good for chronic, nervous affections, skin diseases, gout and rheumatism. Railway as far as Lend (via Munich and Salzbourg or Lintz and Ischl), thence by coach in four hours.

GÉRARDMER. Picturesquely situated in the Vosges. Mineral waters.

GMUNDEN (in the Traunsee, near Ischl). — Saline vapour baths and brine springs.

GRIESBACA (Black Forest, Bade). — Mineral springs, containing iron and carbonic acid, very good against chlorose and anemia, and particularly efficacious in female complaints.

HOMBURG (near Francfort). — Mineral springs, saline and ferruginous, and highly beneficial in restoring the digestive organs.

ISCHL (near Salzburg). — Saline vapour baths. sulphur springs. Beneficial in diseases of the chest. Delightful and fashionable watering-place.

KISSINGEN (Bavaria). — Saline and chalybeate, tonic and aperient, acidulous and alkaline cooling and diuretic.

KRENTH (Bavaria). — Sulphurous and mineral-waters; vapour and douche baths; goat whey and medicinal herbs.

KREUZNACH (Rhenish Prussia). — A favourable watering-place; saline springs, highly beneficial in scrofulous diseases.

LEUK or LEUKERBAD (Switzerland). — Sulphur and saline springs. Excellent for weak nerves, palsy, diseases of the skin, and many chronic complaints.

LIPPSPRINGE (Lippe, near Paderbon). — Warm springs.

LUXEUIL-LES-BAINS. — Mineral springs. Bathing.

MARGARETHEN-INSEL. near Buda-Pest. — These baths, afford sulphurous, alkaline, and warm Artesian springs at 35° reputed to cure gout, rheumatism, muscular, and nervous affections, etc.

MARIENBAD (Bohemia). — Saline purgative springs; 'excellent in bilious complaints. Gazeous baths for diseases of the joints.

MARTIGNY-LES-BAINS. — Well-known place. Cure of gravel.

MENTONE, on the Corniche road from Nice. — Well sheltered; one of the best winter residences on the Mediterrannean.

NAUHEIM (Germany). — Warm saline special treatment.

NEUENAHR, in the valley of the Ahr. near Remagen, on the Rhine; water similar to Vichy and Carlsbad; warm alkaline springs, good for the lungs, liver, gout, etc.

NICE. — On the shore of the Mediterrannean, protected by the Maritime Alps; mild, beautiful climate; fine sea-bathing.

PAU (South of France). — Soft and sedative climate for winter; in view of the Pyrénées.

PETERSTHAL (Black Forest, Baden). — Mineral springs and steel and Lithian baths (via Strasburg and Appenweier, thence by coach).

PFÆFFERS (Switzerland). — Hot saline and sulphurous springs. Beneficial in stomachic debility and for rheumatism, chronic diseases, etc.

PIERREFONDS (near Compiègne). — Sulphur waters. Beneficial in diseases of the lungs.

PLOMBIÈRES (near Lunéville, France). — Warm salines.

PLOMBIÈRES-LES-BAINS. — Vosges. Very celebrated watering-place. Bathing.

POUGUES (France). — Alkaline and ferruginous, efficacious in scrofulous diseases.

PYRMONT (Westphalia). — Chalybeate springs: impregnated with carbonic acid gas; saline and acidulous, tonic and aperient. Good for digestive disorders.

RAGATZ (Switzerland). — Supplied from Pfœffers Baths.

REICHENHALL (near Salsburg). — Saline springs; inhalations of atomized salt water; good for chronic catarrh of the bronchial tubes, etc.

RHEINFELDEN (Switzerland). — On the Rhine, near Bâle; Saline baths; highly beneficial in scrofulous diseases.

RIPPOLSDAU (Black Forest, Baden). — Sulphurous, aperient and diuretic; reputed very good against stomach disease, dyspepsia, hemorrhoïdes, hypochondia, hysterics and nervous complaints.

ROYAT (near Clermont-Ferrand). — Beneficial in anemia, chlorosis, general debility, dyspepsia bronchitis, laryngitis, gravel, rheumatism, gout and cutaneous diseases.

SAXON (Valais). — Halting station between Chamounix and Zermatt. Is the central point for excursions Valaisian and Bernese Alps. Carriages for Chamounix and St. Bernard. Ascent of the Pierre-à-Voir by mules, and descent by sleigh. Bromo-iodurated mineral waters for gout, rheumatism, scrofula, etc. — Grand Hotel des Bains.

SCHINTZNACH (Switzerland). — Contain sulphurated hydrogen, etc. Beneficial in chronic scrofula, various female disorders, diseases of the joints, etc.

SCHLANGENBAD (Fassau). near source of the Rhine. — Possess cosmetic properties, in high repute.

SCHWALBACH (Nassau). — Contain iron and carbonic acid, and highly bracing.

SPA (Belgium). — Chalybeate waters. Beneficial in digestive disorders; in nervous and uterine affections, and in liver complaints they are invaluable.

Sᴛ. Moɴɪᴛᴢ (Switzerland), in the Upper Engadine. — Chalybeate waters, gaseous and sparkling. Said to promote digestion and impart vigour.

Sᴛᴀᴄʜᴇʟʙᴇʀɢ (Switzerland). — Sulphurous and alkaline waters. Beneficial for skin diseases, scrofula, and many chronic complaints.

BEFORE VICHY — AFTER VICHY

Tᴀʀᴀsᴘ-Sᴄʀᴜʟs (Switzerland). — A beautiful spot in the lower Engadine, 4,000 feet above the sea. Powerful alkaline saline springs, and fine gaseous chabyleate waters.

Tᴇᴘʟɪᴛᴢ (Bohemia). — Hot springs of alkali-saline waters, chiefly used for baths taken exceedingly hot. Good for stiff joints and crippled limbs, caused by gout or rheumatism.

Vᴇᴛʟʟ. — Of great repute for the cure of gravel.

Vɪᴄʜʏ (France). — The most frequented watering-place in France. Mineral springs, acidulous and alkaline, for chronic complaints of the liver and digestive organs, kidneys, gout, etc.

Wᴇɪssʙᴀᴅ (Switzerland). — Mineral springs; goat's whey cure.

Wɪᴇsʙᴀᴅᴇɴ (Germany). — Hot waters, aperient and diuretic, for skin diseases, stiffness of the joints and skin.

Wɪʟᴅʙᴀᴅ (near Stuttgart). — Hot springs, for rheumatism, gout, diseases of the joints and skin.

Wɪʟᴅᴜɴɢᴇɴ (Germany). — Mineral springs ; like Vichy, good for diseases of the kidneys, etc.

TO TRAVELLERS

The Editor will be thankful to any traveller who may do him the favour to point out inaccuracies in this work or furnish any information which will be useful to travellers in general. Such information should be addressed to the Editor of Pᴀʀɪs Aʀᴛɪsᴛɪᴄ, 2, rue de l'Echelle, and 182, rue de Rivoli, Pᴀʀɪs.

RIVER STEAMBOATS

First service : From Charenton to the Viaduct d'Auteuil (Point-du-Jour), calling at the following points : —

1. Charenton (Marne), Right Bank.
2. Alfortville (Marne), L. B.
3. Les Carrières, L. B.
4. Ivry, L. B
5. Pont National, R. B.
6. Pont de Tolbiac, L. B.
7. Pont de Bercy, R. B.
8. Austerlitz, R. B.
9. Tournelle, L. B.
10. Grève. R B.
11. Pont-Neuf, L. B.
12. Sts-Pères, Left Bank.
13. Pont Royal. L. B.
14. Concorde, L. B.
15. Invalides, L. B.
16. Alma, L. B.
17. Iéna, L. B.
18. Suffren, L. B.
19. Passy (Ile des Cygnes), L. B.
20. Grenelle (Pont de), L. B.
21 Javel, L. B.
22. Auteuil (Viaduc), R. B.

TRIP TO St-CLOUD BY STEAMER

STEAMBOATS

The steamboats of Paris are extremely convenient. For the small sum of ten centimes on week days or twenty on Sundays, one may go from one end of the City to the other. They are worked by two

THE PLACE DE LA CONCORDE.

companies : 1° the Compagnie des Bateaux-Parisiens which include the *Bateaux mouches* and the bateaux express; 2° the Compagnie des Bateaux-Hirondelles.

BATEAUX-PARISIENS

The service of this Company is divided as follows :

1st SERVICE (Bateaux-Mouches)

From the Pont d'Austerlitz to the quai d'Auteuil (Point-du-Jour). Week-days 10 c. and Sundays and fête-days 20 c. The bateaux depart every ten minutes,

ITINERARY

STATIONS OF THE 1ST SERVICE	STREETS ETC. IN PROXIMITY OF THE STATION
Pont d'Austerlitz	Gares de Lyon and d'Orléans, Jardin des Plantes.
Pont de Sully	Boulevard Henri IV, Ile Saint-Louis.

THE GRAND OPERA - БОЛЬШАЯ ОПЕРА

Hôtel-de-Ville	Hôtel de Ville, Notre-Dame.
Le Châtelet	Les Halles, boulevard Sébastopol, Palais de Justice.
Le Louvre	Faubourg Saint-Germain, Ecole des Beaux-Arts, Institut.
Pont-Royale (chief station for St-Cloud)	Palais-Royal, Louvre, Tuileries, Place and Colonne Vendôme.
Pont de la Concorde	Champs-Elysées, Palais Bourbon.
Pont des Invalides	Palais de l'Industrie, Champs-Elysées.
Pont de l'Alma	Tobacco Manufactury.
Pont d'Iéna	Trocadéro, Champ de Mars, Tour Eiffel.
Quai de Passy	Passy.
Quai de Grenelle	Usine Cail, Anteuil.
Quai de Javel	Grenelle.
Quai d'Auteuil	Point-du-Jour, Bois de Boulogne.

2nd SERVICE

To or from all stations between Charenton and Auteuil. Fares — week-days 20 c., Sundays and fête-days 25 c.

Fares : from Charenton to the Point-du-Jour, 20c. on week-days, 25c. on Sundays and holidays ; from Charenton to the Pont d'Austerlitz 10c. on week-days, and 15c. on Sundays and holidays ; from the Pont d'Austerlitz to the Point-du-Jour, 10c. on week-days, and 20c. on Sundays and holidays.

Second service : From Austerlitz to the Point-du-Jour, calling at the following points : —

1. Austerlitz, Left Bank.	8. Invalides, Right Bank.
2. Sully, R. B.	9. Alma, R. B.
3. Ile Saint-Louis, R. B.	10. Trocadéro, R. B.
4. Châtelet, R. B.	11. Passy, R. B.
5. Louvre, R. B.	12. Grenelle, R. B
6. Pont-Royal, R. B.	13. La Galiote (Auteuil). R. B.
7. Concorde. R. B.	14. Auteuil, R. B.

Fares : 10c. on week-days, and 20c. on Sundays and holidays.

Third service : From the Quai des Tuileries to Suresnes, calling at the following points : —

1. Tuileries, Right Bank.	7. Bas-Meudon, R. B.
2. Concorde, R. B.	8. Sèvres, Left Bank.
3. Alma. R. B	9. Boulogne, R. Br
4. Passy, R. B.	10. St-Cloud, L. B.
5. Auteuil. R. B.	11. Suresnes, L. B.
6. Billancourt, R. B.	Longchamps (R.B.) on racing and review days

Fares : Quai des Tuileries to Suresnes, 20c. on week-days, and 40c. on Sundays and holidays ; St.-Cloud to Suresnes, 25c. on Sundays and holidays.

A boat called *Le Touriste* plies between the Pont-Royal and St. Germain in summer. Meals and refreshments may be had on board. The return fare is 4 fr. 50c.

BATEAUX-HIRONDELLES

From the Quai des Tuileries to St-Cloud and Suresnes. Fares-week-days 20 c. Sundays, fête-days and race-days 40 c. Departures every quarter of an hour in summer and every half-hour in winter. The boats run between stations of the Pont-Royal and Suresnes. On race-days the boats stop at Longchamps.

In view of the enormous and daily increasing trade between America, England and France, and as the value of goods is expressed differently in the three countries both as regards currency and the weights and measures, it may not be amiss to give our readers a few tables, by which they will be enabled to calculate at a glance the comparative values, as near as it can be expressed without going into fractions lower than 1/4 d in English, 1 cent in American and 5 /c in French Money.

THE PANTHÉON — ПАНТЕОНЪ

OMNIBUSES AND TRAMWAYS

Paris is traversed by 75 lines of omnibuses and 35 lines of tramways, and it is possible to gain almost any part of the town by this means of communication. The fare on the omnibuses and tramways, with the exception of some of the lines running into the suburbs, is 15 centimes on the impérial or knifeboard, and 30 centimes in the interior. Passengers can change from one omnibus to another on asking the conductor for a ticket called " une correspondance " when they pay their fare. On changing, the passenger must go to the office and ask for a number for his new destination. Outside passengers taking a " correspondance " must pay full fare, 30 centimes. The advantage of a " correspondance " is that a person can travel from one end of Paris to the other by the payment of a single fare.

THE HOTEL DE VILLE — ДУМА ПАРИЖА

TRAMWAYS

These lines are in three networks or systems : the Tramways de la Compagnie des Omnibus, the Southern, and the Tramways de Paris and du Département de la Seine. The fares are the same as for omnibuses ; 30 centimes inside or on the platform, and 15 centimes on the roof. Those which run to suburban localities make a small additional charge beyond the fortifications. They give *correspondance* tickets, either for their own lines or for the omnibuses.

COMPARATIVE SCALES

OF

AMERICAN, ENGLISH AND FRENCH CURRENCY,
WEIGHTS AND MEASURES

Currency Calculated at the rates [of $\begin{cases} \text{Frcs. } 25.00 = \text{£ } 1.0.0 \\ \text{» } 5.15 = \$ 1. \end{cases}$

Kilogrammes into English pounds

Kilog.	Pounds	Kilog.	Pounds	Kilog.	Pounds	Kilog.	Pounds
1	2.2046	4	8.8184	7	15.4322	10	22.0464
1	4.4092	5	11.0230	8	17.6368	100	220.4642
3	6.6138	6	13.2276	9	19.8414	1.000	2204.6428

English Currency in French

ENGLISH				FRENCH	
£	s.	d.		Francs	Cent.
»	»	» 1/4 d	. . . .	»	2 1/2
»	»	» 1/2 d	. . . .	»	5
»	»	1	. . . .	»	10
»	»	1 1/2	. . . .	».	15
»	»	2	. . . .	»	20
»	»	6	. . . .	»	60
»	1	»	. . . .	1	25
»	2	»	. . . .	2	50
»	3	»	. . . .	3	75
»	5	»	. . . .	6	25
»	10	»	. . . .	12	50
»	15	»	. . . .	18	75
1	»	»	. . . .	25	»
1	10	»	. . . .	37	50
2	»	»	. . . .	50	»
5	»	»	. . . . . .	126	»
20	»	»	. . . .	500	»
50	»	»	. . . .	1.250	»
100	»	»	. . . .	2.500	»

French Currency in English

FRENCH			ENGLISH		
Francs.	Cent.		£	s.	d.
»	5	. . . .	»	»	» 1/2 d
»	10	. . . .	..	»	1
»	50	. . . .	»	»	4 3/4
1	»	. . . .	»	»	9 1/2
5	»	. . . .	»	4	»
10	»	. . . .	»	8	»
15	»	. . . .	»	12	»
17	»	. . . .	..	13	7 1/4
20	»	. . . .	»	16	»
25	»	. . . .	1	»	»
40	»	. . . .	1	12	»
50	»	. . . .	2	»	»
100	»	. . . .	4	»	»

SUPERFICIAL MEASURE

FRENCH ENGLISH

1 Are (100 square Mètres) = 0.898845 rood.
1 Hectare (10,000 sq. Mèt. = 2.471143 acres.
1 Centiare (1 square Mèt.) = 1.196043 sq. yard

Reduced from French into English

Kilom.		Miles.	Frlngs.	Yds.
1	=	0	4	213
2	=	1	1	206
3	=	1	6	199
4	=	2	3	192
5	=	3	0	185
1 myria.	=	6	1	156
2 —	=	12	3	92
3 —	=	18	5	10
4 —	=	14	6	160
5 --	=	31	0	90

MEASURES OF CAPACITY

FRENCH ENGLISH

1 Litre = 1.760773 Pints.
1 Décalitre (10 litres) = 2.2009668 Gallons.
1 Hectolitre (100 litres) = } 22.009!68 Gallons or 2.7512 Bushels.
1 Kilolit., Mèt. cube (1,000 lit.) = 3.426 quarters
1 Décilitre (10 th of a litre) = 0.1760993 Pin.
1 Centilitre (100 th of a litre) = 0.01760773 »

American Currency in French

AMERICAN			FRENCH	
$	Cents		Francs	Cent.
»	1	. . . .	»	5
»	5	. . . .	»	25
»	10	. . . .	»	50
»	50	. . . .	2	55
1	»	. . . .	5	15
5	»	. . . .	25	75
10	»	. . . .	51	50
15	»	. . . .	77	25
20	»	. . . .	103	»
50	»	. . . .	257	»
100	»	. . . .	515	»

Equivalents of Yards in Meters

ENGLISH			FRENCH		
Yards	Inches		Mètres	Centimèt.	Millimètres
»	1	=	»	2	5.00
»	2	=	»	5	n.00
»	3	=	»	7	6.88
»	4	=	»	10	1.20
»	5	=	»	12	7.24
»	6	=	»	15	.2.40
»	7	=	»	17	7.80
»	8	=	»	20	3.20
»	9	=	»	22	8.60
»	10	=	»	24	4 »
»	18	=	»	45	7.20
1	»	=	»	91	4.20
2	»	=	1	82	8 »
3	»	=	1	74	3.40
4	»	=	3	65	7.06
5	»	=	4	57	2 »
6	»	=	5	48	6.04
7	»	=	6	40	n.08
8	»	=	7	31	5.02
9	»	=	8	22	9.0G
10	»	=	9	14	4 »
50	»	=	45	72	» »
100	»	=	91	44	» »

SOLID MEASURE

ENGLISH FRENCH

1 Cubic Inch = 16.386176 Centimètres carrés.
1 d° foot = 0.028214 Mètre cube.
1 d° yard = 0.764502 » »

The unit of Capacity Measure in France is the Litre

English reduced to French

ENGLISH		FRENCH	
Pint..	= ...	0.5675	litres.
Quart..	= ...	1.1359	»
Gallon..	= ...	4.543458	»
Peck..	= ...	9.086916	»
Bushel..	= ...	34.34766	»
Sack..	= ...	1.0904	hectolitres.
Quarter.	= ...	2.90781	»
Chaldron..	= ...	13.08516	»
1 Litre..	= ...	0.2200968	Imp. Gal.

STOCK EXCHANGE

This handsome building commenced in 1808 and completed in 1826 is an imitation of Vespasian's Temple at Rome. The edifice is enclosed by a railing, and approached by a flight of steps at each end. At the corners are four allegorical figures of Commerce, Consular Justice, Industry and Agriculture.

PARIS IN ONE, EIGHT, FIFTEEN AND TWENTY-ONE DAYS

For the convenience of visitors to Paris having a limited length of time at their disposal I have arranged promenades of various lengths which will enable them to get a good idea of the city of pleasure during their stay.

Some of these promenades are to be done partly on foot and partly by cab. None of the instructions are given at hap hazard or without consideration I would recommend visitors to Paris or residents arranging excursions to follow the directions. I give here to the letter as regards the portions to be done on foot and " en voiture ".

The offices of **PARIS ARTISTIC** being situated a stone's throw from the place du Palais Royal, in addition to which the latter is a pretty good centre of Paris, I have chosen this place as the starting point of our daily excursions. Any information desired by tourists or anyone making these excursions will be gladly given gratis at our Foreign Exchange, where we will change your money, supply you with responsible and reliable guides and interpreters (wearing the service uniform, which will assure you courteous consideration and fair treatment everywhere), carriages with English Coachmen by the hour, day or month, arrange and organize pleasure parties to the environs of Paris, personally conducted or otherwise. A Four-in-hand leaves our Office every morning for Versailles, etc., tickets for which must be secured the day before; 15 fr. return fare, or 20 francs box seat. All arrangements are undertaken, sleeping-cars and railway seats secured. Boxes and tickets for the theatres, parties sent by rail or road, or both, and everything done for the convenience and comfort of visitors, or to render their stay in Paris agreeable.

TUILERIES GARDENS   —   ТЮЛЕРІЙСКІЙ САДЪ

PARIS IN ONE DAY

I do not wish to imply that Paris can be properly seen in one day, but, for persons having only that length of time at their disposal, a good glance may be had at the city by following these instructions :

Rise early, have your breakfast (petit déjeuner) at your hotel and be at the place du Palais-Royal at 9 o'clock.

On Foot. Turning your back to the Palais-Royal, the Louvre Stores on the left and the Louvre Palace in front, follow the rue de Rivoli to the right as far as the rue de Rohan. If you require any information call in at our Office, 2, rue de l'Echelle, the next street to the right, and you will be welcome. Facing the rue de Rohan, pass under the archway of the Louvre to your left and you arrive at the place du Carrousel. To your left is the celebrated Louvre Museum, in the square is Gambetta's Monument. Turn to the right, and, facing you is the Arch (Arc du Carrousel), pass under the Arch and cross over the roadway before you go through the Tuileries gardens. Passing the two pieces of water, leave these gardens by the gate leading to the Place de la Concorde through which you see the Obelisk. Arrived at the Place de la Concorde, the magnificent avenue des

Champs-Elysées is before you, surmounted by the Arc de Triomphe. To the left, across the bridge, is the Chambre des Députés, whilst to the right you see the Madeleine. Taking the rue Royale, which leads to the Madeleine on your right, visit the Church. Leaving the Madeleine turn to the right and take the grand boulevards, walking on the right side pavement. You are now in real modern Paris. Follow the boulevards, notice to the left the Grand Café, and the Grand Hotel, then, the Café de la Paix and lastly the Opéra. Place yourself on the refuge in the centre of the Place de l'Opéra, take no notice of anybody, but, have a good look round you.

See the Opera, then, turning your back to this building, you have before you the splendid Avenue de l'Opéra, leading down to the place du Palais-Royal, from whence you started. On the right is the rue de la Paix leading to the Vendôme column, on the left the rue du 4-Septembre, leading to the Bourse (Stock Exchange). It is now about 12 o'clock, lunch either at the place or in the avenue de l'Opéra.

After lunch continue the boulevards, the back to the Place de l'Opera, now on the left hand pavement. Remark in the boulevard des Capucines, at the corner, the Vaudeville Theatre, and at the end of the fine street terminating at this point of the Boulevard, the Trinity church. Continue along the boulevards des Italiens and Montmartre, bordered by numerous shops and splendid Cafés. This is the most lively and animated part of Paris. Notice on the boulevard des Italiens the Crédit Lyonnais Bank, and a little farther on the Parisiana Concert, and on the left the celebrated restaurant the Maison Dorée, and the Nouveautés Theatre. When in the boulevard Montmartre take a seat on the terrace of one of the numerous cafés, and some refreshment.

YOU ARE IN THE HEART OF PARIS

About three o'clock, take a hackney carriage by the hour, telling the coachman to take you to the Bastille by the grand boulevards, returning by the rue Saint-Antoine, rue de Rivoli, avenue Victoria, place du Châtelet, quai de la Mégisserie, rue du Louvre, rue Etienne-Marcel, place des Victoires, rue des Petits-Champs, and the rue Vivienne. Here passing the Bourse you will return to your point of departure on the boulevard Montmartre. On this route you will pass on the grand boulevards to the left the Porte Saint-Martin and the Porte Saint-Denis, and after them the theatres of the Renaissance (Sarah Bernhardt's), the Porte-Saint-Martin, and the Ambigu. Immediately after this you arrive at the place de la Republique, in the centre of which stands a statue of the Republic. You then go on to the Bastille, passing about halfway on the left the Winter circus. Arriving at the Place de la Bastille, ascend the colonne de Juillet in the centre. The next thing of note is the Hôtel de Ville, in the rue de Rivoli; tell the coachman to stop here. Descend and cast an eye over this palace. Turning your back to the rue de Rivoli you have before you, on the other side of the Seine, the belfry and towers of Notre-Dame, and farther away the dome of the Pantheon. You now return to your carriage, and in a few minutes find yourself before the Tour Saint-Jacques. Then place du Châtelet. In the centre is a fine fountain. To the right the Chatelet, the largest theatre in Paris, and on the left the Opéra-Comique. From here you can see on the other side of the river the Palais de Justice and the Sainte-Chapelle. Continuing the journey you pass the Pont-Neuf, and shortly after, following the quai, you see before you the gilded railings of the colonnade of the Louvre palace. Here remark, on the other side of the river, the Mint, and farther on to the right, the Institut de France ; and still farther down the river the noble ruin of Napoleon's Cour des Comptes, burnt during the commune. You now take the rue du Louvre ; pass the church Saint-Germain de l'Auxerrois (where the signal-bell tolled for the Saint-Bartholomew massacre), pass the central markets and the New General Post-office.

At the Place des Victoires note the equestrian statue of Louis XIV, and in the rue Vivienne, one of the entrances of the Bibliotheque Nationale, and just before arriving at the grand boulevard, to the right, the Paris Stock Exchange, a building in the form of a Greek Temple, surrounded by 66 Corinthian columns.

Having now arrived at the end of your journey, *pay* (two francs per hour and gratuity) and dismiss your coachman, and, presuming you to be somewhat fatigued, again repose on a seat of the terrace of one of the cafés on the boulevard Montmartre until 6.30, to get an idea of the movement and customs of true Paris.

At half past six to seven dine at the Restaurant Universel, 9, boulevard des Italiens, if you wish to dine at " prix fixe ", or at the Restaurant Joseph or Maison Dorée if " a la carte ".

At 7.30, dinner being finished, if in the summer, take a cab and have a turn in the Bois-de-Boulogne, finishing up at one of the Café-Concerts in the Champs-Elysées, or at the Folies-Marigny summer theatre.

If in the winter, go and see the piece in vogue, or, if an unmarried man, pass the evening at he Folies-Bergère or the Casino de Paris.

Next thing : BED.

PARIS IN EIGHT AND FOURTEEN DAYS

FIRST DAY

SATURDAY

Morning. — Promenade to the Buttes-Chaumont, visit to the Churches of Saint-Vincent-de-Paul and Saint-Laurent. If a good walker this can be done on foot, otherwise a hackney carriage should be taken.

Mid-Day. — Lunch on the grand boulevards at Duval Restaurant.

After Lunch, take a carriage. and following the grand boulevards by the place de la Bastille, visit the Père-Lachaise cemetery, return by the rue de Rivoli, place des Vosges (statue of Louis XIII), then to the Palais Royal, for dinner.

For the evening, either a carriage drive or walk in the Bois de Boulogne, or consult the play-bills.

SECOND DAY

SUNDAY

Presuming this day to be a Sunday, and as English Churches exist in the environs as well as in Paris, it would be well perhaps to devote the day to a visit to Versailles. The first Sunday of every month the grand fountains play. Lunch and dine in the town, returning to Paris in the evening. Trains after church time for those who desire to attend the services.

THIRD DAY

MONDAY

Morning. — (On foot) : Leaving the place du Palais Royal visit the rue de Rivoli, church of St-Roch return to the statue of Joan of Arc and follow the rue de Rivoli, rue Castiglione, column Vendôme to the place de l'Opéra.

Lunch. — Then take a carriage and visit the Champs-Elysées, Bois de Boulogne, Jardin d'acclimatation and the Parc Monceaux. Tell the coachman to follow :

Les Champs-Elysées, l'avenue du Bois-de-Boulogne, la route de Suresnes, chemin de ceinture du Lac, le rond des Cascades, route de la grande Cascate, allée de Longchamps, Jardin d'acclimatation, barrière de l'Etoile, avenue Hoche, parc Monceaux, place de l'Opéra.

Arrived at the top of the Champs-Elysées, ascend the Arc de Triomphe. Very fine view. Gratuity to attendant. When in the Bois de Boulogne, at the Lake, take a boat and visit the Chalet des Iles, if you have an hour to spare. Return to the carriage and descend again at the Grand Cascade. Pass under the rock and waterfall and mount the platform. A splendid view to be had from here. On the boulevard Malesherbes visit the Church of Saint-Augustin.

6 O'clock, dinner. — *EVENING* : Stroll along the boulevards or consult the play bills.

FOURTH DAY

TUESDAY

Morning. — Visit the Bibliothèque Nationale and the Musée des médailles and antiquites. Then Lunch.

Afternoon. — Visit the place du Carroussel, Chambre des députés, Palais des Invalides,

Artillery museum, Napoleon's Tomb, Church of Sainte Clothilde and the Trocadero Palace. Dinner at one of the restaurants in the Palais-Royal.

Evening. — Stroll on the boulevards, or consult the play bills.

FIFTH DAY

WEDNESDAY

Morning. — Visit the Louvre Museum picture galleries.
Then Lunch at a Restaurant in the neighbourhood or in the Palais-Royal.

Afternoon. — Finish the Louvre. Having finished visit the Church Saint-Germain-l'Auxerrois and stroll along the avenue de l'Opéra and the grand boulevards until dinner.

Dinner. — At the Restaurant Universel, boulevard des Italiens. We would mention to our readers that special attention is paid in all restaurants to persons noticed carrying this book. (Any discourtesy or inattention on the part of an employé in any restaurant we should be glad to hear of. All such communications are treated as strictly confidential and only noted for the benefit of other travellers).

Evening. — Visit the Buttes Chaumont. Omnibuses pass the boulevard at end of rue Vivienne every few minutes. The park should be thoroughly gone over on foot. The effect of the moonlight or electric light is fairylike.

SIXTH DAY

THURSDAY

Morning. — Visit to the Sorbonne, the Church of Saint-Etienne-du-Mont and to the Pantheon.
Leaving the Palais Royal about nine o'clock, follow the rue de Rivoli to the Tour Saint-Jacques turn to the right, cross the Seine, take the boulevard du Palais, cross the Pont St-Michel, boulevard St-Michel to the place de la Sorbonne. Visit the Sorbonne, then continue the boulevard to the Luxembourg gardens. At this point you will see to the left the Pantheon. Visit the Pantheon and the church of Saint-Etienne-du-Mont, returning to the boulevard Saint-Michel to take lunch in the vicinity of the Musée de Cluny.

On this route you will pass : the Tower Saint-Jacques, the Chatelet Theatre, the Opera-Comique (doing duty pending the construction of the new one on the boulevard), the Palais de Justice and the Sainte-Chapelle.

Do not visit any of these monuments, as they form part of Saturday's route.

After lunch, visit the Musée de Cluny. Leaving the Cluny Museum, take the boulevard St-Michel and the rue Racine to the Odéon Theatre. Making the tour of the Odeon, cross the rue de Vaugirard and enter the Luxembourg Gardens. Visit the Luxembourg Museum and gardens ; pass the Palace, then return through the Saint-Sulpice church ; visit the church. Remark the splendid fountain facing it, then taking the rue Buonaparte, visit the church Saint-Germain-des-Prés, see Diderot's statue facing it, and then return to the Palais Royal by the rue Buonaparte, and place du Carrousel.

A stroll round the Palais-Royal gardens, and dinner in one of the restaurants. After dinner consult the affiches des spectacles.

SEVENTH DAY

FRIDAY

Excursion to Versailles by mail-coach, starting from Campbell's Grill Room, rue St-Honore at 10. a. m. returning to Paris for dinner.

These excursions are universally pronounced the great feature of a visit to Paris, and should not be missed. Tickets should be taken at least the day before, if possible.

For those desirous of remaining in Paris I would suggest a second visit to the Louvre.

At eleven o'clock, lunch at one of the Duval establishments.

1 o'clock. — Visit the Palais de l'Institut (Académie française) before which is a statue of the Republic, then turn to the right, pass the statue of Voltaire, and take the rue Buonaparte to the

FAÇADE OF NOTRE-DAME CATHEDRAL

The Façade of Notre-Dame, the finest part of the Cathedral, dates from the 13th century and is the earliest of its kind. It has served as a model for the façades of many other French Churches. It is divided into three vertical sections by buttresses, and consists of three stories exclusive of the towers.

Palais des Beaux-Arts. — This is worth a visit. Return to the Institut and following the quai Conti, visit the Mint. Leaving the Mint, cross the Pont-Neuf (remark equestrian statue of Henry IV) to the Central Markets (Halles Centrales). The sous-sols of the Halles are very curious and should be seen. After the markets, visit the church of Saint-Eustache, returning to the boulevards by the rue Montmartre, one of the most animated streets in Paris. Notice **en route** the new General Post Office.

Dinner at the Café Riche, from the dining-rooms of which a good view may be had of the boulevards. After dinner consult the playbills.

EIGHTH DAY

SATURDAY

Morning. — Visit the churches of Notre-Dame de Lorette and la Trinité, returning to the grand boulevards by the gare St-Lazare and the rue Auber.

Lunch. — Then, visit the Pont-Neuf, follow the quai des Orfèvres, and visit the Palais de Justice and the Sainte-Chapelle. After visiting these monuments, make your way by the rue de Lutèce, then turn to the right, and in a few moments you will be facing Notre-Dame Cathedral. Visit the cathedral; then, by the rue du Cloître, see the Morgue.

Devote the remainder of the afternoon to a visit to the Jardin des Plantes. From here return to the grand boulevards either by omnibus or hackney carriage.

Stroll on the boulevards until seven o'clock, Dinner, then go to the Cirque des Champs-Elysées in summer or Nouveau Cirque in winter.

I have endeavoured in the preceding pages to give as complete a Guide to Paris as possible, considering the length of time at my disposal. For those having 14 days to spare, I would say follow the preceding itinerary for the first eight days, being careful to arrange excursions according to the days at their heading, on account of the fact that certain Monuments and Museums are only open on certain days and hours.

For the remaining seven days go :

9th DAY (THURSDAY). — To the forest of Saint-Germain; visit the Museum.

10th DAY (WEDNESDAY). Excursion to Fontainebleau; visit the palace and drive in the forest.

11th DAY (THURSDAY). — Excursion to Saint-Cloud and to Sèvres.

12th DAY (FRIDAY). — Excursion to the Château de Pierrefonds and to Compiègne.

13th DAY (SATURDAY). — Excursion to Vincennes, visit to the Museum of arms (with permission) and to the fort, and promenade in the wood.

14th DAY (SUNDAY). — Excursion to Saint-Denis; visit the Cathedral. From there to Enghien and Montmorency.

A month could well be passed in excursions into the environs of Paris, visiting different villages, each having its peculiar and individual features and attractions, never visiting the same neighbourhood twice, and continuing the excursions every month throughout the year never seeing a village twice under the same conditions, owing to the change in the seasons and the corresponding change in the general aspect and surroundings.

In the foregoing excursions I have included the principal places having a special interest for the tourist. A whole volume would, however, be required to give a complete guide and description to the environs of Paris

At the end of this guide is a detailed description of some of the principal Parisian holiday resorts.

For tourists desirous of doing Paris on foot, I have arranged a series af skeleton promenades, to cover a period of twenty days.

PARIS IN TWENTY WALKS

FIRST WALK

Today we have rather a long journey before us, part of which may be done on foot and part by driving as the inclination may dictate.

It would be well to start by driving to the Parc de Montsouris, descend here, discharge your carriage, and visit the park on foot.

Close to the Parc de Montsouris is one of the entrances to the catacombs.

Visit these in detail.

Leaving the catacombs and continuing along the exterior boulevards, we shortly after reach the Montparnasse cemetery, containing tombs of many celebreties.

After visiting the cemetery, continue along the boulevard until you reach the Abattoir des Fourneaux.

From here return home by the boulevard Montparnasse, rue de Rennes, boulevard Saint-Germain, rue du Bac, Pont Royal, crossing the Louvre, home.

SECOND WALK

Commencing this walk from the Palais Royal, in good time, we make our way by the rue de Rivoli and boulevard Saint-Michel to the rue Saint-Victor, in which is the Bouding warehouse for wine (Halle aux vins). This market covers an area of 109 acres.

At the junction of the rue Saint-Victor and the rue Cuvier is a very elaborately ornamented fountain, known as the Fontaine du Jardin des Plantes.

We next see the Hopital de la Pitié, the prison of St. Pelagie, the leather market, the great central bakery for the hospitals and asylums of Paris, and lastly the amphitheatre of anatomy.

Next visit the Jardin des Plantes.

From the Jardin des Plantes a hackney carriage should be taken along by the terminus of the Orleans Railway, cross the Pont d'Austerlitz, and taking the boulevard Bourdon by the side of the canal, pass the place de la Bastille, boulevard Beaumarchais, boulevard du Temple, place de la République to the grand boulevards.

THIRD WALK

Our third walk commences with the manufacture nationale des Gobelins (Gobelin Tapestry Manufactury).

Then taking the rue Mouffetard, we see the church of St. Medard, and in the boulevard du Port Royal the Hopital du Midi. In this boulevard is also the old Port Royal Abbey, now used as a house for accouchements, known as " la Maternite ".

Then visit in rotation : the Hopital Cochin, in the Faubourg St. Jacques; the convent of the Dame de St. Joseph; the Prison de la Sante; and the Observatory, rue Denfert-Rochereau.

After this we pass the Hospice des Enfants Assistés; then the Infirmerie de Marie-Thérèse; farther on the place Denfert-Rochereau, in the centre of which is a bronze model of the Lion of Belfort.

Near here is the Ball Bullier, a Ball something after the style of the Moulin Rouge, frequented largely by students and their gay lady friends, facing which is the statue erected to Marechal Ney on the spot where he was executed, and a beautiful fountain, adorned with 8 horses and a group of goddesses.

In the rue de l'Observatoire you pass the Ecole de Pharmacie (School of Chemistry) and further on, in the rue d'Assas, is a free hospital for accouchements, containing 130 beds.

Striking the rue Val de-Grace, we soon come to the church of that name and the Military Hospital of Val de-Grace.

Farther on, at N° 254, is the national institution for the deaf and dumb (Institution Nationale des Sourds-Muets).

From here proceed to the church St. Jacques-du-Haut-Pas, after which we gain the rue des Irlandais, at N° 5 of which is the College des Irlandais, in which the government of Napoleon embodied all the British Colleges of Paris.

This will finish to day's promenade, so far as the monuments and public buildings are concerned.

From the rue des Irlandais we make our way to the boulevard St. Michel, descending which we cross the two bridges of the Seine, finding our way into the rue de Rivoli.

Turning to the left by the Tour St. Jacques, and passing the Halles, a few minutes walk will bring us to the avenue de l'Opera.

FOURT.H WALK

Leaving the Palais-Royal we cross the Pont de la Concorde, facing the place of that name, and taking the boulevard St.-Germain to the left, then the rue des Ecoles and the rue Monge, we pass at the junction of the two latter streets a small square adorned with statues of Voltaire and François Villon.

A little farther on is the place Monge, where is a statue of Louis Blanc.

Then following the rue de Pontoise, we enter by the rue St. Victor the church of St. Nicolas-du-Chardonnet. After which follow the rue des Carmes, in which is a Gothic chapel and several old colleges. You are now in the centre of the Latin quarter, one of the oldest parts of Paris.

Next visit the church of St. Séverin, and from here take the rue St. Jacques to the College de France, in front of which is a statue of Claude Bernard.

In the rue St. Jacques, to the left, is the Lycee Louis the Grand, the largest and most important college in France.

Near here is the Pantheon.

After visiting the Pantheon, see the Bibliotheque St. Genevieve, on one of the sides of the square, and, behind the Pantheon, the church of St. Etienne-du-Mont.

Next visit the Lycée Henry IV (part of the abbey of St. Genevieve), and at N° 65, rue Clovis, the ancient college des Ecossais.

Returning by the rue Clovis, we finish our day's promenade by a visit to the Ecole Polytechnique, rue Descartes, a building with a fine monumental front, overlooking the square Monge. This school is in the ancient college de Navarre, founded by Joan of Navarre in 1304.

We now make our way home by the boulevard St. Germain, rue de Sevres (passing the Bon Marché), Pont des Arts and rue de Rivoli.

FIFTH WALK

This day can well be devoted to an excursion into the country.

A mail-coach leaves the Daily Messenger Office, 4, rue de l'Echelle, every day, at 10 a m. weather permitting, for Versailles.

Seats should be booked in advance, if possible. Prices : 15 francs each person, box-seat 20 francs.

SIXTH WALK

Starting as usual, we take an omnibus which proceeds along an interesting route to the church of St. Sulpice Visit this.

Fronting the church is the Fontaine de St. Sulpice, a fine work.

Leaving the fountain behind us, we make our way to the Luxembourg Museum, which is worthy of a visit, and should not be missed.

Then visit the Luxembourg palace and chapel.

Leaving the Luxembourg gardens we strike the rue de Vaugirard, at N° 74 of which is the Catholic College, from whence the rue de Rennes will conduct you to the boulevard Montparnasse, the Western Railway terminus and Montparnasse station.

Now proceed to the Lycée Saint-Louis, nearly opposite which is the college de la Sorbonne. Visit these buildings, and then descend the rue de la Sorbonne to the Cluny Museum.

This walk will have taken a good day, and the visitor will no doubt be glad to avail himself of the omnibus, which will take him back to the grand Boulevards.

SEVENTH WALK

This morning we will start by a visit to the church of St-Thomas d'Aquin, situated in the place St-Thomas d'Aquin, near the rue du Bac and boulevard St-Germain.

This church was founded by Cardinal Richelieu in 1683 as a Jacobin convent, and contains a number of very fine pictures and frescoes. Taking the rue de Grenelle, we soon come to the fountaine de Grenelle, one of the finest in Paris.

Then taking successively the rue de Sèvres, rue du Dragon, rue des Saints-Pères, rue Jacob and the rue Buonaparte, we pass the church of Jesus, the Académie de médecine, the Hôpital de la Charité, and finally at the end of the latter street the church of St-Germain-des-Prés. This church contains some fine mural paintings and monuments.

Continuing the rue Bonaparte to the banks of the Seine, and turning to the right, you see before you the statue to Voltaire and the Institut de France, and farther on the Mint (Hôtel des Monnaies).

Retracing our steps to the quai Malaquais, you will see the Palais and School des Beaux-Arts, near which is the Pont des Arts, and farther on the Pont du Carrousel.

Along these successive quays, on the walls of the Seine embankment are the stands of the celebrated dealers in prints and second-hand books.

Cross the Pont-Royal, the next bridge, then take the rue des Tuileries, and rue des Pyramides, home.

EIGHTH WALK

Starting as usual we retrace our steps of yesterday's return journey to the quai d'Orsay, following which, to the right, we soon arrive at the Esplanade des Invalides, a magnificent square extending from the Palais des Invalides down to the quai d'Orsay.

Visit the Palace, the Church, Napoleon's Tomb, Place Vauban, a semicircular place facing the Church, and then return to the Esplanade and rue de Grenelle.

At N° 127 is the residence of the Archbishop of Paris, the Hôtel du Châtelet.

N° 110 is the Hotel of the Minister of Public Instruction. N° 106, Calvinistic church, built on the site of an ancient convent.

At the place Bellechasse is the Church of Ste-Clotilde.

In the rue St-Dominique is the War Office, fronting the boulevard St-Germain, and formerly, a convent.

At 231 boulevard St-Germain is the Dépôt de la guerre. The library may be visited by permission from M. le directeur du Dépôt de la guerre.

Returning from the boulevard St-Germain by the rue and Pont de Solferino, cross the Tuileries Gardens, home.

NINTH WALK

Our ninth walk will commence from the Palais-Royal and lead us across the rue de Rivoli to the Pont-Royal.

Crossing this and turning to the right we pass the Caisse des Dépôts et Consignations, the ruins of the Cour des Comptes, burnt during the Commune, and the Palais de la Légion d'honneur.

A little further on is the Chambre des Députés, formerly known as the Bourbon Palace, now the seat of the Legislative assembly. Visit this, then see the Palace of the Presidency, next the Residence of the Minister of Foreign Affairs, the Manufacture Nationale des Tabacs and then on to the Champ de Mars. Here are remaining some of the buildings of the great Exhibition of 1889. Remark the Central Dome, the Eiffel Tower, the Palaces of the Liberal and Fine Arts and the Machine Gallery.

Near here is the Panorama of the Compagnie générale Transatlantique, from Havre to New-York, and the Ecole Militaire.

In the place de Breteuil is the Artesian Well of Grenelle. (Interior may be viewed).

N° 39 avenue de Breteuil is the church of Saint-François Xavier, and n° 56 the National Institution for the young blind.

Take the rue de Sèvres. No 151, the Hôpital Necker, and adjoining, the Hôpital des Enfants malades.

From here the best way to return home is by taking the rue de Sèvres, to the rue de Saint-Pères, Pont du Carrousel, and crossing the Louvre.

TENTH WALK

Once again we start from our old point, and, turning to the left into the rue de Rivoli, we follow the latter street until we come to the rue du Pont-Neuf, on the right. Striking this street, we cross the Seine by the Pont-Neuf, and commence a visit of the Paris Islands, now known as the « Ile de la Cité ».

First of all we see the place Dauphine, then the Palais de Justice, Conciergerie, Ste-Chapelle, Pont au Change, Tribunal de Commerce, Pont St-Michel, Notre-Dame cathedral, interior and

THE WESLEYAN METHODIST CHURCH
4, rue Roquépine, Paris.
PASTOR : Rev. H. Bramley Hart.

exterior, Ile St-Louis, ponts de la Tournelle and Sully, church of St-Louis en l'Ile, ponts Marie and d'Arcole, returning to the extreme point of the island to finish up our visit with the Morgue.

ELEVENTH WALK

Leaving the Palais-Royal we turn into the rue de Rivoli to the left and walk on, passing the Tour St. Jacques, to the Hôtel de Ville. Visit this and then continue the rue de Rivoli to the rue de Jouy, in which we shall pass the Hotel d'Aumont (N° 7) and the passage Charlemagne (N° 14).

Taking this passage we come to the rue St. Antoine. Here (N° 120) is the Lycée Charlemagne, and adjoining the latter, the church of St. Paul and St. Louis. At N° 143 is the Hotel occupied by Sully.

In the rue de Sully is the Arsenal. Library open from 10 to 3 excepting Sundays and holidays.

Leaving the rue de Sully and striking the rue du Figuier, you will see, at N° 1, the Hotel de Sens. Return to the rue de Rivoli home.

TWELFTH WALK

We usher this walk in with the *boulevard Voltaire*, crossing the spacious *boulevard Richard-Lenoir*, built over the canal, the arched roof of which is about a mile in length.

Continuing the *boulevard Voltaire* we pass successively the church of *St. Ambroise*, the mairie of the 11th arrondissement and the *place Voltaire* (bronze statue of *Ledru Rollin*, the famous tribune). Then the *passage Richard-Lenoir, rue de Charonne*, and *rue St. Bernard*. In the latter street is the church of *Ste Marguerite*. At 184 is the St. Antoine Hospital, and farther on, the *place de la Nation* (two lofty Doric columns).

Now take the boulevard Diderot, rue de Picpus (N° 12, maison d'Enghien and N° 2 Hospital for Jews) rue de Reuilly (church of St. Eloi). Descending the boulevard Diderot, we see the Mazas Prison, and, opposite, the terminus of the Lyons and Mediterranean Railway.

We now see in rotation the pont de Bercy, the pont Tolbiac and the pont National, and returning to the pont d'Austerlitz we visit the Panorama close by.

Continuing our walk we soon arrive at the place de la Bastille, where rises the pedestal of the July column on the site of the ancient Bastille Prison.

On this square is the terminus of the Vincennes Railway.

Entering the rue de Charenton the memory of the visitor will recall the terrible massacre of several hundred Protestants here in 1621, as they were leaving their church at Charenton. In this street are the Trousseau Hospital for children, and the Hospital for the blind known as the Hopital des Quinze-Vingts.

Omnibuses leave the place de la Bastile every two minutes for the Madeleine, passing the commencement of the avenue de l'Opera. Descend here.

THIRTEENTH WALK

This promenade may be commenced from the boulevard de Sebastopol, proceeding down which, towards the Seine, we see the Tower St. Jacques.

Adjoining this is the place du Chatelet, in the centre of which is a fountain 58 feet in height, surmounted by a gilt statue of Victory. On one side of this square is the Châtelet Theatre, and on the other the Opéra-Comique.

Following the rue de Rivoli and taking the rue des Archives to the left we arrive at the Palais des Archives Nationales. Visit this palace in detail.

Behind the Hotel de Soubise, in the rue Charlot, is the church of St. Jean St. François, and in the rue Vieille-du-Temple we see the Imprimerie Nationale.

At N° 12, rue des Francs-Bourgeois, is the chapel of Notre-Dame-des-Blancs-Manteaux. At N° 23, rue de Sévigné, is the Carnavalet Museum.

The rue de Sévigné leads eastwards to the place des Vosges, in the centre of which stands an equestrian statue of *Louis XIII*.

At the corner of the rue St. Claude is the church of *St. Denis du St. Sacrement*, containing some excellent paintings.

On the *boulevard des Filles-du-Calvaire*, stands the *Winter Circus*, for equestrian performances.

Return by the grand boulevards and the *avenue de l'Opéra*.

FOURTEENTH WALK

Starting, we proceed along the avenue de l'Opéra, taking the boulevards to the right to the triumphal arch of the Porte St. Martin, about one minute from the Porte St. Denis which we saw yesterday: we pass this, and see the Theatre de la Rénaissance (Sarah Bernhardt's Theatre) and by the side of it the Theatre de la Porte St. Martin, then retracing our footsteps we take the boulevard de Strasbourg to the right, passing the Eldorado and Scala Music Halls, as well as the church of St. Laurent.

At the top of the Eastern boulevard is the Railway Terminus.

By the rue de Strasbourg we enter the Faubourg St. Martin. Crossing the canal in the rue des Recollets, we find the Hopital St. Louis, rue Bichat.

From the rue Bichat we enter the Faubourg du Temple. Again crossing the canal, we find the Entrepot of the Compagnie des Douanes.

In the rue des Marais stands the chapel of St. Martin.

We now proceed to the boulevard St. Martin by the rue de Lancry. To the right is the Ambigu Theatre.

Now visit in rotation : the caserne du Château-d'Eau, the Temple (from whence Louis XVI, was led to the scaffold), the chapel of Saint Elizabeth, the synagogue, 15, rue Notre-Dame-de-Nazareth, and finally the Conservatoire des Arts and Metiers.

In front of the Conservatoire is a fine square, to the left of which is the Gaity Theatre. Further down is the church of St. Nicolas des-Champs.

Return by the grand boulevards.

FIFTEENTH WALK

Starting from the Palais-Royal, we cross the rue de Rivoli, bearing towards the left, and 2 minutes walk takes us to the celebrated church of St. Germain-l'Auxerrois from whose belfry the fatal signal was given for the commencement of the massacre of St. Bartholomew, the bell being kept tolling throughout the whole of that dreadful night.

Next the church is the Mairie of the 1st arrondissement, which has been built on the site of the house where the Duchess of Beaufort, Henry IV's mistress, died in 1599.

Following the rue du Louvre, we pass the Bourse de Commerce and continuing our walk by the rue Sauval and along the rue St. Honoré, we pass the square and fountain des Innocents.

Close to this are the new central markets (Halles), and opposite these, at the corner of the rue Montmartre, is the church of St. Eustache.

The rues Coquillière and Jean-Jacques-Rousseau lead to the new General Post Office.

Following the rue Turbigo we see on the left the square feudal tower built by Jean sans Peur after the murder of his cousin the duc d'Orléans.

Turning off the rue Turbigo we take the rue St. Denis. At N° 182 is the church of St. Leu and St. Gilles. This was at one time the chief street of Paris.

Still following the rue St. Denis we take the grand boulevards to the left, returning by the rue de la Paix to the place Vendôme.

SIXTEENTH WALK

Starting out from our usual point, we visit first of all the Banque de France, then the place des Petits-Pères, the church of Notre-Dame des-Victoires, rue de la Banque, passing the stamp office en route, cross the place de la Bourse to the right, following the grand boulevards to the rue du Faubourg Poissonnière on the left, in which we pass the Conservatoire of Music, and the rue Ste-Cécile in which is the church of St-Eugène.

After the Faubourg Poissonnière we gain the rue Lafayette, following which to the right we pass the church of St-Vincent-de-Paul, and further on the Northern Railway terminus.

Then turn into the Faubourg St-Denis, in which at the junction of the boulevard Magenta we find the St-Lazare prison, and at the end the triumphal arch of the Porte St-Denis raises itself.

We now turn westwards seeing the Gymnase Théâtre on our right and a little farther on the Théâtre des Variétés on the left, from whence we return by the boulevards and the rue de Richelieu to the Palais Royal our starting point.

SEVENTEENTH WALK

Commencing our walk as usual from the Palais Royal, we make the tour of the gardens and shops.

Leaving the Palais Royal by the place du Théâtre Français, and proceeding westwards along the rue St-Honoré, we pass first of all the avenue de l'Opéra, then on the right the church of St-Roch, and farther on the Marché St-Honoré, the latter erected on the site of the ancient convent of the Jacobins. The large arched gate still visible in the rue St-Hyacinthe was the actual entrance to the famed Jacobin club.

We then visit the fountain Louis-le-Grand, and enter the boulevard by the rue du Port-Mahon.

We pass the Théâtre du Vaudeville, then the Grand Opéra, facing the avenue de l'Opéra; further on the Grand Hôtel, and to the left the rue des Capucines, from the corner of which the eventful shot was fired on the 23rd February 1848 which commenced the great revolution and the overthrow of the monarchy.

Turning down the rue Caumartin opposite, we see the Lycée Condorcet, the church of St-Louis d'Antin and the rue de la Victoire, at N° 60 of which Napoleon and Josephine once lived.

A few steps will now take us to the chaussée d'Antin, and turning to the right, we perceive the Trinity church, place de la Trinité, and to the right facing the rue Laffitte is the church of Notre-Dame-de-Lorette.

Returning to the boulevard by the rue Drouot we pass the public auction rooms, and crossing the boulevard des Italiens we make our way to the Bourse (Stock Exchange) via the rue Vivienne.

Leaving the Bourse we continue our promenade to the rue Richelieu where is the Bibliothèque National.

Continuing southwards along the rue Richelieu at N° 40 is the house in which Molière is said to have died, and nearly opposite this the visitor will notice the handsome fountain erected to his memory.

EIGHTEENTH WALK

Starting as usual we make our way to the Arc-de-Triomphe, surmounting the Champs-Elysées. From this point twelve spacious avenues branch out in different directions, the principal of which are : the avenues des Champs-Elysées, avenue du Bois-de-Boulogne, avenue Hoche, avenue Victor-Hugo and avenue de la Grande-Armée.

Taking the latter magnificent avenue we arrive at Neuilly, a picturesque village on the banks of the Seine, a favourite English residence and resort.

Returning by the avenue des Ternes, we pass at the corner of the rue Armaillé the église St-Ferdinand and continuing along the faubourg St-Honoré, we find at 208 the Hôpital Beaujon.

At N° 21 rue de Berry is the American church, and a few steps farther on, in the faubourg St-Honoré is the church of St-Philippe-du-Roule.

Farther down in the place Beauveau is the Home Office, opposite which is the Palais de l'Elysée, the residence of the President of the Republic.

At N° 5 rue d'Aguesseau is the Anglican church, and almost facing this street, in the faubourg St-Honoré, at n° 39 is H. B. M's Embassy.

A few steps will now bring you to the rue Royale, facing which is the Madeleine.

East of the Madeleine a flower market is held every Tuesday and Friday.

Taking the boulevard Malesherbes we pass on the left the rue Roquepine, at N° 4 of which is the new Wesleyan church, in the English gothic style of the 15th. century and opposite, the French Calvinist church. Further on in the boulevard Malesherbes is the church of St-Augustin.

NINETEENTH WALK

Leaving the Place du Palais Royal, the visitor commences his nineteenth walk by the Place de la Concorde, where he will see the obelisk of Luxor, the two fountains, the horses of Marly, and from whence a view may be had of the Madeleine, the Pont de la Concorde and the Legislative Palace, and towering behind the latter, the Dome of the Invalides; on the east side the Tuileries, and on the west the beautiful avenue des Champs-Elysées.

Passing along the Champs-Elysées, he will see to his left the Palais de l'Industrie, and to the right the President's Palace. In these gardens are the celebrated open air Café-Concerts, the Palais de Glace (real ice skating rink) and the pretty little theatre of the Folies Marigny.

Turning to the left along the quai de Billy, we meet the Pont de l'Alma. Four statues, a zouave and soldier of the line by Dieboldt, and an artilleryman and a chasseur by Arnaud.

Continuing our route we pass at N° 4 the Pompe à Incendie de Chaillot, at N°s 32-36 the subsistence militaire and then the Pont d'Iéna, opposite which is the military school and the Champ-de-Mars. Four splendid equestrian statues.

At the corner of the avenue d'Iéna is the Guimet Museum of ancient art and eastern religions.

In the avenue du Trocadéro is the Galliera Museum and then the Trocadéro Palace.

Southward the road now leads to that charming suburb of Paris, Passy.

Returning from Passy, passing the rue Gallilée, at N° 59 of which is the United States Legation.

TWENTIETH WALK

Leaving the Palais Royal we take the rue de Rivoli and the Champs-Elysées, to the Arc-de-Triomphe. Finding our way to the boulevard de Courcelles and continuing along the exterior boulevards, we soon see to our left Montmartre, surmounted by the church du Sacré-Cœur.

Near here is the Montmartre cemetery, containing tombs and monuments of many celebreties, among them several Englishmen.

In the rue Affre the church of St-Bernard should be seen.

We now continue the boulevard, strike the rues de Marseille, de Meaux, and de Puebla, shortly after arriving at the beautiful parc des Buttes-Chaumont.

Leaving this park by the rue de Puebla, we enter Belleville, the Parisian Whitechapel.

In the rue Lassus is the church of St-John the Baptist.

Returning again to the boulevard, we continue until we arrive at the cemetery of Père-Lachaise, visit this.

Near here is the celebrated prison de la Roquette, in front of which the guillotine is erected for public executions.

Mounting the omnibus for the Place de la Bastille, ask for a " correspondance ". Arrived at the Place de la Bastille change omnibus for that going to the Madeleine, alighting in front of the Opéra. Two minutes on foot down the Avenue de l'Opéra and turning to the right down the rue de l'Echelle, you are once again at our starting point.

PALACES

PALAIS DES TUILERIES (Tuileries Palace). — The ancient Tuileries Palace was burnt down during the communist struggle and its site is now occupied by a beautiful square preceding the Tuileries Gardens and facing the Arc de Triomphe du Carrousel and Gambetta's Monument.

PALAIS DU LOUVRE (Louvre Palace). — The present Louvre Palace was commenced by François Ist, in 1541, on the site of an ancient fortress, constructed by Philip Augustus, of which some remains were discovered in 1883 under the salle des Cariatides.

Continued by the successors of François Ier the Louvre Palace, inhabited by Catherine de Médicis, Charles IX. and Louis XIII remained for a long time unfinished and at last threatened to fall into ruins. In 1805 Napoleon Ist ordered the restoration of the Palace, but time did not allow him to complete this enormous undertaking. After him, Louis XVIII. Charles X. and Louis-Philippe did little towards its completion and it was finished by Napoleon III. from the plans by Visconti. It is said that the ancient castle above referred to was used as a hunting seat by Dagobert, as at that time the woods extended down to the water's edge and over the present site of Northern Paris.

In 1200 Philip Augustus used it as a state prison. Charles IX. inhabited the old Louvre and it was from its windows that he fired upon the victims during the perfidious massacre of St. Bartholemew. It also served for some time as the residence of Queen Henrietta of England, widow of the unfortunate Charles I. The magnificently worked bronze gates were made by order of Napoleon Ist.

A small garden on the south-western side is called the Garden of the Infanta, from the Spanish Princess who came into France, in 1721, to marry Louis XV. Similar gardens run all round the palace.

Interior — Almost all the interior of this palace is devoted to the museums collectively known under the name of *Musées du Louvre*, for which it is so celebrated.

PALAIS ROYAL. — The galleries of the Palais-Royal are open to the public every day.

The Palace itself is now occupied by the Counsel of state and the interior is no longer opened to the public. The elegant façade of columns has been restored and serves as an " entrée d'honneur "

The Palace, which played so important a part in the political annals of France, was, for a long period, the property of the Duke of Orleans (Louis-Philippe) and was used, during the last Empire, as the residence of Prince Napoleon, cousin of the Emperor. On the side of the rue Saint-Honoré the façade is monumental and in harmony with the new Louvre, facing it. The best view is to be had from the square in front of the Louvre.

After the death of Louis XIII. in 1643, Anne of Austria, with the young king. Louis XIV. made it her abode during the turbulent times of the *Fronde*. In 1692, it was ceded by Louis XIV. to Philippe of Orleans, his nephew, as part of his apanage on his marriage with Mlle. de Blois. In 1763,

THE LUXEMBOURG PALACE AND GARDENS

This palace was begun by Marie de Medicis, from the designs of Desbrosses in 1615. Since the revolution, it has successively been used by the Peers and Senate.

Le petit Luxembourg, in the « rue de Vaugirard » is the residence of the President of the Senate, and contains a cloister with fountains as well as the old chapel of the convent of the Filles-du-Calvaire, work of the XVI century.

THE TUILERIES GARDENS

Our view shews these gardens as seen from the site of the ancient Palace.

In the distance, is the Avenue des Champs-Elysées, surmounted by the Arc de Triomphe, which was the highest point in Paris from which a view of the city might be had before the erection of the Eiffel Tower.

the theatre, built by the cardinal, was destroyed by fire; and, on this occasion, the entire front of the palace, with its two wings, was rebuilt after the designs of Moreau. The debts of the duke having become so enormous that he once meditated a declaration of insolvency, it was determined, by the advice of the brother of Mme de Genlis, to erect buildings with shops and places of amusement, in the garden of the palace, as a means of augmenting his revenue. These were begun in 1781, upon the designs of the architect Louis: the houses and arcades, as they now stand were finished in 1786. The plan succeeded. After the execution of the duke in 1793, his palace, then called *Palais Egalité*, was confiscated. and soon converted into salerooms, ball-rooms, cafés, etc. The Palace was taken and devastated by the mob on Feb. 24, 1848, and in that and the following year, it became, under the name of *Palais National*, a place of meeting for some of the republican members of the Constituent Assembly. In 1850, 1851, and 1852, it was used for exhibitions; but immediately after the revival of the Empire, it was assigned to Prince Jerome for a residence. The commune set fire to it on the 23d of May, 1871.

PALAIS DE LA BOURSE (Stock-Exchange), rue Vivienne and place de la Bourse. — Open free to the public every day, excepting Sunday, from 12 to 3 for Stock Exchange business and from 3 to 5 for ordinary commercial transactions.

In order to have a good idea of the Bourse one should go about 2 o'clock to the first floor.

Advice. – **Do not go well dressed or with a tall hat** as the stock-brokers are not so orderly as we are accustomed to see in London, in fact, some unfortunate visitors get **very roughly handled**, especially if foreigners. One should make up a party of 5 or 6 gentlemen before intruding into the stock-brokers' sanctuary.

The Bourse contains two admirable imitations of bas-reliefs representing the opening of the Bourse by Charles X. and France receiving tribute from the five parts of the earth, the Union of Commerce, Sciences and Arts, and the principal towns of France.

The building erected by the architects Brongniart and Labarre, has the form of a Greek Temple, and is surrounded by 66 Corinthian pillars. It was opened in 1826.

BOURSE DE COMMERCE (Chamber of Commerce of Paris), 2, place de la Bourse. — In the same building is the well selected Bibliothèque de Commerce, open daily, holidays excepted from 11 to 4.

A **BRITISH CHAMBER OF COMMERCE**, sits at 25, boulevard des Italiens.

The **AMERICAN CHAMBER OF COMMERCE** is situated at **3, rue Scribe.** Open daily from 11 to 2, Sundays excepted.

PALAIS DES INVALIDES. Esplanade. — Open free to the public every day, from 12 to 3, in winter and 12 to 4 in summer. The military mass is celebrated here every Sunday at 12 o'clock, in the Saint-Louis church.

Napoleon's Tomb.—Visible to the public Mondays, Tuesdays, Thursdays and Fridays (holidays excepted, from 12 to 3 in winter and 12 to 4 in summer. — The entrance is flanked by two sarcophagi resting upon plinths, and surmounted by two Corinthian columns crowned with segmental pediments; one is dedicated to Marshall Duroc, the other to Marshal Bertrand, the Emperor's friends during his adversity. A bronze door gives access to the crypt; over it, on a black marble slab, are the following words, quoted from the Emperor's will :

> " Je désire que mes cendres reposent sur les bords de la Seine,
> au milieu de ce peuple français que j'ai tant aimé ".

Two colossal bronze caryatides, by Duret, at the entrance, hold the globe, sceptre, and imperial crown. A gloomy gallery, running under the high altar, now leads to the crypt, dimly lighted by funereal lamps of bronze, and adorned with bas-reliefs, designed by Simart, and executed by Lanno, Petit, and Ottin, representing : 1. The Termination of Civil War; 2, the Concordat; 3, the Reform of the Administration; 4, the Council of State; 5, the Code; 6, the University; 7, the Court of Account; 8, the Encouragement of Trade and Commerce; 9, Public Works; 10. the Legion of Honour : all due to the reign of Napoléon III. The pavement of the crypt is decorated with a crown of laurels in mosaic, within which, on a black circle, are inscribed the names of the following victories : — Rivoli, Pyramids, Marengo, Austerlitz, Iena, Friedland, Wagram, and Moskowa. Twelve colossal statues, by Pradier, representing as many victories, stand against the pilasters, facing the tomb, which consists of an immense monolith of porphyry, weighing 135,000 lbs., and brought from Lake Onegain Finlan 1 at a cost of 140,000 fr. It covers the sarcophagus, also a single block, 12 feet long and 6 in breadth, resting upon two plinths, which stand on a block of green granite, brought from the Vosges. The total height is 13 1/2 feet. In the gallery which encircles the crypt is a recess, called the *Chapelle Ardente*, containing the sword the Emperor wore at Austerlitz, the insignia he wore on State occasions, the crown of gold voted by the town of Cherbourg, and the colours taken in different battles.

At the farthest end of the recess stands the statue of the Emperor in his imperial robes, due to the chisel of Simart. This reliquary is closed with gilt doors. Special permission must, however, be obtained from the Minister of War in order to visit this part of the monument. The crypt is only visible from the circular parapet above. The marble cost 2,000,000 fr.: the whole expense amounted to 9,000,000 fr.

In a vault beneath the pavement of the dome are deposited the bodies of Marshal Mortier and the other fourteen victims of Fieschi's attempt.

Hôtel des Invalides. — This part of the Palais des Invalides owes its existence to Louis XIV.. who founded it 1670 to assure a happy existence to wounded or infirm military men, who found themselves without resources after having fought for their country. But the establishment was not really organized until the time of Napoleon I.

Originally intended to lodge 5,000 pensioners, this immense structure, occupying a superficial area of 120.985 sq metres, only now contains about 250, the old soldiers preferring to live independently with the pension allowed them.

Lodged, fed, warmed and clothed by the State, the invalid soldiers are taken the greatest care of. The food is good, wholesome and sufficiently abundant, their sleeping apartments are light and airy, and the most irreproachable cleanliness everywhere.

Remark, in the exterior court, 18 cannons, souvenirs of Napoleon's victories. now used to herald fêtes, etc.

At the side of these batteries are various pieces of different calibre, and to the right and left, small gardens, favourite walks of the old warriors.

In front, at the entrance of the Hotel, statue of the Prince Eugene.

There is something majestically imposing in the façade which developes on to the garden. It is 200 ft in length and is composed of three floors. A portico, surmounted by an equestrian statue of Louis XIV. and near which are two stone statues, marks the entrance to the Palace.

PALAIS DES BEAUX-ARTS, 14, rue Bonaparte. — Open free Sundays from 12 to 4. Other days it may be visited from 10 to 4. (Saturday from 10 to 3) under the conduct of a guardian, to whom a small gratuity (25 c.) should be given. Apply for a conductor to the concierge, to the right on entering the courtyard. Public Exhibition of the Grand Prix de Rome, every year, during the month of August.

In this school 14 professors teach the history of art and aesthetics, anatomy, perspective, mathematics, the natural sciences, practical architecture, and archæology. There are three class-rooms for painting, three for sculpture, three for architecture, one for plate-engraving, and one for engraving medals and precious stones, all superintended by eleven professors. Pupils are admitted between the ages of 15 and 25. An annual competition takes place for the *Grand prix de Rome*: the successful candidates, who need not be pupils of the school, but must be French subjects, and not older than 25, are sent to Rome and maintained there at the expense of the Government for four years (engravers for three). An exhibition of the works of the students here, as well as of those sent by the students at Rome, takes place every year in September.

The exhibition rooms are specially set apart for the works sent by the students at Rome, or the prize works executed by the pupils in Paris. The ceiling of the great hall is decorated with copies from the Vatican, by Sigalon and Boucoiran, of the twelve large frescoes severally representing the Persian, Cumean, Erythræan, Libyan, and Delphic Sibyls, and the prophets Daniel, Isaïah, Zachariah. Jonah, Johel, Ezekiel, and Jeremiah.

In the rue Bonaparte we find the principal entrance to the Palais des Beaux-Arts, which we will now describe.

There are two courts in front of the palace. The first is entered through a gateway adorned with busts of Poussin and Pujet. It is flanked by two buildings of Ionic design : the northern one contains the offices of the Director and two amphitheatres for students; the southern which masks part of the ancient buildings of the convent *des Petits Augustins*, displays in its intecolumnations the sculptured ornaments of a door, and other interesting fragments of the *Hotel de la Trémouille*, or *Maison de la Couronne d'Or*, a splendid specimen of the architecture of the 14th century. On the same wall there is a copy in mosaic of Raphael's picture of God blessing the World, executed by MM. Balze. There is also a monument to the memory of Henri Regnault, the distinguished artist killed at Buzenval during the siege of 1870-71. Adjoining the porter's lodge is the

Sixtine Chapel. — The front is formed of the portal of the *Château d'Anet*, built in 1548 for Diana of Poitiers, by Henry II. It is adorned with bas-reliefs and statues, the finest of which is a Cupid in the act of stringing his bow. Over the top arch runs this inscription :

> Bræsæo hæc statuit pergrata Diana marito
> Ut diuturna sui sint monumenta viri.

SOCIÉTÉ
INDUSTRIELLE ARTISTIQUE

SPÉCIALITÉ	SPECIALITY
d'Objets pour Cadeaux	**of Objects for Presents**

EXPOSITION	EXHIBITION
des Œuvres des plus grands Artistes	of Masterpieces by the greatest Artists in
(Bronzes, Marbres, Terres cuites, Étains, etc.)	Marble, Bronzes, Terra cotta pewter, etc.

ŒUVRES ORIGINALES	**ORIGINALS**
du Salon	from the great Exhibitions

DÉPOT DE PORCELAINES	OFFICIAL DEPOT
DE LA	OF THE
MANUFACTURE NATIONALE DE SÈVRES	**SÈVRES PORCELAIN MANUFACTORY**

Ernest Gouarne & Fils

184, Rue de Rivoli et 1, Rue de l'Échelle

PARIS

House celebrated for its Large and Varied Choice of Souvenirs of Paris at all prices

The Editor specially recommends this Society on account of the good taste and large choice of articles displayed, and as being one of the rare houses where the prices of all goods are plainly marked in known figures.

The interior consists of a single nave with an arched roof. The wainscoting at the entrance is the same that adorned the chateau d'Anet. At the end is a copy of Michael Angelo's Last Judgment, by Sigalon, on canvas, occupying the whole wall. In a chapel to the left, are casts of the Moses of Michael Angelo, two tombs, by the same, one of which is that of the Medici ; and also a fine cast of the bronze gates, by Ghiberti, of the Baptistery at Florence. The twelve pictures here are copies from Michael Angelo's frescoes in the Sixtine Chapel at Rome.

Returning to the court, the visitor will observe in the centre a Corinthian column of red marble, on the top of which is the figure of an angel in bronze one of several saved from a group, abstracted by the mob from the tomb of Cardinal Mazarin. Immediately behind it is the beautiful front of a château erected at Gaillon in 1500 by Cardinal d'Amboise, and transported hither by M. Lenoir. Its western surface is studded with brackets supporting antique statues, and medallions. The second court is flanked by two arched screens, the one to the left florid Saxon, with three arches ; the opposite one with four; the two central ones supported by a colossal pendant keystone, the whole in the style of the time of Francis I. Beyond this, in a garden, a fountain, surmounted by four figures, was sculptured by Paolo Poncio. Underneath is an escutcheon by Jean Goujon, and two seated figures by Germain Pilon. On the walls of the court, forming the curves, we perceive interesting specimens of old architectural and sculptural fragments. There is a curious monolith basin of the 13th century, brought from the Abbey of St. Denis, 12 feet in diameter, and ornamented with quaint heads of Ceres, Bacchus, Pan, Neptune, Avarice, and various of animals.

Interior. — In the spacious Corinthian vestibule are staircases right and left leading to the upper stories. Next is a rectangular court, where the visitor will see medallions with the portraits of Leo X. and Francis I., the restorers of the art ; and facing them, corresponding likenesses of Pericles and Augustus. Round the walls are engraved the names of famous artists of all countries. On the walls to the right and left are fragments of antique tombs, etc., also a curious bas-relief, représenting a sacrifice. On the opposite side is the entrance to what is properly the *Ecole des Beaux-Arts*. The galleries on the ground-floor contain casts and copies of architecture from the antique, Grecian, Roman, and of the Middle Ages. The amphitheatre for the distribution of prizes, etc., on the western side of the inner court, is semi-circular, and besides richly gilt compartments in the cupola, contains one of the finest productions of modern art, by Delaroche, representing groups of the most celebrated artists of every age and country, assembled and presided by Zeuxis, Phidias, and Appelles, for the purpose of awarding prizes to successful competitors. It contains seventy-five figures, of which seventy are those of artists. One of the female figures, arreyed in a green mantle, is the portrait of the gifted painter's wife. From the ample amphitheatre the visitor is conducted to *Salle Louis XIV*, containing the first part of a series of portraits of the most eminent members of the Academy, among whom are Vanloo, Servandoni, Lemoine, etc. A gallery filled with busts leads hence to the *Salle du Conseil*, where the series of portraits is continued. Passing through a corridor, painted with copies of arabesques from the Vatican, we enter the *Gallery of Prizes*. Here may be seen the prize-works of the most eminent artists, such as Fragonard, David, Ingres, Heim, Hesse, Pujol, etc. The collection begins with a painting by Natoire. of the year 1721. Open to the public on Sundays from 12 to 4, on other days from 12 to 4, but visitors must be accompanied by an attendant. Saturdays, to 2, on application at the porter's lodge. A fee is expected.

In the rue Visconti, not far from this palace No. 21, stands the house where Racine died in 1699, and Adrienne Lecouvreur in 1730.

PALAIS DU LUXEMBOURG (Luxembourg Palace). — This Palace is now occupied by the Senate and is only opened to the public during the vacation, from 9 or 10 to 4 or 5. Admission is free, but a small gratuity (25 c.) is usual to the guardian. Apply at the end of the court of Honour to the left, where there are always guardians on hand. During the session of the Senate, the Council Chamber may be visited with permission from the secrétaire de la questure, to whom a written application for a ticket should be addressed.

Historical. — This Palace, built for Marie de Médicis, in 1612, by Jacques Desbrosses, upon the model of the Pitti palace at Florence. It was then called by her name. On being bequeathed to Gaston de France, Duke of Orleans. her second son, it assumed the name of *Palais d'Orléans*. In 1795 the sittings of the Directory were held there, and it was then called *Palais du Directoire*. When Bonaparte came into power, it was at first devoted to the sittings of the consuls, and received the name of *Palais du Consulat*, and, shortly after, that of *Palais du Sénat Conservateur*. This senate held its sittings there till its dissolution in 1814, when the Chamber of Peers was created. In March and April 1848 Louis Blanc held his socialist meetings of workmen there. In the subsequent month of May, the Executive Commission occupied it during its ephemeral existence. In 1852 it resumed its old destination and name of *Palais du Sénat*, and has since been the hall of sittings of the senate, excepting from 1871 to 1879, when the seat of Government was at Versailles.

Exterior. — The court forms a parallelogram of 360 feet, by 300. The front towards the rue de Vaugirard consists of two large pavilions, connected together by terraces, in the centre of which rises a cupola, surrounded with statues. The clock pavilion is ornamented with allegorical figures, 8 feet high, of Eloquence, Justice, Wisdom, Prudence, War, and Peace, by Pradier.

Interior. — On entering the State apartments, we find, in the first room, called *Salle des Gardes*, several good statues of Greek and Roman Celebrities. Next follows the *Salle d'Attente*, where the ceiling, by Jadin, represents Aurora. The walls of the adjoining *Salon* are decorated with paintings representing : Charles IX. receiving the keys of Paris from de l'Hôpital, who refuses his consent to the massacre of St. Bartholomew, by Caminade; St. Louis, by Fiandrin; the Duke of Guise (Le Balafré) proposing the League to Harlay, by Vinchon; Louis XIII. and Richelieu, by Cabanel, and Charlemagne dictating the Capituleries, by Bouchot. The ceiling, by Decaisne, represents Union, Force, and Abundance; and, in a small medaillon, a portrait of the Duke de Reichstadt. Next follows the *Salle des Pas-Perdus*, formerly *Salle du Trône*, formed out of the old throne and Senate rooms, and the *Salle des Conférences*. This splendid saloon is gorgeously gilt and sculptured. A door to the right leads into the *Galerie des Bustes*, which runs parallel to the *Salle du Trône*, and is filled with busts of the great generals and statesmen of the first Empire.

PALAIS DE LA MONNAIE, Quai Conti. — The monetary Museum and the workshops can be visited every Tuesday and Friday, from 12 to 3. A special authorization from the Directeur Général des Monnaies is absolutely necessary, and when writing the application, a stamped, addressed envelope should always be enclosed for reply.

Entrance quai Conti. The sale rooms are to the left on entering and the Museum on the first-floor, to the right. (See Mint and Monetary Museum).

PALAIS DE L'ELYSEE, (Elysée Palace). — Faubourg Saint-Honoré and avenue Gabriel and Champs-Élysées.

Since this palace has become the official residence of the President of the Republic, visitors are no longer admitted.

The Elysée, built in 1718 for the comte d'Evreux, was bought by Louis XV. for Madame de Pompadour, after which it became the residence of extraordinary ambassadors.

Inhabited, in turn, by Louis XV, Madame de Pompadour, Napoleon I, the Duke of Wellington, Murat, and the Duchess de Berri, this Palace has witnessed two most stirring events in the History of France, viz. The abdication of Napoleon, after the battle of Waterloo, and the coup d'Etat of 2nd December 1851.

It was the official residence of Napoleon III, while President of the French Republic. During the Great Exhibition of 1867 it was tenanted by the Sultan, by the Emperors of Austria and Russia, and by other princes. The *Cour d'Honneur*, leads to the entrance of the palace, adorned with a portico of four Doric columns. A broad flight of steps, overspread by a verandah, gives access to a vestibule opening into the suite of apartments on the ground floor, commencing with a dining-room. The walls of this apartment are painted by Dunouy with landscapes, some of the figures of which are by Vernet, and were executed for Murat. The views represented are : the Pyramids of Egypt, the passing of the Tiber, the Château de Benrath, on the Rhine, near Dusseldorf, once occupied by Murat (the carriage in the foreground contains Murat's children), and a view of the château de Neuilly at that time also Murat's property; is said to be a good portrait of Mme. Murat, the sister of Napoleon. This room gives access to a *Ball-room* of recent erection, in the new wing of the palace, towards the avenue de Marigny. Returning to the Dining-room, a door to the left leads to the State-apartments. The *Salle de Réception* was used by Napoleon I. as a council-chamber. This room is now adorned with portraits of the Pope, Victor Emmanuel, the Queens of England and Spain, the Emperor of Austria, etc. There is also a beautiful mosaic representing the map of France in 1684. Adjoining is the *Chambre de Napoléon I.* This was his favourite bed-room, where he last slept in Paris after the battle of Waterloo. Next comes the *Salle des Souverains*, formerly the *Salon de Travail*, where Napoleon I. signed his last abdication. Here Her Majesty Queen Victoria partook of a splendid collation on the 20th Aug. 1855. It is furnished in Louis XV. style with Beauvais tapestry.

Now completely restored it is one of the richest and most graceful monuments of Paris; extending from the rue du Faubourg Saint-Honoré to the avenue Gabrielle, it forms, with the enormous garden and hot-houses, a complete parallelogram isolated on all sides.

PALAIS DE JUSTICE, Boulevard du Palais. — Open every day, excepting Sundays and holidays.

Note. — To visit the Conciergerie and the « cuisines de Saint-Louis », application must be made, either personnally or by letter, at the Préfecture de Police, bureau n° 3. The cell of Marie Antoinette is to be seen, transformed into an expiatory chapel.

The Palace of Justice is the ancient Residence of the Kings of France. Reconstructed at the side of the place Dauphine, it is composed of four buildings, the whole forming one block.

The Palais Royal is formed of two distinct parts, the Palace proper (at present occupied by the Conseil d'Etat, to which the public are not admitted) with its facade in the square, and the garden, surrounded by galleries, behind. Erected by Cardinal Richelieu in 1629 it was named the Palais Cardinal. Occupied after his death by Anne of Austria, widow of Louis XIII. with her two sons Louis XIV. and Philip of Orleans, the building has since been called the Palais Royal. The South wing was set on fire and destroyed by the communists in May 1871, but it has now been completely restored. (For fuller description see page 43).

These buildings are : The Palais de Justice proper, — the Tour de l'Horloge (Clock Tower), — the Conciergerie, remarkable on account of its three turrets, giving on the quays; — the Prefecture of Police, situated on the quai des Orfèvres; and the Sainte-Chapelle, enclosed by the Palais. Partly burnt during the Commune, the Palais de Justice has since been completely restored, and counts amongst the most beautiful of the Parisian edifices.

A magnificent façade, with gilded railings facing the large clock of the Palace, indicates the principal entrance.

Remark, at the angle of the guay, facing the Tribunal of Commerce, a tower with clock, blue framed, restored in 1852 and 1882. It was from this tower tolled the famous silver bell which, in company with that of Saint-Germain-l'Auxerrois, gave the signal for the perfidious massacre of Saint-Bartholemew's Day 1572.

PALAIS DU CORPS LÉGISLATIF (or Chambre des Députés), Quai d'Orsay,
facing the place de la Concorde.

This palace, occupied by the parliament, may be seen, during the sittings, with tickets to be obtained by a written application to the secrétaire de la questure de la Chambre. (Entrance from the quai, to the right of the grand staircase). — During the vacation the Chamber may be visited in company of a quardian (gratuity).

The palace, formerly the Bourbon Palace, which dates from 1722, has two façades, one fronting the quai and the other, place du Palais-Bourbon.

The principal façade, facing the quay, is preceded by a large flight of steps, measuring 34 meters in width. There are 12 Corinthian colums, supporting a front on which France is represented, holding the constitution in her hand, surrounded by Liberty, Peace, War, the Fine Arts, Eloquence, Industry and Commerce. The flight of steps is decorated with colossal statues representing Justice and Prudence and the scated figures of d'Aguesseau, Colbert, l'Hospital and Sully.

The façade of the place du Palais-Bourbon is preceded by a marble statue representing Law. (FEUCUÈRES, 1855).

The edifice at the side of the Palace is the residence of the President of the Chambre des Députés.

PALAIS DE L'INSTITUT, 21, quai Conti, facing the Pont des Arts. Open daily, excepting Sundays, from 11 to 1. Apply to the concierge. The Palais de l'Institut occupied the site of the ancient Tour de Nesle. It is surmonted by a fine cupola, and ends in two pavillions resting on arcades. The Mazarine Library contains 300,000 printed volumes, and about six thousand manuscripts. The library is open daily, excepting Sundays, from 11 to 4 or 5. Well worth a visit. The visitor will be shewn the ink-stand used by the great Prince de Condé; also busts of Cardinal Mazarin and of Racine. The Institute, which was created by Buonaparte, when first consul, is divided into five sections or academies :

The Academie française ;

The Academie des Inscriptions et des Belles Lettres ;

The Academie des Sciences ;

The Academie des Beaux Arts ;

The Academie des Sciences Morales et Politiques.

Every year, on the 25th October, the whole of the 5 Academies unite in a solemn meeting. Permission to be present at the receptions and annual meeting of the French Academy may be obtained on application for special tickets to the chef du secrétariat de l'Institut.

PALAIS DE L'INDUSTRIE, Carré Marigny, Champs-Elysées. — Open during the
annual and other exhibitions.

The Palais de l'Industerie was erected for the universal exhibition of 1855 by a limited liability company. After the exhibition it was acquired by the State. It is 250 metres long and 110 metres in width, covering a superficial area of 32,000 metres.

The principal entrance, facing the splendid avenue des Champs-Elysées, is surmonted by a colossal statue representing France distributing golden crowns to Industry and Art, who are seated at her feet.

The building possesses a magnificent stained-glass window at the extremity of the grand nave, representing France inviting all the nations of the earth to the universal exhibition.

The annual exhibition of paintings and sculpture, known as the Salon, is held in this palace every year from the 1st of May to the 20th June. Entrance fee : week days : 2 francs in the morning and 1 franc during the afternoon (Fridays afternoons 5 francs); Sundays : 1 franc in the morning afternoons 50 c.

This year (1896) is probably the last one which will see the celebrated Salon held in this building, as the demolition of the Palais de l'Industerie has been decided upon, to make room for some of the buildings of the great exhibition to be held in Paris in 1900.

PALAIS DE L'HOTEL DE VILLE, Rue de Rivoli. — Certain parts of this palace are open to the public on Tuesdays, Thursdays and Saturdays. Tickets obtained at the Hotel de Ville, bureau de la Direction des travaux, first floor, cour du Nord.

Note. — Visitors should present themselves at 2 or 2.30 precisely at the Salle des Prévots, cour du Nord, where a *guardian* is in attendance, who will show the rooms and give explanations.

In 1357 the municipality purchased for 2,880 livres de Paris, the *Maison de la Grève*, or *Maison aux Piliers*, which had formerly belonged to Philip Augustus, and was frequently the abode of royalty. Upon the site of this, the original Hôtel de Ville was erected. It was a monument the interior of which vied in splendour with the Tuileries. Princely festivals were given here to Queen Victoria in 1855, and to various other crowned heads at different periods. The Hôtel de Ville was burnt down by the Commune on the 24th of May, 1871, together with its valuable library of 65,007 volumes. It was quickly decided, however, that the building should be reconstructed, while utilising as far as was possible those portions of the original edifice that were not destroyed by fire. It was considered especially desirable to retain the façade by Godde and Lesueur, fronting the Place Lobau; but this portion of the scheme was abandoned, and it was eventually decided to pull down the whole of the ruins and to build on the site an Hôtel de Ville identical in all important features with the former edifice. Designs were advertised for in July, 1872, and those of MM. Ballu and de Perthes were accepted. Subsequently the architects were requested to introduce certain alterations into their plan, so as to allow of greater internal accomodation than that which existed in the old building. The cost of the work was set down at 25,500,000 francs. Although still incomplete, especially as regards the interior fittings, the new Hôtel de Ville was publicly opened with great ceremony on the occasion of the National Fête, July 14, 1882. It contains 368 rooms. One of the most noticeable features of the façade is the clock and its ornamentation. The design has been copied from that of the original. The two winged figures supporting the upper part of the dial are by M. Charles Garnier, architect of the Opera House. The seated figure immediately below, representing the city, is by M. Gautherin, and the two recumbent figures on either side of the clock are by M. Aimé Millet. The building is at present used for municipal purposes.

PALAIS DE LA LEGION D'HONNEUR, Quai d'Orsay. — Under the Commune of 1871, the Palace of the Legion of Honour was burnt down, in company with many other beautiful monuments of Paris. The present building was erected by subscription among the members of the Order, and is an exact reproduction of the old Palace.

PALAIS DU TROCADERO. — The Trocadéro Palace, erected for the Exhibition of 1878, is the work of the two clever architects Davioud and Bourdais. The building is constructed on an eminence, and is a mixture of all styles of architecture. It is composed of a central edifice, built in the form of a rotunda with colonnade, surmounted by a statue of Fame, by Mercié, and two semicircular galleries joined to the principal building by two pavillions with towers. The central part contains the grand « Salle des Fêtes », used at present as a concert hall. It contains a colossal organ, and is decorated with splendid paintings by Lemeire. The stage accommodates 400 musicians, and the auditorium 5,000 persons. Open Tuesdays, Thurdays and Saturdays from 12 till 5, excepting on concert rehearsal days.

Admission by ticket furnished by the secrétariat du Ministère des Beaux Arts or by the Administrator of the Palace. A lift conveys visitors to the summit of one of the towers, from whence a good view may be had.

The two gal'eries or wings of the Palace, contain the Musée de Sculpture comparée, and the Musée Ethnographique. The garden on the south of the Palace contains many rare shrubs and plants, and, being well protected against cold winds, is a charming place of resort.

In the Trocadéro Gardens, on a site just below the right wing of the Palace, we find the *Institut Populaire du Progrès*, a newly opened establishment for popular scientific instruction. Lectures are delivered here on physics, astronomy, chemistry, etc., the premises being fitted with all the appliances necessary to these studies.

A large *Aquarium* has been established under the garden, its entrance being in the main avenue parallel to the Seine. It is a circular grotto of about 500 feet in circumference, adorned with all kinds of ferns.

The elegant new building at the top of the hill to the right, is the *Dépôt des Phares*, or storehouse for all the lighthouses of the State. It contains a museum of all the inventions made in this line, and an immense mural map of all the lighthouses of France.

MUSEUMS

LOUVRE MUSEUM

The Museums of Paris, containing a world of marvels, have each a special catalogue which changes frequently, and of which it is impossible to give full details in a volume of this size. We refer you, therefore, for complete details to the official catalogues.

The richest collection of paintings and marvels in the world. Open to the public every day (excepting Monday) during the summer from 9 to 5; winter, Sundays and holidays from 10 to 4.

Ground Floor (rez-de-chaussée). — Sculpture, antique, modern, middle ages and renaissance styles. Egyptian and assyrian museums.

First Floor. — Paintings, Campana Museum, Greek, Etruscan, Egyptian, Babylonian and Chaldean antiquities. The Lenoir, Davillier, and Dieulafoy collections. Middle ages and renaissance Museums. Thiers collection, etc.

Second Floor. — Marine, Ethnographic and Chinese Museums. A supplementary room of paintings.

Note. — The Louvre Museum being a veritable labyrinth, I would advise strangers to follow ont my itinerary to the letter, which will permit them to see the Louvre in a single day.

The Louvre Museum has three entrances; 1st Pavillon Denon (the new Louvre) ; 2nd. Pavillon Sully (the Cour d'Honneur) entered by the escalier Henri II ; 3rd. Colonnade du Louvre (rue du Louvre).

This itinerary being traced from the Pavillon Sully, I advise visitors to start from that point.

Note. — Every object in the Louvre is distinctly labelled. Visit to the galleries of the 1st floor. Itinerary. Having arrived under the clock of the Pavillon Sully, enter the Louvre and leaving the Museum of antiquities to the left ascend the staircase Henri II, leading to the 1st floor : Museum of Paintings. There you will enter, by a green door, the « Musée La Caze ».

Musée La Caze. — This museum contains a rich and beautiful collection of 275 paintings of different schools, generously given by M. Louis La Caze on condition that the collection should not be dispersed. His portrait (n° 275) is to the right on entering. Also on the right are :

991 Jupiter and Antiope, by *Watteau*; 376, Head of a young Girl, by *Greuze* ; 448, Portrait of Président Laage, by *Largillière* ; 1311, Death of Seneca, *Giordano*; 2120, 2121 and 2127, Rubens ; 1945, The Provost of the Guilds and the Sheriffs of Paris, *Philippe de Champaigne ;* 2550, Woman bathing, *Rembrandt :* 292, The Happy Hour, *J. T. Tragonard,* 2174, Village festival. *Teniers le Jeune;* 2513, Pig-Stye, *Van Ostade ;* 983, Clowns, *Watteau ;* 2385, Portrait, *F. Hals ;* 1925, Falavera Bridge, *Breughel ;* 103; The Card house, *Chardin;* 2009, Landscape, *Huysmans;* 491, Portraits of Largillière, wife and daughter, *Largillière;* 491 Gascon punished (Lafontaine's fables) *Lancret ;* 2177, Smoking-room, *Teniers ;* 2170, Kermesse, *Teniers ;* 659, Portrait of Mlle de Lambesc; and Count de Brionne, *Nattier;* 1468, Suzannah bathing, *Tintoretto ;* 293, Fair bathers, *Fragonard,* 2515 Winter landscape, *Van Ostade ;* 1980, St-Joseph, *Van Dyck.*

Returning by the left:

2393, Home, *Heemsherk ;* 2579, Family at Dinner, *Stenn :* 2502-2503 The Drinker-The Reader, Van Ostade, 1725, Man with club-foot, *Ribera ;* 1946, Portrait, *Ph. de Champaigne;* 2549 Woman bathing, *Rembrandt ;* 2406, The White Turkey, *Hondecœter;* 2504-2505, Reading the Newspaper, *Van Ostade;* 769, The Three Graces, *Regnault ;* 692, Conversation in a Park, *Pater;* 1735, The Infanta, Maria Theresa (afterwards Queen of France), *Velasquez;* 2109, Marie de Medecis as Gallia, *Rubens;* 2551, A man, *Rembrandt;* 987, The Conjurer, *Watteau,* 987, Triumph of Flora, *Callet ;* 986, Gay company in a Park, *Watteau ;* 2132, Young woman playing the Mandoline, *School of Rubens ;* 1469, Madonna and Child, with Saints, *Tintoretto,* 46 Venus in the Forge of Vulcan, *Boucher;* 2384, Gipsy Girl, *Hals ;* 791, Cardinal de Polignac *Rigaud ;* 2435, Landscape, *K. Dujardin ;* 1916, The Smoker, *Brawer;* 2707, A Woman, *Denner.*

Through the door to the left is the Salle Henri II, where are exhibited the French painters of the 19th century.

Beginning on the right :

406, Human Comedy, *Hamon ;* 955, Deer-Stalking, Charles Xth's time, *Vernet;* 206, Bulldog and Terrier, *Descamps ;* 771, Execution without trial under the Moorish Kings of Graenda, *Regnault;* Suzannah the chaste, *Chassériau ;* 145, Spring, *Daubigny ;* 143, Burial in Ornans. *Courbet;* 420, Joan of Arc at the coronation of Charles VII, Ingres ; 833, Flowers, *Saint-Jean ;* 361, Sleep of Endymion, *Geraudet-Trioson ;* 120, The Tepidarium, *Chassériau ;* 125, Sunshine and Rain, *Chantreuil ;* 359, The Slave-Merchant, *Girand.*

The ceiling, by *Blondel;* represents the quarrel between Neptune and Minerva.

This Hall communicates with the

Salle de sept cheminées; which contains the masterpieces of the Modern French School.

To the right: 396, Pyrrhus taking Andromacha and Astyana under his protection, *Guérin;* 393, The return of Marcus Sextus, *Guérin;* 322. Isabey, by *Gérard;* 388, Bonaparte visiting the plague-stricken at Jaffa, *Gros;* 756, The abduction of Psyché, *Prud'hon;* Aiaia at the tomb, *Girodet-Frioson;* 328, Psyché receiving the first kiss from Eros, *Gérard;* 395, Phedrus and Hyppolitus, *Guérin.*

At the bottom of the Hall: 526, Mme Molét-Raymond, *Mme Lebrun;* 343, Carbinier, *Géricault;* 248, Epsom Races, *Géricault;* 202, David, by himself; 202 *bis,* Coronation of Napoléon I, *David;* 198, Pius VII, *David;* 381, Bonaparte at Arcole, *Gros;* 622, Mme Lebrun and her daughter, *Mme Lebrun;* 746, Assumption of the Virgin, *Prud'hon.*

To the left: 396, Clytemnestra and Aegystheus preparing to strike Agamemnon, *Guérin;* 338, The raft of the « Medusa », *Géricault;* 747, Justice and Divine vengeance pursuing Crime, *Prud'hon;* 75, Empress Joséphine, *Prud'hon;* 360, The Deluge, *Giraudet-Frioson;* 341-342 Wounded Cuirassier, *Géricault;* 188, The Sabine women interposing between the Romans and the Sabines, *David;* 339, Charge of a Cavalry Officer, *Géricault;* 187, Leonidas at the Thermopyles, *David.*

We next enter « *Salle de Bijoux* » by a door opening on the right of painting n° 188.

The Salle de Bijoux contains a precious collection of jewels discovered in excavations. The ceiling represents *Time* pointing out the Ruins he causes and the treasures he brings to light.

To the right: in the case near the window; Antique bracelets and fibulae in gold and bronze.

To the left: first case; silver vases from the treasury of Notre-Dame d'Alençon. Second case: gold rings with engraved seals, gold necklaces and ear-rings. 4th case. Gold and bronze rings and cameos. Wall centre case: Silver objects, a *Ceres* with movable arms; antique marks from N.-D. D'Alençon, Greek and Roman Rings and Etruscan ear-rings. Centre of the Hall: Case containing a magnificent Greco-Etruscan Diadem of almost inimitable execution, Iron Helmet, gilded and enamelled, of the Roman epoch, found at Amfreville (Eure), an Etruscan helmet with golden crown and wings, golden quivers, necklaces, etc., etc.

From this hall you cross a vestibule with beautiful modern mosaic and large white marble vase, copy of an antique in the Vatican. Ceiling: The Sun and the four elements.

Turn to the right and enter the Gallery of Apollo by the superb wrought-iron gate.

Gallery of Appollo. — This Gallery is one of the marvels of the Louvre. It is the work of the celebrated painter *Lebrun* (17th century), restored by *Duban.*

The paintings on the upper part of the cupola represent: Apollo vanquishing the serpent Pytho (Delacroix) Night and Evening (Lebrun), the morning star (Renon) Aurora (Muller). On the sides are the four seasons and the months of the year. On the vaulting above the entrance is the triumph of Sybele, the goddess of the earth (Guichard after Lebrun), The painting opposite of The Triumph of the Waters is by Lebrun himself. Remark portraits of celebrities in Gobelin tapestries.

In the centre are four magnificent tables of cases which explain themselves.

At bottom of Saloon is table-map of France in mosaic 1684. to right of this table; case containing armour, helmet and buckler of Charles IX and the casque of Anne of Austria; to the left, a case containing an arm of St-Louis of Toulouse and a statuette of the Virgin holding the infant Jesus.

In the centre of this Room are what remain of the Crown Diamonds. The case contains the Regent diamond (estimated value: 12 millions of francs); the petit Mazarin diamond, Napoleon's sword, the crown of Charlemagne, crown of Louis XV, Marie-Antoinette's Brooch. Ruby animal having belonged to Anne de Bretagne, very valuable, watch ornamented with diamonds presented to Louis XIV by the Dey of Algiers. etc., etc.

This case descends into a safe under the floor every night.

Leaving this Saloon we enter the Salon Carré, situated at the bottom, to the right. This room contains master pieces of painters of all schools.

Making the tour of the room by the right: 1564, Virgin and child with St-Rosa, St-Catherine and angels (Perugino); 1198, Jupiter hurling thunder-bolts at criminals (This painting decorated the ceiling of the Assembly Hall of the Council of Ten in the Doge's Palace, at Venice) *Paolo Veronese;* 1584, Entombment, *Titian;* 1706, St-Basil's Discourse, *Herrera;* 1118, Antiope and Jupiter, *Correggio;* 1454, Dejanira and the centaur Nessus, *Guido;* 2496, The Schoolmaster, *Van Ostade.*

Above the door giving access to the Salle Duchatel: 723, St-Francis-Xaxier restoring the daughter of a Japanese to life, *Poussin.*

Passing the door of the Salle Duchatel:

2547, A Woman, *Rembrandt;* 2587, The gallant soldier, *Terbourg;* 2459, Officer receiving young lady, *Metsu;* 1352, The Visitation, *del Piombo* 2348, The Dropsical woman, *Gérard Dow;*

This enormous monument surpasses everything
of the kind hitherto erected. Powerful lifts are
available to all three platforms, from whence
magnificent views may be obtained of Paris
and its environs. On the first platform is a
theatre and cafés with room for hundreds of
visitors. The height of the second platform is

ЕЙФЕЛЕВСКАЯ БАШНЯ

THE

EIFFEL

TOWER

376 feet, (the height of Strasburg cathedral
Spire) and the third platform is 863 feet
high; the total height of the tower being
985 feet. It is open to the public from the
1 st. of April to the end of October. Built by
the celebrated engineer M. Eiffel for the great
Exhibition of 1889, it has justly become a
favored resort of both visitors and Parisians.

1184, A Sculptor, *Bronzine*; 1709 The immaculate conception ; bought by the state for 615,300 francs, *Murillo* ; 1193, The feast of Simon the Pharisee, *Paolo Veronese* ; 1590, Alphonso de Ferrara and Laura of Dianti ; 1497, The Virgin with the Crown, *Raphael* ; 1321, Visitation, *Ghirlanjo* ; 1601, Golconda, *Léonardo da Vinci* ; 1067, Charles I, *Van Dyck* ; 1530, The Virgin with the Green Cushion, *Solario* ; 1219, The Virgin appearing to St-Luke and St-Catherine, *Carracci* ; 1503, St-George and the Dragon, *Raphael* : 1498, The famous picture The Holy Family, by *Raphael* ; 1221, The dead Christ on the knees of the Virgin, *Carracci* ; 1502, St.-Michael, *Raphael* ; 1496, The Beautiful Gardener, *Raphael* ; 1932, Christ dead, *Philippe de Champaigne* ; 437, Descent from the Cross, *Gouvenel* ; 1986, The Virgin, *Van Eyck*.

Above the door, communicating with the grand galerie : 737, Portrait of Bossuet, *Rigaud* ; 3013, Infancy of Jupiter, *Jordaens*.

After the door of the grand gallery : 3074 and 3075 (in the same frame) St John and the Magdalen, *Hans Memling* ; 2715, Erasmus of Rotterdam, *Hollein the younger* ; 1598, The Virgin, Child, and Saint Anne, *Leonarda da Vinci* ; 1134, The Coudottieri, *Ant. da Messina* ; 1143. The Protectors of Modena, *Barbieri* ; 777, St. Paul's Vision. *Poussin* ; 1197, The Marriage feast of Cana (the largest picture in the Louvre, 36 feet by 71), *Paolo Veronese* ; 1117, Marriage of St. Catherine, *Correggio* ; 1136, Village Concert, *Giorgione* ; 1713, Holy Family, *Murillo* ; 1464, Susannah at the bath, *Tintoretto* ; 2105, The Virgin and Child, *Van der Weyden* ; 1383, Jesus on the way to Calvary (attributed to *Simone di Martino* ; 1504, St. Michael overcoming the Demon, *Raphael* ; 1139, Raising of Lazarus, *Barbieri* ; 1435, The Nativity, *Francia* ; 2027, Marriage of St. Catherine, *Memling* ; 2718, Anne of Cleves, *Holbein the Younger*. You will now leave this Hall and enter the

Salle Duchatel, containing pictures given by Mme. Duchatel. Commencing on the right side corner of the Gallery : 2480 and 2481, Portraits by *A. Mor*. Then come the portraits by *Luini*, of which we will speak farther on.

In the opposite corner : 422, The Spring, *Ingres* ; 421 (near the entrance) Œdifus solving the riddle of the Sphinx, *Ingres* ; 2026, Virgin and Child, *Memling*.

Frescoes by *Luini* : in the centre of the right side of the gallery : 1359, The Nativity ; 1361, Christ giving His-Benediction ; 1360, Adoration of the Magi ; 1357 and 1358, Children in an arbor ; 1364, Christ surrounded by the instruments of the Passion ; 1363, The Annunciation ; and 1365, Curius Dentalus refusing the presence of the Sammites.

The Salle Duchatel communicates with the sale-room of the photographs of the Louvre, inaugurated in 1885 where reproductions of any of the pictures may be obtained.

From this gallery we return to the Grande Gallery via the Salle Duchatel by a door under the two pictures : 783, the portrait of Bossuet, and 2013 Gordaens.

Note. — Be careful to follow the Grand Gallery without staying to examine the Salle de Sept Mètres and the old Salle des Etats, which you should visit last of all.

Grande Galerie. — This great gallery, which some day will connect the Louvre with the Pavillon de Flore, is subdivided into eight galleries, and contains the masterpieces of the Italian, Spanish, German, Flemish and Dutch schools.

First Gallery : Italian School.

On the right. after the door of the Salle des Sept Metres : 1114, Madonna with Child, *Albertinelli* ; 1334, The coronation of the Virgin, *Ghirlandajo* ; 1553, The slumber of the infant Jesus, *Garofalo* ; 1513, Madonna of Loretto, after *Raphael*, the original being lost ; 1603, The Lords supper, after *Leonardo di Vinci* ; 1350, St. Jerome in the wilderness, *L. Lotto* ; 1586, The Council of thirty, *Titian* ; 1514, Charity, *Andreas del Sarto* ; 1242, Visitation, *Carrachi* ; 1399, Annunciation to the Shepherds, *Palme le Vieux* ; 1465, Paradise, *Tintoretto* ; 1580, The Holy Family, *Tittian* ; 1607, Bacchus, *Leonardo da Vinci* ; 1506, Joan d'Aragon, *Romain* (head attributed to Raphael) ; 1190, Holy Family, *Paul Veronese* ; 1197, St. Mark and the three Cardinal Virtues, (ceiling-painting from the Doge's Palace at Venice), *Paul Veronese* ; 1597, John the Baptist, *Leonardo da Vinci* ; 1501, St; Margaret, *Raphael* ; 1179, Portrait of a young mother, *Veronese* ; 1191, Holy Family, *Veronese* ; 1588. Francis I, *Tittian* ; 1170, Resurrection of Lazarus, *Bonifacio* ; 1500, John the Baptist in the wilderness, *Raphael* ; 1183, Christ and Mary Magdalene, *Bronzino* ; 1575, Annunciation, *Vasari* ; 1594, A. Man, *Tittian* ; 1195, Calvary, *Veronese* ; 1188, Susannah bathing, *Veronese* ; 1577, Madonna and Child with Saints, *Tittian*, 1438, Circumcision of Christ, *Bagnacavallo* ; 1440, ditto, *Barocci*.

Left wall, beginning again from the entrance ; 1318. Madonna, Child, John the Baptist and Angels, *Girolamo Dai Libri* ; 1433, Concert, *Primatici* ; 1171, Holy Family, *Bonifacio* ; 1508, 2 male portraits known as Raphael and his fencing master, *Raphael* ; 1604, Madonna with the scales, school of da Vinci ; 1593, the Gloved Man, *Tittian* ; 1135, Holy Family, *Giorgione* ; 1587, Jupiter and Antiope, known as « Venus del Ppardo, *Tittian* ; 1591. A. Man, *Tittian* ; 1154, Madonna enthroned, with Saints, *Fra Bratolommeo* ; 1351, Holy Family, *Lotto* ; 1581, Christ and the Disciples at Emmaus, *Tittian* ; 1418, Nativity of Christ, *Romain* ; Holy Family, known as « Vierge aux Rochers », *da Vinci* ; 1172, Holy Family, *Bonifacio* ; 1196, Christ and the Disciples at Emmaus, *Veronese* ; 1583, Christ crowned with thorns, *Tittian* ; 1505, Balthasar Castiglione, *Raphael* ; 1153, Annunciation, *Fra*

Bartolomeo; 1506, A young man, *Raphael*; 1194, Christ falling under the Cross, *Veronese*; 1578, Virgin with the rabbit, *Tittian*; 1600, A. wom an called « La Belle Feronese », *da Vinci*; 1589, Alph. d'Avalos and his wife, *Tittian*; 1125, Holy Family, *Andreasi*; 1150, Coronation of the Virgin, *Barocci*.

Second Gallery : Italian and Spanish Schools

On the right : 1230, Diana discovering the pregnancy of Calisto, *Carrache*; 1165, Romulus and Remus, *de Cortone*; 1164. Madonna and Christ with St. Martina, *de Cortone*; 1228, St. Sebastian, *Carrache*; 1111, Diana and Actœon, *Albani*; 1450, St. Sebastian. *Guido Reni*; 1419, Mary Magdalen, *Guido Reni*: 1227, Martyrdom of St. Christopher, *Carrache*; 1490. Assumption, *Sassoferrato*; 1456, Abduction of Helen, *Guido Reni* ; 1460, Polyxenes Sacrificed, *Ricci* ; 1110, Venus and Adonis. *Albani*, 1408, Interior of St. Peter's at Rome, *Fanini*; 1495, Annunciation, *Sassoferrato* ; 1716, Miracle of St.-Diago, *Murillo*; 1708, Immaculate Conception, *Murillo*; 1714, Christ in the Garden of Olives (painted on marble), *Murillo*; 1721, Worship of the Shepherds, *Ribera*.

Left wall, beginning from the entrance : 1133, Madonna with St. Stephen and John the Baptist, *Anselmo*; 1217, Virgin and the cherries, *Carrache*; 1445, Peter receiving the keys of Heaven, *Guido Reni*; 1161, Nativity of the Virgin, *de Cortone*; 1121, Death of the Virgin, *Caravage*; 1379, A Woman, *Maratta*; 1233, The Hunt, *Carrache*; 1440, Annunciation, *Reni*; 1447, Ecce Homo, *Reni*; 1448, Mary Magdalen, *Reni*; 1616, Triumph of Eros; *Dominichino*; 1203, Venice, *Canaletto* : 1613, St. Cecilia, *Dominichino*; 1479, A Battle, *Salvator Rosa*; 1283, Melancholia, *Feto*; 1547, Lord's Supper, *Tiepolo*; 1127. Little Drummer, *Angeli*: 1727, Philip IV of Spain, *Velasquez*; 1710, Nativity of the Virgin, *Murillo*, 1723, St. Paul the Hermit, *Ribera*; 1705, Spanish Girl, *Goya*; 1717, The Young Mendicant, *Murillo*; 1734, 13 portraits, by *Velasquez*; 1334, Coronation of the Doge at Venice. *Guardi*; 1722, Christ in the tomb, *Ribera* ; 1717, Madonna with Rosary, *Murillo*: 1704, Guille-Mardet, French Ambassador at Madrid in 1798, *Goya*.

Third Gallery : 16th. Century French School.

On the right : 1013, Diana, *Fontainebleau School*; 155, Last Judgment, *J. Cousin*, 1035, Ball at the Court of Henry III, 1032. Henry III.

On the left : 998, Christ taken from the Cross, 15th century French School; Two portraits of Francis I; 995, Martyrdom of St. Denis; 15th century; 365, The Nativity, *Gourmont*.

Fourth Gallery : German, Flemish and Dutch Schools.

On the left : 20-30, Christ imparting a Blessing, *Quinten Matsys*; 1957, Marriage feast of Cana, Flemish School, 14th century; 20-28, Ressurection and Ascension of St. Sebastian, *Memling School*; 27-37, Descent from the Cross. Cologne School; 27-13, Nicolas Kratzer, Astronomer to Henry VIII, *Holbein the Younger*; 2714, William Warham, Archbishop of Canterbury, *Holbein Junior*; 2732, Death of Adonis, *Rottenhammer*; 1961. Madonna and Child with St. Magdalen, David and John the Baptist, *Van Dych*. 2107, Jane of Austria, *Rubens* ; 2111, Henry de Vicq, Dutch Ambassador, *Van Dych*: 2554, Portrait of Rembrandt by *himself*.

We now proceed to examine the series of large paintings by Rubens of the history of Marie de Medicis.

Gallery to the left : 2085, The three fates spin the fortunes for Marie Medicis ; 2086. Birth of Princess Marie, 2087, Her education conducted by Minerva, Apollo, Mercury, and the three graces; 2088, Cupid shows the Princess the portrait of Henry IV, above are Jupiter and Juno, beside the King appears Gallia ; 2089, The Nuptials; 2090, The Queen lands at Marseilles; 2091, Wedding Festivities at Lyons; 2092, Birth of Louis XIII. : 2093, Henry IV. starting on his campaign against Germany; 2094, Coronation of the Queen at St. Denis by Cardinal le Joyeuse ; 2075, Aposthcosis of Henry IV.; 2096, Regency of the Queen under the protection of Olympus.

Gallery on the right : 2097, The Queen's journey to Ponts-de-Cé; 2098, Treaty between France and Spain ; 2099, Prosperity during the Regency : 2100, Majority of Louis XIII ; 2101, Flight of the Queen ; 2102, Reconciliation of the Queen with Louis XIII ; 2103, The Queen conducted to the Temple of Peace ; 2104, Marie de Médicis and Louis XIII, in the Olympus; 2105, Triumph of Truth.

Further paintings to be noted on the same side : 2108, Marie de Medicis, *Rubens*; 1637, Louis XIII, crowned by Victory, *de Champaigne* ; 2072, Marie de Médicis, *Porbus Junior*; 2305, Amsterdam Harbour, *Bakhuisen* ; 2011, Jesus chasing the merchants from the Temple; 1941. A Child. *Champaigne*; 2340, Craesbeke painting a portrait by himself; 2144, Hunting the wild boar, *Snyder*; 1975, Duke of Richmond, *Van Dyke*; 2433, Landscape, *Dujardin*; 2106, François de Médicis, *Rubens*; Thomas Moore, Chancellor of Great Britain, *Holbein junior*; 2703, Landscape with Venus, *Cranach*; 2196, Descent from the Cross, *Van der Weyden*; 2616, A Man, *Holbein junior*; 2029, The Banker and his wife, *Matsys* ; 2739, The adoration of the Magi, German School, 16th century; 2479, The dwarf of Charles V, *Moor*; 1998, Madonna with Child, *Nabuse*; 2202, Annunciation, Flemish School, 16th century.

Fifth Gallery

Table of *Beham* ; — painting of subject from the Holy Scripture : Entrance of Saul into Jerusalem, after the defeat of the Philistines; David and Bethsabe; Siege of Rabbath; the prophet Nathan before David.

Sixth Gallery : Flemish and Dutch Schools.

On the right :

2527, The prairie. *Potter*; 2548, Interior of a butchery, *Rembrandt*; 2159, Kermesse, *Teniers*; 2142, Entrance of the animals into the ark, *Snyders*; 2544, An old Man, *Rembrandt*; 2548, The Music lesson, *Terburg*; 2553, Portrait of Rembrandt, by himself; 1934, Two nuns *Champaigne*; 2314, Landscape, *Berghem*; 1954, Ferdinand of Austria, *Crayer*; 2497, Fish Market, *Van Ostade*; 1966, Renaud and Armides, *Van Dyck*; 2543, Venus and Cupid, *Rembrandt*; 2083, Triumph of Religon, *Rubens*; 2392, Fruit, de *Heem*; 2016, The Dutch Admiral, *Jordaens*; 2272, Young Girl, *Fictoor*; 2370, Isaac blessing Jacob, *Fictoor*; 2463, Dutch Cook, *Metsu*; 2462, Dutch woman, *Metsu*; 2332, Landscape, *Both d'Italie*; 1971. Marquis d'Avtona, *Van Dyck*; 2112, Elisabeth of France, *Rubens*; 1970, Elisabeth of Austria, *Van Dyck*; 2323, Landscape, *Berghem*; 2331, A man, *Bol*

. On the left, recommencing at the other extremity : 2,538, St. Matthew, *Rembrandt*; 2403, The Watermill, *Hobbema*; 2141, Terrestrial Paradise, *Snyders*; 2044, Fontainebleau, *Van der Meulen*; 2145, The fishmongers, *Snyders*; 2341, Landscape, *Cuyp*; Lady whith her daughter, *Van Dyck*; 2343 The promenade, A. *Cuyp*; 1928, The Lord's Lupper, de *Champaigne*; 2015, The after-dinner Concert, *Jordaens*; 2076, Elias in the Wilderness, *Rubens*; 2342, Starting for a Walk, A. *Cuyp*; 1973, Man with child, *Van Dyck*; 2557, The forest, *Ruisdael*; 2130, Diogenes with his lantern, *Rubens*; 1985, Jean Grusset and his son, *Van Dick*; 2498, Interior of a cottage, *Van Ostade*; 2598; A frozen canal, *Van den Velde*; 2078, Madonna with angels, *Rubens*; 2113; The second wife of Rubens, *Rubens*; 2068, The Lord's supper, *Porbus*.

Seventh Gallery: 2 Sèvres Vases.

Eighth Gallery; Flemish and Dutch Schools.

On the right :

2115, Kermesse, *Rubens*; 2327, Nativity, Bloemaert; 2117, Landscape, *Rubens*; 1920, The Air, *Breughel*; 2487, Lesson on the Bass-viol. G. *Netscher*; 2486, The singing-lesson, *Netscher* ; 2487, Mountain-Landscape, *Ruysdael*; 2067. The plague at Milan, V. *Oost*; 2163, Interior of a tavern, *Teniers* ; 2528, A white horse, *Potter*; 1969, The Bavarian Duke, Charles-Louis, and his brother Robert, Duke of Cumberland, *Van Dyck*; 2410 and 2411, The same persons, *Honthorst*; 2321, Landscape, *Berghem*; 2383, Descartes, *Hals*; 2609, Vanquished pirates, *Weenix*; 1953, St. Augustin, *Crayer*.

To the left; recommencing at the other end : 1962, Madonna, *Van Dyck*, 2647, Landscape, *Wynants*; 2540 and 2541, Two philosophers in profound meditation. *Rembrandt*; 2578, Roisterers, a humourous and joyful scene, J. *Lteen* ;2510, Frozen canal in Holland, *Van Ostade*; 2595, Landscape with animals, *Van den Velde*; 2558, Stormy sea on the Dutch Coast, *Ruysdael*; 2082, Christ on the Cross, *Rubens*; 2538, The Good Samaritan, *Rembrandt*; 2313, Environs of Nice, *Berghem*; 2726, Flowers, *Mignon*; 2476, The Cook, *Miéris*.

Now return to the nearest door and enter on the left the

Salles Françaises (French School).

1 st. Room :

71, Descent from the Cross, *Bourdon*; 152 and 153. Cavalry fight, *Courtois*; 652, Royal magnificence, *Mosnier* ; 165 Appolon, *Coypel*; 459 and 460, Landscapes, *La Hyre*; 539, Nativity, *Le Nain*; 541, The village meal, *Le Nain*; 74, Julius Caesar, *Bourdon*.

2nd Room : 22 pictures by Eustache Lesueur illustrating the life and death of St. Bruno.

3rd Room : Mythological scenes and other works by *Lesueur*; 454, St. Peter healing the sick, *La Hyre*.

4th Room : Views of French seaports by *Joseph Verney.*

5th Room : Five sea-pieces by *Vernet*; several English works, amongst which is a portrait of Lord Withworth, British Ambassador, by T. *Lawrence*; (no number) landscapes by *Constable*, and a collection by Coutan.

Leaving the fifth room, you arrive at the landing of the Mollien Pavillion staircase, where are some Egyptian tombs. Enter, by the green door to the right, the French Galleries.

Galerie Française. — In this room are exhibited the chief works of Mignard, Poussin, etc.

Commencing on the right, and making the round of the room, we see: 730, Bacchanale, by *Poussin*; 57, Solomon's Judgment, by *Valentin*; 513, The entrance of Alexander the Great into Babylon, by *Le Brun*, 56, The innocence of Susan recognized, by *Valentin* ; 504, The martyr of St. Étienne, by *Lebrun*, 558, Jesus appearing to Mary Magdalen, by *Le Sueur*; 494, The adoration of the Shepherds, by *Lebrun*; 710, The Philistines smitten by the pestilence, by *Poussin*; 740, Orphelia and Eurydice, *Poussin*; 507, Christ dead on the knees of the Virgin, *Lebrun*; 434, The resurrection of Lazarus, *Jouvenet*; 560, St. Paul preaching at Ephesus, *Le Sueur*; 511, Darius's tent, model of tapestry, *Lebrun*; 715. The blind of Jerico, *Poussin*; 313, Sunset at a seaport, *Claude Lorrain*; 312, The village fête, *Claude Lorrain*; 726, The young Pyrrhus saved, *Poussin*; 433, The miraculous draught of fishes, *Jouvenet*; 724, The abduction of the Sabine women, *Poussin*; 529, Portrait of a master and his pupil, *C. Lefèvre*; 315, David anointed king, *Claude Lorrain*; 456, The pope Nicholas before the body of St. François d'Assize, *La Hyre*; 510, Battle of Arbelles *Le Brun*; 317, A seaport, *Claude Lorrain*; 790, Portrait of Robert de Cotte, *Rigaud*; 557, The descent from the cross, *Le Sueur*; 636, Hope, *Mignard*.

Between the two doors at the extremity of the gallery: 555, The angelic salutation, *Le Sueur*; 52, St. Benedict reviving an infant, *Boulogne*; 736, The terrestrial paradise, *Poussin*; 780, The presentation at the temple, *Rigaud*; 977, Wealth, *Vouet*; 517, Alexander the Great and Porus, *Le Brun*; 739, The deluge, *Poussin*; 629, Jesus and the Samaritain, *Mignard*; 545, Portrait of Henri II., Duke of Montmorency, *Le Nain*; 851, St. Cecile, *Stella*; 314, The landing of Cleopatra at Tarsus, *Claude Lorrain*; 735, Time protecting Truth from Envy and Discord, *Poussin*; 734, The arcadian shepherds (very beautiful), *Poussin*; 628, The Virgin and the grapes, *Mignard*; 781, Louis XIV, *Rigaud*; 705, Moses in the bullrushes, *Poussin*; 70, Christ and the little children, *Bourdon*; 440, The high altar at Notre-Dame of Paris, *Jouvenet*; 505, Mary Magdalen, *Lebrun*; 530, Portrait of a gentleman, *C. Lefebvre*; 540, The forge, *Le Nain*; 311, The Campo Veccino at Rome, *C. Lorrain*; 66, Adoration of the shepherds, *Bourdon*; 732, The triumph of Flora, *Poussin*; 509, The passage du Granique. *Le Brun*; 69. The presentation at the temple, *Bourdon*; 634. Saint Cecile, *Mignard*; 483, Portrait of the Count of la Châtre, *Largillière*; 704, Eliazer and Rebecca, *Poussin*.

Return on your steps and at the end of the Gallery, enter the Denon Room.

Denon Room. — This room is, above all, remarkable for its ceiling, which represents: St-Louis and the Saint Chapelle; François 1st visiting one of his artists; Louis XIV continuing the Louvre and Napoleon 1st ordering its completion.

On the walls are 104 portraits of artists, sculptors, architects, many of which were executed by themselves; in the centre of the room is a superb blue Sèvres Vase.

Note. — In this room, a door to the left opens into the ancient State-Room, where was held the opening of Parliament under Napoleon III. This room, completely transformed, joins the Denon Room to the Grand Gallery.

Enter next the State-Room (Salle des Etats) which is devoted to the masters of the modern School. The splendid decoration of this room was executed under the able direction of M. Guillaume.

Making the tour of the room from the right, remark: the small pictures by Corot, Diaz, H. Regnault and T. Rousseau; 250, Birth of Henri IV, *Deveria*; 415, Christ delivering the keys of Paradise, *Ingres*; 207, Dante and Virgil, *Delacroix*; 419, Roger delivering Angelica, *Ingres*; 145, The Kid's stable, *Courbet*; 363, The lost illusions, *Gleyre*; 156, The Romans of the Decadence, *Th. Couture*; 702, Rouget de Lisle singing the Marseillaise, *Pils*; 841, St-Augustin and St-Monic, *Ary Scheffer*; 615, Ruins of a Mosque at Cairo, *Marilhat*; 390, Francis 1st and Charles Quint, *Gros*; 423, The Bather, *Ingres*; 189, The oath of the Horaces, *David*; 138, A Matinée, *Corot*; 417, Apothesis of Homer, *Ingres*; 145, Combat of the Stags, *Courbet*; 306, Arab encampment, *Fromentin*; 744, Christ on the Cross, *Prud'hon*; 191, The lictors bringing to Brutus the bodies of his sons, *David*; 643, Spring, *Millet*; 956, The Clichy Barricade, *H. Vernet*; 889, Oxen at work, *Troyon*; 610, The death of Virginia, *Lethière*; 305, Hunting with falcons, *Fromentin*; 817, Return from the pilgrimage, *L. Robert*; 748, Interview between Napoleon I. and François II. *Prud'hon*; 958, Raphael at the Vatican, *H. Vernet*; 827, A promenade in the forest at Fontainebleau, *Rousseau*; 284 and 285, Portraits by *Flandrin*.

Above the door communicating with the Grand Gallery: The Levite of Ephraim, by *Couder*.

Continuing the tour of the room you will see, 184, The Wineharvert in Bourgogne, *Daubigny*; 216, Death of Queen Elizabeth of England, *Delaroche*; 840, The temptation of Christ, *Ary Scheffer*; 816, The Reapers, *L. Robert*; 847, The young Courtesan, *Sigalon*: 609, Brutus condemning his sons to death, *Lethière*; 890, The Return to the Farm, *Troyon*; 416, The Virgin to the host, *Ingres*; 210, Algerian women, *Delacroix*; 50 bis, the 18th Brumaire, *Bouchot*; 213, The taking of Constantinople by the Crusaders, *Delacroix*; 141, Landscape, *Corot*; 199, Madame Recamier, *David*; 389, Napoleon on the battle-field at Eylau, *Gros*; 409, Charles X distributing rewards to artists, *Heim*; 217, The children of Edward, *Delaroche*; 957, Judith and Holopherne, *H. Vernet*; 212, Don Juan's Barque, *Delacroix*; 641, The Church of Gréville, *Millet*; 643 bis, The Gleaners, *Millet*; 208, The Massacre of Scio, *Delacroix*.

Above the door communicating with the Danon Room: Portrait of General Prim, by *Regnault*.

Return by this door to the Danon Room and visit the second gallery of the French School, situated to the right.

2ⁿᵈ French Gallery. — In this gallery are exhibited the works of Boucher, Greuze, Oudry, etc., etc.

THE MADELEINE

This church forms a parallelogram surmounted by columns of Corinthian order and recalls the ancient roman temples. Noteworthy : the *high alatr* in white marble representing the *Assumption* by Marchetti, the *Baptism of Christ*, and the *Marriage of the Virgin*, groups by Pradier, the *bronze doors* by Triqueti.

Behind the high altar is a large painting by Ziegler of *Magdalen at the feet of Jésus*, surrounded by some evangelists and historical personages, Constantine, Clovis, Joan of Arc, Raphael, Napoléon I., Pope Pius VII., etc.

CHURCH
AT THE PALAIS DES INVALIDES

The Palais des Invalides built during the reign of Louis XIV. is the asylum for old soldiers, wounded and maimed in war and contains the church Saint-Louis where repose the remains of Napoleon.

The entry to the tomb is Place Vauban at the back of the Invalides.

To the right : 411, Dog attacking some Geese, *Huet* ; 701, Aglawre turned into stone, *Pierre* ; 672. Landscape, *Oudry* ; 42, le But, *Boucher* ; 671, Dog à la niche, *Oudry* ; 654, The three Graces, *Natoire* ; 462 to 465, Spring, Summer, Autumn and Winter, *Lancret* : 655. Juno. *Natoire* ; 168, Atti'a chased from the temple, *Coypel* ; 224, Portrait of a hunter, *Desportes* ; 905, The toilette of a Sultana, *Van Loo* ; 896, Diana and Endymion, *Van Loo* ; 657, Mary Magdelen, *Nattier* ; 374 and 375, Heads of Young ladies, *Greuze* ; 900, Portrait of Marie Leczinska, *Van Loo* ; 32 and 33, Pastoral subjects by *Boucher* ; 30. Diana leaving the bath, *Boucher*, 906 the Sultana and her attendants, *Van Loo* ; 2722, Portrait of Madame de Krüdner and her danghter, *Kaufmann* ; 820, Damsel ornamenting the statue of Love with a garland of flowers, *Roslin* ; 797, the truimphal arch of the town of Orange, *H. Robert* ; 666, Blanche, pet dog of Louis XV, *Oudry* ; 170, Esther and Ahasuerus, *Coypel* ; 863 ; The triumph of Amphitrite, *Jaraval* ; 97, The Monkey antiquarian, *Chardin* ; 668, Dog Guarding game, *Oudry* ; 913, Moonlight, *C. Vernet* ; 667, Wolf-Hunting, *Oudry* ; 241 and 242, Game, *Desportes* ; 658, Portrait of Adelaide of France, *Nattier* ; 261, Interior of a kitchen, *Drolling* ; 520, Peace bringing back plenty, *Le Brun* ; 766, Pygmalion, *Raoux* ; 291, The Music-lesson, *Fragonard* ; 761, Christ taken down from the Cross, *Regnault* ; 43, The toilette of Venus, *Boucher* ; 194, Paris and Helen, *David* ; 370, the Paternel Curse, *Greuze*.

To the left of the door leading to the Daru Pavillion staircase :

371. The Son Punished, *Greuze* ; 44, Venus disarming Love, *Boucher* ; 34 and 35, Pastoral Subjects, *Boucher* ; 922, Returning from fishing, *C. Vernet* ; 925, Moonlight effect, *C. Vernet* ; 469, Innocence, *Lancret* ; 369, l'Accordée de village, *Greuze* ; 468, The Music-lesson, *Lancret* ; 884, The toilette of Esther, *Troy* ; 101-102, Dead Natures, *Chardin* ; 450, Melancholy. *Lagrenée* ; 899, Hunting Hall, *Van Loo* ; 867, Marie Leczinska, *Tocqué* ; 982, Embarcation for Cytheria (very pretty) *Watteau* ; 91-92, The Benedicite and the laborious mother, *Chardin* ; 372, The broken pitcher, *Greuze* ; 923, Landscape, *C. Vernet* ; 45, Pastoral, *Boucher* ; 638, The Great Dauphin, *Mignard* ; 921, The Bathers, *C. Vernet* ; 36, Vulcan presenting to Venus arms for Aeneas, *Boucher* ; 237-245, Dead Natures, Desportes, 226-230, Dogs, *Chardin* ; 89, Interior of kitchen, *Chardin* ; 869, Portrait of Madame de Graffigny, *Tocqué* ; 180, Perseus delivering Andromeca, *Coypel*.

Between the two doors : Suzanne at her bath, by *Santerre*.

Return to the extremity of this gallery, and, near to the picture 370, The Paternel Curse, leave the gallery by the landing of the Daru pavillion staircase. Here are some beautiful frescoes. Turn to the right, and, instead of descending the staircase visit the room called, « La Salle des Sept Mètres ».

Salle des Sept Mètres. — This room contains a collection of the masters of the old Italian school (since the 14th century).

To the right : 1260, The Virgin and Angels, *Cimabué* ; 1319, Triumph of St. Thomas d'Aquin, *B. Gozzoli* ; 1279, The Virgin and Child, *Gentile da Fabriano* ; 1394, Three infants executing a Concert, *Bart Montagna* ; 1367. The Virgin Mary, the Child Jesus and little St. John the Baptist, *Mainardi* ; 1303, The coronation of the Virgin. *Garbo* ; 1437, The Virgin and Child, *Ecole de Franzia* ; 1482, The Virgin glorified, *Roselli* ; 1295, The Magnificat, *Botticelli* ; 1290, The coronation of the Virgin, *Fra Giovanni da Fiebole* ; 1296, The Virgin, Jesus and St. John, *Filipepi*, 1181, The Presentation, *Borgognone* ; 1488, The four Doctors of the Church, *Sacchi* ; 1532, Jesus on the Cross, *A. Solario* ; 1416, The coronation of the Virgin, *Piero Lorenzo*, (called *Cosimo*) ; 1539, The Nativity, *Lo Spagna* ; 1259, The Virgin and Child with John and Mary Magdelen, *Cima-da Conegliano* ; 1567, Love and Chastity, *Le Perugin* ; 1526, The adoration of the Wise Men, *Signorelli* ; 1167, The Virgin and Infant, *Bianchi*.

Above the entrance to the Grand Gallery is the celebrated frescoe by la Magliana : God the Father and angels, Ecole de Raphaël (Lo Spagna).

Returning, near the entry : 1372, The Holy Family, *Manni* ; 1174, The Virgin and Infant, *Bonini* ; 1375, Parnassus. *Mantagna* ; 1263, The Virgin, Child and Saints ; *Lor di Credi* ; 1211, Prophesy of St. Etienne, *V. Carpaccio* ; 1384, The Virgin of the Victory, *Mantegna* ; 1158, The Virgin, Infant and Saints, *B. Bellini* ; 1373, Calvary, *Mantegna* ; 1565, The Holy Family, *Le Perugin* ; 1175-1176, Four Saints, *A. Bonvicino*, 1182, St. Peter of Verona and a woman, kneeling, *Le Borgognone* ; 1344, The Virgin and Child, with angels and Saints. *Fra Filippo Lippi* ; 1120, Set of three compartments containing six subjects, *Alunno* ; 1436, Christ on the Cross, with the Virgin. St. John. and Job, *Le Francia* ; 1417, Virgin and Child, *Le Penturricchio* ; 1161, Virgin, children and four Saints, *Florentine School* ; 1345, Virgin and Child, *Lippi* ; 1316, Virgin and Child, *Biotto* ; 1665, Calvary, *Siena School* ; 1312, St. François d'Assize receiving the stigmas, *Giotto*.

From the gallery des Sept Mètres return to the landing of the Daru Pavillion staircase.

To the left, on issuing from the Salle des Sept Mètres, are frescoes of the villa Lemmi, *Boticelli* ; and of Christ, by *Giovanni*.

Pavillion Daru Staircase or Grand Staircase of the Louvre. — The decoration of this staircase is not yet finished. It will ultimately, become, from its size, style and crnamentation a veritable model of its style.

Built from plans by M. Guillaume, it will be. in a way, a résumé of the whole Museum of the Louvre. All the great painters. of all countries and all schools, whose masterpieces are exhibited in the Louvre will have their names engraved in gold letters on its walls.

Four large designs in mosaic, representing respectively France, Italy, Flanders and Germany are under the central cupola, lighted by a gigantic window in coloured glass.

In the four arches of the dome are, in mosaic, portraits of Poussin (France), Raphaël (Italy), Rubens (Flanders), and Albert Dürer (Germany).

Passing the cage of the staircase, gain the opposite landing, where you will remark, on the prow of a gallery, the Victory of Samothrace, detaching itself from a frescoe in the wall. There mount seven steps, bearing to the left and enter a door which will bring you back to the Rotunda Room. Leaving the Apollo Gallery on the right, return directly to the Room of the seven chimneys (Salle des sept Cheminées), passing through the Antique Jewellry Room.

Important Note. — If you are fatigued or it is getting late, put off the rest of your visit to the morrow, and redescend into the grand court of the Louvre by the Salle Henri II. and the Musée La Caze (La Caze Museum) placed to your right.

If, on the contrary, you intend to see the whole Museum in one day, follow the following instructions to the letter :

Note. — Our itinerary has been prepared with a view to satisfying either arrangement.

SECOND DAY

Or rest of the itinerary for those persons desirous of completing the Louvre Museum the same day.

From the Salle des Sept Cheminées (which serves as our point of departure for this itinerary), open two parallel galleries, one, to the right, contains the Campana Collection and the other, to the Museum of Roman, Greek and Egyptian antiquities. These two galleries are alike.

Visit, to the right, the Campana Museum.

THE CAMPANA MUSEUM, composed principally of vases and earthenware, includes a portion of the important Campana Collection, bought by the Papal Government in 1861 and increased considerably since that epoque. It occupies nine rooms, the ceilings of which are decorated with magnificent paintings, dating from the time when thise rooms were devoted to paintings of the French School.

First Room. — Statuettes and vases from Phoenecia, Cyprus, Asia Minor, Rhodes and Greece. — Ceiling: Richelieu presenting the artist Le Poussin to Louis XIII. *Alaux*.

Second Room. — Earthenware from Italy, Smyrna, and Greece. Statuettes coming from exavations at Myrina. — Ceiling : The Battle of Ivry and the Clemency of Henri IV. *Steuben*.

Third Room. — Etruscan pottery, black and brown. — Ceiling : Le Puget presenting to Louis XIV his groupe Milon de Crotone. *Devéria*.

Fourth Room. — Etruscan ceramic, from Caeré. In the centre of the room is a funeral pile is earthenware, on which are a man and woman in a half reclining position, painted flagstones from Etruscan tombs. — Ceiling: François I. receiving the statues and pictures bronght back from Italy by the Primate. *Fragonard*.

After this room, a passage gives entrance to room N° 5. This passage contains a collection of earthenware, masks of men and women.

Fifth Room. — Corinthian Vases, found at Cadré, and Greek Vases. Ceiling : — The Renaissauce of Art in France, and eight scenes from French History, from the time of Charles VIII. until the death of Henri II., *Heim*.

After another passage, decorated with Greek vases, black figured, you enter the.

Sixth Room. — Greek vases discovered at Caeré. — Ceiling : François Ist created knight by Bayard. *Fragonard*.

Seventh Room. — Red figured Greek vases, a number of which are signed by the artists who executed them. — Ceiling : Charlemagne receiving manuscript books from Alcuin. *Schnetz*.

Eighth Room. — Black varnished pottery, Greek and Italo-Greek drinking vases. Red and Green varnished pottery from Arezzo. Figured Cups. Large Showcase containing small statuettes and small animals. — Ceiling : Louis XII. proclaimed father of the people in the general States of Tours. *Drolling*.

Ninth Room. — Paintings from Herculaneum and Pompeii. Antique glasses and pottery from Pompeii. Celisia, Dalmatian and Gaulois. — Ceiling ; The Egyptian expedition under the orders of Bonaparte, *Cogniet*.

From this last Room, return on your steps through the Salle des Sept Cheminées, and, turning to the right, under the painting of the Deluge, No 360, enter the Museum of Roman, Greek and Egyptian antiquities, parallel to the Campana Museum.

The Roman Greek and Egyptian antiquities Museum also comprises nine rooms remarkable not only on account of the precious collections they contain, but also by their beautifully painted ceilings.

1st Room. — Salle d'Homère. Statuettes in marble and stone. Central glass case: Greek plasters, fragments of pottery, antique and middle-age ivories. Glasses from Tarsus.

Ceiling: Apothéosis of Homer.

2nd Room. — Greek vases — date Greek decadence. 2 cases of lamps.

Ceiling: Vulcan receiving from Jupiter the fire which will consume Pompeii, etc. (*Heim*).

3rd or Greek Room. — Greek terra-cottas. In the centre case are painted plates, dolls and medallions in terra-cotta.

Ceiling: The nymphs of Parthenope carrying their Penates arrive at the bank of the Seine, *Meynier*.

4th Room. — Greek vases and terra-cottas from Tarsis.

Ceiling: Cybele protecting Herculaneum and Pompeii from the fires of Vulcan, *Picot*.

5th Room or Salle des Colonnes. — Egyptian mummy-cases of painted wood. Glass cases: bronze statuettes, archaic papyrus (before the time of Alexander the Great), Arabic papyrus, etc.

Before the windows: Royal papyrus 18 metres in length out of the book of the dead (in perfect preservation although upwards of 3,000 years old.

Ceiling: In the centre G'ory being supported by Virtue; to the right: Time placing Truth under the protection of Wisdom; to the left: Mars crowned by Victory and stayed by Moderation; at the sides: the centuries most celebrated in Art.

6th Room (Salle des Dieux), — Statuettes and various Egyptian religious objects. Mummy cases, cameos, etc.

Ceiling: Study and Genius unveiling Egypt to the Greeks, *Picot*.

7th Room. — Mummy cases painted with alegorical subjects; mummies of men and animals, masks, manuscripts, etc. Immense Mss. from the Book of the dead.

Ceiling: Egypt saved by Joseph, *Pujol*.

8th Room. — Monuments, domestic objects, rings, necklaces, etc.

Ceiling: Julius II, giving orders for the construction of the Vatican and St-Peters to Bramante, Michael Angelo and Raphael *Vernet*.

9th Room. — Interesting historical objects.

Ceiling: The Genius of France encouraging the Arts and taking Greece under her protection.

Leave this room by the door to the right of the one communicating with the Campana Museum. Turn to the right and enter the rooms of the ancient Musée des Souverains.

Vestibule. — Ceiling: Medallions and paintings.

Above the fireplace: Portrait of Anne of Austria; opposite, her husband Louis XIII. Facing the entrance: « Peace », silver statue by *Chaudet*.

1st Room. — Alcove where Henry IV. breathed his last. Gilded ceiling, portraits of Henry IV. and Marie de Médecis. Marquetry in colour, gift of E. Piot.

2nd Room (formerly the chapel of the Holy Ghost, founded by Henry III, 1578). Portrait of Henry II.

3rd Room. — Cases containing ancient snuff-boxes and Lenoir miniatures. Tapestry, curtains., etc.

4th Room. — Glass case containing statuettes, chandeliers and coffers.

5th Room (Dieulafoy collection). — Persian and Chaldean antiquities. Fragments of various monuments.

6th Room (Dieulafoy collection). — Capitals from the palace of Artaxerxes. Mnemon, Chaldean, Assyrian and Parthian seals. Enamelled bricks from the palace of Artaxerxes.

7th Room. — Babylonian and Assyrian antiquities. Statuettes in terra-cotta, stone and marble; bronze gods, etc.

Important Notice. — Into this room opens a narrow passage containing a fine collection of designs by the old masters. At the end of this gallery is a small staircase leading to the second floor, where are located: 1° The Marine Museum, Ethnographic and Chinese Museums, and the « Salle du Canal de Suez »; 2° Supplementary room containing paintings.

Note. — Visitors not desirous of seeing these last-named rooms, should next inspect the museum of the Middle Ages and the Renaissance museum.

MUSEE DU MOYEN-AGE ET DE LA RENAISSANCE:

1st and 2nd Rooms. — Collections of Italian Faience.

3rd Room. — French Faience (Bernard Palissy). To the left : Ivories of the Sauvageot collection.

4th Room. — Is being reorganized.

5th Room. — Cases containing precious glass. To the right : « The Triumph of Amphitryon », and to the left : « Autumn ».

6th Room. — Carved Ivories, Sauvageot and Lenoir collections, a large carved coffer.

7th Room. — In the cases : Venetian glass. A g'ass mosaic : « The Lion of Venice ».

8th Room. — Pastels and portraits of the celebrated pastelists Latour and Rosalba Carriera.

From this room enter the

Thier's Museum. The Thier's collection, left to the Louvre by the first President of the 3rd. Republic, occupies two rooms. This fine collection comprises Egyptian and Greek antiquities, Renaissance and modern terra-cottas, bronzes, marble statues, carvings, Venetian glass, French and foreign porcelains, water-colours, Chinese paintings, Japanese and Chine-e bronzes, enamels and Oriental jewel-work and jewels. Notice in the first room to the right, the celebrated portrait of Thiers by *Bonnat.*

9th Room (marked Salle XIII).— Historical portraits ; design on silk offered by Charles V. to the Cathedral at Narbonne.

10th Room (Salle XII). — Interesting miniatures froom 15th to 19th century. Unfinished painting by *David.*

11th Room (Salle XI). — Sketches by *David, Gerard, Gerichault, Girodet, Gros, Isabey, Prudhon, Ingres,* etc.

12th Room (Salle X). — Framed designs by *Watteau, Boucher,* Van Loo, etc.

13th Room (Salle IX). — Designs by *Van der Meulen, Lebrun, Girardon, Coypel, etc.*

14th Room (Salle VIII). — Designs by *Lesueur.*

15th Room (Salle VII). — Designs by *Poussin, Lesueur, Lorrain, Bourdon.* etc.

16th Room (Salle VI). — Framed pastels.

The small door leads to the marine museum.

17th Room (Salle V). — Designs and sketches by German, Flemish and Dutch painters : Durer, Teniers, Van Dyck and Rubens.

Ceiling : Triumph of Marie de Médicis, *Duran.*

18th Room (Salle IV). — Italian sketches and designs. Ceiling : Divine Wisdom giving laws to kings and legislators, Immense porcelain vase from the Sèvres manufactory.

19th Room (Salle III). — Italian designs ; sketch by Jules Romain. Ceiling : The Law descending to Earth.

20th Room (Salle II). — Designs by the great Italian masters. Large paintings by J. Romain. Ceiling : France receiving the charter from the hands of Louis XVIII.

21st Room (Salle I).— Designs of the early Italian masters. Painting by J. Romain. Ceiling : France victorious at Bouvines.

Outside this room is the staircase leading to the Salle des Boites.

Salle des Boîtes. — Containing designs by Raphael, Michael Angelo, etc., is open every day, excepting Sundays and Mondays, from 2 to 4.

Salle des Bronzes Antiques. — Leaving Salle I. (21st room); and passing the staircase to the right leading to the second floor, enter the collection of antique bronzes. This hall was formerly the Louvre chapel, but now contains a fine collection of statuettes, vases, helmets, and shields of Greek and Roman art.

From this room descend the staircase Henri II and visit, on the ground-floor to the right, the museum of antique sculpture.

THE GROUND FLOOR

The ground floor contains the following collections : Antique sculpture, modern sculpture, middle ages and renaissance sculpture, Egyptian museum, and the Assyrian and Asia Minor Museums.

NAPOLEON'S TOMB — ГРОБНИЦА НАПОЛЕОНА

ANTIQUE SCULPTURE

Salle des Cariatides. — This is the first room to be visited on the ground floor. It derives its mame from the magnificent caryatides carved by Jean Goujon.

It was in th's room that Henri IV. was married to Marguerite de Valois, and on the tribune supported by the Caryates, that he lay in state after his assassination by Ravaillac. Molière played his first pieces here, and here at one time the « Institut » held its sittings.

Among the most remarkable objects exhibited, notice to the right : a statue of Hercules and a lion in bay-salt.

In the middle of the salle going towards the door are two statues of Bacchus, the Borghese vise, and two large antique alabaster vasques found at Marmosala. Their position in the hall is the cause of a curious echo. If you speak into one of them, even in a low tone of voice, any person at the other one will hear everything you say.

On the left : Venus Aphro lite, Jupiter, Nymphe of Diana, Pluto-Jupiter, Child and Goose, Alexander the great, Venus stooping.

At the bottom between two pillars : Jupiter of Versailles ; a Greek philosopher ; Demosthenes.

At the end of the hall of the carytides is a magnificent modern chimney piece ; before this latter is a fine statue of Hercules and to the right before the window The Borghese Hermaphrodite.

Into the Salle des Cariatides opens the corridor de Pan, where on the right is the entry to the vaults, or

Salles Souterraines. — These vaults were excavated by Mr. Guillaume in 1883 for the installation of heating apparatus.

The first stroke of the pickaxe brought to light traces of the Louvre Francis I. ; then a vast hall called the Salle de Philippe Auguste, and on continuing the excavations at right angles in the direction of the Pont des Arts, the ancient rampart of the Seine, the foundations of a tower corresponding to those of which one sees the traces in the Cour du Louvre, and finally a sewer, upon the walls of which may still be seen a caricature of a trumpeter of the time of Charles IX. Thanks to the ability of M. Guillaume who has preserved these important vestiges, the extent of the ancient Louvre may yet be traced.

In these subterranean halls have been found traces of human remains, and fragments of a floor of the 13th. century, which may be seen in a case in the Salle de Philippe Auguste. These vaults may be seen every Monday from 1 to 3 by special permission from the conservateur du Louvre.

From the corridor of Pan you will see to the right the back of the statue of the Borghese Mars, and to the left the celebrated Venus de Milo, the marvel of the sculpture museums of the world.

Cross this corridor and enter the

Salle du Tibre. — Notice in this hall, to the right on entering, four Satyrs supporting the architrave of the scene of a theatre. Before this monumental sculpture is the colossal statue of the Tiber, represented as protecting Romulus and Remus suckled by the wolf. Finally in the centre of the hall is a statue of Diana on a pedestal ornamented by fine bas-reliefs.

Salle du Gladiador. — In the centre the Gladiator, Venus Genitrix ; to the right : Mercury, Hygeia ; to the left ; Mercury, Cupid, Marsyas and Psyche.

Salle de Minerve. — Statues of Polyhymnia and Minerva, called the Pallas de Velletri. In the centre : Apollo, Venus of Arles, Venus leaving the bath, the genius of repose, and the masked vase.

Salle de Melpomère. — Colossal statue of Melpomene the Muse of tragedy. To the right, Apollo ; to the left, Mercury. Before the statue is a modern mosaic by Belloni, and to the left is the

Salle de la Venus de Milo. — In the centre is the admirable masterpiece of antique sculpture, discovered in 1820 in the Isle of Milo, and presented to Louis XVIII, by the Marquis de Rivière. Turning to the right you pass into the :

Salle de la Psyché. — Statues of Bacchus, Psyche, Ceres, and Attalanta. Between these two halls are statues of Venus Aphrodite.

Salle d'Adonis. — To the left : Hercules reposing, and a magnificent sarcophagus on which is carved Tritons and Nereids. Adonis wounded in the chase by a boar, dying in the presence of desolate Venus. To the right : Sarcophagus, bas reliefs and Bacchus. In the centre ; Venus stooping.

Salle de l'Hermaphrodite de Velletri. — Juno on the right ; sleeping Hermaphrodite, and Venus. To the left : Minerva and Venus.

Salle de la Médée. — In the middle : Venus stooping, found in Vienne, (France) ; on the left : the three Graces. Bas-relief representing Medea, Flora and Mercury.

Corridor de Pain. — To the right, Naiade, Minerva and Pan seated.

Salle Grecque. — Fine ceiling by Prudhon : Diana imploring Jupiter. On the walls : Bas-reliefs from the temple of Jupiter : In the middle : Juno and two statues of Apollo. Now enter the

Salle de la Rotonde. — Statue of Mars (formerly called Achilles). Notice to the right : a Nymph and Mars ; before the window Mercury and Apollo ; at each end, Polla and Apollo, then a Bacchante and Ceres. Ceiling by Mauzaisse.

From the Salle de la Rotonde, you pass into the

Salles des Empereurs Romains.

1ˢᵗ **Room** (Salle de Mécène). — On entering notice Silene and Bacchus, and some bas-reliefs ; to the left, enormous head of Carecalla, colossal bust of Mecœnas, and a statue of Nero. To the right : Roman bas-relief ; Scylla. In the centre five antique bas-reliefs. Ceiling by Meynier.

2ⁿᵈ **Room** (Salle des Saisons). — This hall contains numerous bas-reliefs representing the worships of Mithras, God of the Sun. The principal one, to the right : Mithras slaying the bull. Numerous busts of Emperors and Empresses. To the right Constantine the Great and Germanicus. In the middle : Hadrian and Sabine as Mars and Venus. Ceiling by Romanelli.

3ʳᵈ **Room** (Salle de la Paix). — In the centre : Statue in red porphery of Minerva. Statues of Roman Emperors. Ceiling by Romanelli.

4ᵗʰ **Room** (Salle de Septime Sevère). — Ceiling by Romanelli. Statues of Mammaca, Mother of Alexander Severus, Pertinax, Julian (called the apostate), Geta, Antinous, and Septimus Severus.

5ᵗʰ **Room** (Salle des Antonius). — Roman Emperors. Colossal statue of Marcus Aurelius. Trajan. Colossal head of Lucilla. At the end of the hall : Window of Charles IX.

6ᵗʰ **Room** (Salle d'Auguste). — Ceiling by Matout. Colossal bust of Antinous. Magnificent statue of a Roman orator, formerly called Germanicus. Colossal group of Rome, Romulus and Remus, and the wolf. Statues of Augustus, Nero, and Julian.

Now retrace your steps and enter the :

Vestibule Daru. — This vestibule is filled with statues, columns and sarcophagi.

Now enter the *Galerie Denon ;* which contains various reproductions of antique bronzes and treasurus from the Vatican, and some mutilated statues. Then visit the

Galerie Molien ; where are exhibited antique sculptures, for the most part mutilated.

From the Galerie Molien, return to the vestibule Denon, go out into the Cour du Caroussel, repass under the pavillon Sully and turn immediately to the left in the Cour du Louvre ; in order to visit the Museum of modern sculpture (2nd door to the left).

MUSEUM OF MODERN SCULPTURE

The Modern works are found on the ground floor in the following six halls :

Salle du Puget. — Hercules, Milo the Crotonean, Perseus and Andromeda, Cariatides (two, copies of those in the Hotel de Ville at Toulon) by *Puget ;* Phaetusa, by *Theodon ;* Busts of *Boileau, Mansard, Colbert.* Bas-relief, Alexander the Great and Diogenes.

Salle de Coysevox. — Magnificent mausoleum of Mazarin. Busts of Richelieu, Mazarin, Bossuet, Colbert, Le Brun, and Mignard, the Rhone, and Venus stooping by Coysevox.

Salle des Coustou. — Statues of J. Caesar, Diana, Venus, Hannibal, Louis XV ; Marie Leczinska, Mercury, and Amalthea, Adonis, Prometheus, and Cupid.

Salle de Houdon. — Diana statue in bronze, by *Houdon*, Cupid and Psyche, by *Delaistre ;* Bacchante, by *Clodion ;* another Bacchante, by *Pajou ;* Cupid, by *Bouchardon ;* Psyche, by *Pajou ;* The Duke de Richelieu, The Death of Abel, by *Stouf ;* Busts of Mirabeau, Madame Du Barri, J.-J. Rousseau and Buffon, etc.

Salle de Chaudet. — To the right and on making the tour, Victory (in Bronze) ; Caton d'Utique, *Rude ;* The soldier of Marathon, *Cortot ;* Epaminondas, *Bridan ;* Biblis transformed into a fountain, *Dupatey ;* Salmacis, *Bosio ;* Zephyr and Psyche, *Paxtiel ;* Nisus and Euryale, *Romain ;* Daphne and Chloe, *Cortot ;* Homer, *Roland :* — In the centre of the Room : Phorbas and Œdipe, *Chaudet ;* Cupid and Psyche, *Canova ;* Bust of Madame Dumont, *Dumont ;* Mucius Scævola. *Deseine ;* Arista, *Bosio.*

Salle de Rude. — To the right and on making the tour : Spartacus, *Foyatier ;* Christ, *Rude ;* Joan of Arc and Neapolitan fisher, *Rude ;* The adieux, *Perraud ;* Philopoemen, *David ;* Fisher Dancing (bronze), *Duret*; Chiidhood of Bacchus, *Perraud*; Psyche, *Pradier*, Theseus combatting the Minotaure, *Ramey*; The improvident wine harvester (bronze) *Duret*.

In the middle of the room : The four quarters of the World, *Carpeaux*; Mercury (bronze), *Rude* ; Despair, *Perraud*; Sappho, *Pradier*.

From the salle Rude return by the salle Pujet.

CHALCOGRAPHY MUSEUM. — Those strangers who wish to purchase choice engravings may do so at the Chalcography museum, which is situated to the right of the Musée des sculptures modernes.

Itinerary. — On leaving the Museum of modern sculpture, direct your steps to the right to the Pont des Arts.

To the left of this Pavillion, in the same square, are the Middle Age and Renaissance sculpture Museums.

MUSEUM OF SCULPTURES OF THE MIDDLE AGES AND RENAISSANCE

On the ground floor, on the left of the guichet du pont des Arts, court of honour of the Louvre.

At the entrance of the vestibule to the left :

Salle de la cheminée de Bruges (Bruges Chimney Room). — Model of the monumental chimney piece of the Palace of Justice at Bruges, tombs of Charles the timorous and Marie of Bourgogne; Florentine statue by *Olivieri*.

Leaving the above room we enter another, now being installed, which will contain some of the works of *Anguier*.

To the right of the vestibule :

Salle Chrétienne (Christian Room). — Bas-reliefs, saracophagus and inscriptions. Roman and Tunisian mosaics, fragments of pottery, christian lamps.

To the right of this room, another one is being organised. If unable to cross, return to the vestibule and enter the salle Jean Goujon.

Salle de Jean Goujon. — In the centre is the famous group, Diana Huntress, with stay and dogs, from the Château d'Anet; — The group of the three Graces, on the theological Virtues, for the monument of Henri II. and of Catherine of Medicis; Group of 4 statues in wood, made to support the frame of St. Geneviève; — magnificent chimney piece from the Château of Villeroy; — funeral column with statues erected to the memory of the Constable Anne de Montmorency; a Mausoleum erected to the memory of the family de Cossé-Brissac; busts of Henri II., Charles IX., Henri III., etc.; — to the right, in the first window. no. 98, The judgement of Daniel, small and very curious bas relief.

To the right of the Jean Goujon Room :

Salle de Michel-Ange (Michel-Angelo Room). — Monumental Portal, 15th century, from the Stagna palace at Cremona; bas reliefs of the Milan, Italian and Florentine Schools; Christ Dead, 16th century; Two slaves, Michael Angelo; Hercules, victor of the Hydre, and Jason (bronzes) The Nymph of Fontainebleau (bronze) by *Benvenuto Cellini*.

To the right :

Room 6. — Busts of Roman emperors (16th century) Friendship, *Olivieri*; Louis XII., statues of the Italian School.

Return to the salle Jean Goujon and enter the salle Michel Colombe, which communicates with it.

Salle de Michel Colombe. — Bas-reliefs and statues of the 15th century, St. George and the Dragon, bas-relief by *Michel Colombe*; the Virgin and child Jesus; bronze busts of François 1st and of Jean d'Alesso; in the middle of the room : Mercury and Psyche.

Salle du Moyen Age. (Middle Ages Room). — Marble Statues of The French School of the 14th century; Door of a home in Valencia, 15th century, communicating with the new room.

Salle d'André Beauneveu. — Marble statues of the 14th and 15th century, amongst others : Philippe VI (attributed to *André Beauneveu*), of the comte d'Evreux and of Catherine d'Alençon; — on columns, busts of Charles VII and of Marie d'Anjou ; — a brass statue of Blanche de Champagne (executed at Limoges, 14th century) and last of all, the tomb of Philippe Pot, from the Abbey of Citeaux, a very remarkable piece of work of great artistic value.

Behind Philippe's tomb is a passage giving access to the Egyptian Museum, near the grand staircase leading to the Egyptian Antiquities and the ancient Sovereigns' Museum.

Turn to the left and enter the Egyptian Museum on the right. Remark, in the vestibule, statues, tombs and Egyptian inscriptions.

EGYPTIAN MUSEUM

ON THE GROUND FLOOR, TO THE RIGHT, UNDER THE COLLONADE

Egyptian Museum. — Collection of sphinx, bas-reliefs, columns, inscriptions, and saracophagus. Worthy of note : A Monolith Chapel, The saracophagus of Rameses III, and that of Horus; statue of Sebekhoton III. (more than 2000 years before the christian era); statue of Seti II., the base of the Lougsor obelisk, statue of Rameses II.; A saracophagus of the XXVI. dynasty and of Tako, the sphinx of Tapio, 2400 years B. C. ; chapel of the temple of Philoe; base of a colossal statue of a king of the 12th dynasty.

Note. — If the Algerian Gallery, parallel to the Egyptian Museum, is open to the public, visit it, then :

Leaving the Egyptian Museum, cross the archway and enter, in front, the Museum of Asiatic Antiquities.

MUSÉE ASSYRIEN ET DE L'ASIE MINEURE

ON THE GROUND FLOOR, TO THE LEFT, UNDER THE COLLONADE

In the vestibule, bas reliefs of Nineveh and from the palace of the king Largon (13th century).

1st Room : Assyria. — Four immense fantastic animals, winged with men's heads; gigantic figures of men, numerous bas-reliefs, tables and stones bearing unreadable inscriptions, fragments from the palace of king Sardanapale at Nineveh (700 years B. C.) and fragments of Chaldean statues.

2nd Room : Assyria and Phoenecia. — Saracophagus, bas-reliefs with inscriptions and designs. In the cases : Agate and coral necklaces, statuettes, etc., etc.

In the vestibule, at the foot of the staircase leading to the Dieulafoy Rooms, are some Phoenecia Saracophagus of great antiquity and busts from Carthage.

To the right of the staircase, new room containing Jewish antiquities, saracophagus, stones, inscriptions, bas-reliefs, etc., many of which belonged to the de Sauley collection.

To the left of the staircase are three hals i

1st Hall : Phoenecia and Cyprus. — Fragments of Architecture, inscriptions etc.; an immense vase from Amathonte (Isle of Cyprus) ; a saracophagus from Kneifedk, near Tyre.

2nd Hall : Salle Millet. — Collection of curiosities presented to the Louvre by the Rothschild family, discovered in excavations made on their account in Asia-Minor.

This collection comprises Archaic objects, many of them from the ruins of the temple of Apollo, a massive lion. in white marble; etc., etc., etc.

3rd Hall : Salle de Magnésie. — This room contains many sculptures by Magnésie from Meandre, near Ephesus and some fragments of the temple of Arthémis Leucophryne, notably the frieze (one of the most vast compositions remaining to us from antiquity) representing a combat against the Amazons. In the centre of the room is an immense vase discovered at Pergamus. You have now finished the Louvre.

After the exhaustive description I have given of the Louvre, on account of its importance, I shall confine myself to a general description of the other museums and refer you, for full details, to the special catalogues, which are issued periodically, and, being official, can be relied upon for correct information. They are always to be obtained at the doors or from the officials in attendance.

THE LUXEMBOURG MUSEUM, known formerly under the name of the museum of contemporean artists and which was formerly in the Luxembourg palace, occupies, at present, the ancient orangery of the Luxembourg gardens, to which several new buildings have been added. Situated on the right side of the Seine, it is open every day to the public (excepting Monday); in the summer from 9 to 5, winter 10 to 4 ; Sundays and holidays all the year round from 10 to 4. Entrance by the gate in the rue de Vaugirard, facing the rue Férou.

This museum, the distribution and lighting of which is arranged in the most perfect manner possible, includes, really, two museums, viz :

The Museum of Sculpture, which occupies a space of 432 metres surface, superficial; and

The Museum of Paintings, comprising eleven halls of different sizes.

Passing through the gate which gives access to the small courtyard preceding the museum you arrive before the facade, surmounted by a pediment representing France offering palms and crowns to Painting and Sculpture (Crauk), beneath which you will read the inscription : Musee National du Luxembourg (Luxembourg National Museum). Then, mounting the eleven steps and crossing the vestibule, you will be in the sculpture gallery.

The Tomb of Napoleon I was constructed by *Visconti* and consists of an open circular crypt. Its walls are of polished granite, ornamented with 10 scenes in relief. Between these reliefs are 10 colossal victories, by Pradier. The 6 trophies consist of 10 flags each, brought from the Luxembourg Palace, where they had long lain concealed. On the pavement are recorded the names of important battles. viz. : Moscow, Wagram, Friedland, Iena. Austerlitz, Marengo, Pyramids and Rivoli. (For fuller details see page 43).

Note. — Many changes being constantly made in the Luxembourg museum on account of the continual acquisition of new works and the transfer of certain others to the Louvre and to provincial museums, I find it impossible to give you, here, an exact description, and would recommend you to procure a copy of the current catalogue, which will cost you 45 c (4 1/2 d.) and with it to visit the rooms in their numerical order.

MUSEE DES THERMES ET DE L'HOTEL DE CLUNY. Boulevard Saint-Michel; entrance: 24, rue du Sommerard. — This museum contains rich collections of National and foreign antiquities, of the Middle-âge and Renaissance periods.

Days and hours of admission. — Every day (excepting Mondays and reserved holidays) from 11 to 5 from 1st April to 30th. September and from 11 to 4 from 1st October to 31st March.

The entrance to the gardens is by the large door of the Cluny museum.

Note. — Cards for study should be asked for from the secretarial département of the museum.

Historical notice. — The Thermes Palace, on a part of the ruins of which has been built the Cluny museum and of which the grand hall still remains intact, with its immense antique arch, is the most ancient monument in Paris. It appears that its erection dates from the reign of Constance Chlore and the chroniclers declare that Julien the Apostate was proclaimed Emperor there, (a. d. 360).

The ruins of the palace were acquired in 1340 by the Abbey of Cluny. Later on the buildings known as the Hotel de Cluny were erected for the monks; and these constructions, continued by Jacques d'Amboise, were only completed about the commencement of the sixteenth century.

Becoming National property at the Revolution, it was lost by the state until 1843, when it was again acquired together with the Sommerard collections which were placed there in 1832.

The Hotel de Cluny is the only civil monument in Paris which has retained its primitive aspect owing to the works of restoration, having for their sole object the preservation of the delicacy and originality of the building. Constituted a museum by law of 1843, the Musee des Thermes et l'Hotel de Cluny contained 1,400 objects. This number has now increased to over 12,000 most interesting curiosities.

For the nomenclature of objects exhibited and description of interior, consult catalogue. Space will not permit me to give details here. A few words on the chapel and Palace of Thermes before leaving the building.

Chapel. — This delightful monument of the fifteenth century is extremely elegant and in a perfect state of preservation. The lacework of the belfry, the bands covered with leaves and foliage in high relief, the thousand details of a thin, fine architecture have been discovered, thickly covered with plaster, and the Chapel of the Hotel de Cluny remains as a most complete specimen of the Renaissance period.

Worthy of note, a figure of Christ on the Cross (12th century) a chorister's desk and lighting apparatus in wrought iron, of the 15th century, and a large Flemish altar-piece of the 15th century.

A light staircase, opening in an angle of the Chapel, descends to the ground floor, from whence access may be had to the garden by a sort of covered passage, of which the central pillar supports the crowned K of Charles VIII (Karolus) and the arms of the Amboise family.

From here, descend a few steps to the left and you will be in the middle-ages exhibit room, cross this and enter, by the door facing, the Palace des Thermes.

Palais des Thermes. — It is here, under these imposing arches, that all the antique monuments are placed; the Gaulish altars found at Notre-Dame and the marble statue of the emperor Julien proclaimed here in the year 360.

The gardens of the Palace are decorated with numerous pedestals and statues, the greater part of which come from the ancient résidence of the monks. You will remark particularly the iron cross taken from the Church of St.-Vladimir of Sebastapool, the doorway of the ancient Church of St.-Benoit and the three Roman arcades from the Argenteuil Abbey.

On leaving the Hotel de Cluny mount the few steps of the rue de la Sorbonne and see, to the left, at the angle of the rue des Ecoles, the magnificent building of the Academy of Paris; then descend to the right the rue des Ecoles to the boulevard St.-Michel, the favourite evening resort of the students of the Latin Quarter. Nobody should leave Paris without having spent an evening in this quarter, to get a true idea of the life of the Parisian student. From the fountain at the end of this boulevard, omnibuses and trams may be obtained to any quarter of Paris.

NATIONAL CONSERVATOIRE OF ARTS AND TRADES. MUSEUM OF MACHINES AND INDUSTRIAL ARTS. (Conservatoire National des Arts et Métiers) 292, rue Saint-Martin. — The exhibition is open free to the public Sundays, Tuesdays and Thursdays, from 10 to 4. One may visit the collections on other days from 12 to 3 with a special authorization from the director of the establishment.

The Conservatoire des Arts and Metiers occupies the site of the ancient Priory of St.-Martins in the Fields (St-Martin des Champs).

The body of the actual building is composed of three principal wings, the central, northern and southern. It will be completed by another wing, of which the south-east end is already finished.

This building is well worth a visit. It is one of the most important industrial museums in the world and very interesting to engineers and manufacturers.

MUSÉE D'ARTILLERIE (Artillery museum). Situated at the Palais des Invalides the artillery museum is open Tuesdays, Thursdays and Sundays, from 12 to 3, from the 1st Nov. to 31st. Jan. and from 12 to 4 from 1st Feb. to 31st Oct. This museum contains specimens of firearms, large and small, from date of first invention to present day.

MUSEUM OF NATIONAL ARCHIVES, au Palais des Archives, 60, rue des Francs-Bourgeois. — Open free every Sunday, from 12 to 3. (Thursdays from 12 to 4, with card). In the elegant palace of the Princes of Rohan-Soubise, which became national property at the time of the great Revolution, have been collected the original documents of the authentic history of France.

Having crossed a large courtyard ornamented with flower beds and surrounded by a graceful collonade, you mount a staircase and arrive at the vestibule, from whence another stairway leads to the first floor.

On the ground and first floors are arranged, in the different halls, under glass cases, the most important maps and historical documents. Every thing is labelled and there are catalogues in every room, free for public use.

MUSÉE CARNAVALET. — Library and historical museum of the town of Paris, 23, rue de Sévigné. — Open Thursdays and Sundays, from 11 to 4.

Historical. — The Hotel Carnavalet, built by Pierre Lescot in 1550, was decorated with some admirable sculptures by Jean Goujon, who executed the interior and exterior decoration of the principal entrance. It is also to the school of this celebrated artist that the collosial figures of the four seasons decorating the façade at the bottom of the interior court, are due. The other eight figures are by Van Obstal, a sculptor of the 17th. century.

Restored in 1661 by Mansart, this edifice forms an almost regular " quadrilatère ", with courtyard in the centre and garden behind, the whole having a superficial area of about 2,500 mètres. Constructed for Jacques de Lignerio, president of the Parliament of Paris. it was bought in 1572 by M. de Kernevenoy (by corruption Carnavalet).

Inhabited by the Marquis de Sévigné, who took possession of it in October 1677, the Hotel Carnavalet, was the resort of all the greatest celebrities of the 17th century, which, under the influence of the vivacious and charming mistress of the place, gave the tone to all the Societies and Courts of Europe.

After the revolution of 1789, the offices of the Direction of the Public Library were installed in the Hôtel for several years; the school of Bridges and Roads was afterwards established there by Napolean 1st. In 1829 it was replaced by one of the principal institutions of the Charlemagne College.

M. Verdot. who was chief of this College in 1864, sold the Hotel to the town of Paris in February of that year. The town then had the building restored, giving it, as much as possible, its 16th century style and character, at the same time preserving the souvenirs of Madame de Sévigné. The building was considerably enlarged in 1889.

THE MINT AND MONETARY MUSEUM, 11, quai Conti; at the hôtel des Monnaies. Open Tuesdays and Fridays, from 12 to 3, with permission (which should be written for in advance) from the Director. (When writing add a stamp for reply).

Precious collections of coins and stamps, medals, pleasure pieces and jetons, struck since the time of Charles VIII down to present day.

For the purchase of medals included in the catalogue, apply at sale office (Bureau de vente) of the Hôtel, on the left, on entering.

Note. — In the court, busts of Henri II., Louis XIII., Louis XIV. and Louis XV.

The Coinage Museum, which you will reach by the staircase opening to the right of the vestibule, comprises : 1° Medals, struck since the time of Charles VIII. until the present day; 2° Private tokens; 3° French and foreign monies; 4° Models of matrices and other apparatus used in coining money; 5° Coins. punches of medals and tokens, etc., etc.

CHATEAU D'AUTEUIL, 16, rue d'Auteuil, Paris (près du Bois de Boulogne)

PENSIONNAT DE JEUNES FILLES	YOUNG LADIES COLLEGE
Préparations à tous les Examens. Langues Étrangères. Prix modérés	Comfortable home. Large garden. Good Lessons. Moderate terms. Good references
Dirigé par Mlles BOURÉ	Principals: Mlles BOURÉ
DEMANDER LE PROSPECTUS	PROSPECTUS ON APPLICATION

NATIONAL PRINTING WORKS, — TYPOGRAPHICAL MUSEUM, 87, rue Vieille-du-Temple. — Open every Thursday at 2 o'clock precisely. Admission by ticket granted by the director. (After 2 o'clock visitors are no longer admitted).

To visit the paintings by C. Huet, and the punches, a special authorization must be obtained from the administration.

The National Printing Works (Imprimerie Nationale) occupies the ancient residence of the Cardinal de Rohan (then known as the Hotel de Strasbourg). The bulletin of laws, and other works executed at the expense of the treasury, also all ministerial and administrative printing for the state, is executed here. In the works, about twelve hundred employés, of both sexes, are occupied in all the operations relating to the productions of books, from the founding of the type to binding, photogravure and lithography.

The establishment possesses 288 different characters, of which 153 are foreign, the latter permitting printing in fifty eight oriental languages. It also possesses a library, containing copies of all the most remarkable books from its presses, a drawing-room ornamented with pictures by C. Huet (1745) and the door of the ancient stables, with magnificent bas-relief by Robert le Lorrain, etc.

NATURAL HISTORY MUSEUM (Musée d'Histoire naturelle) (See Jardin des Plantes, page 77).

MUSÉE MINÉRALOGIQUE, at the National School of Mines, 60-62, boulevard Saint Michel. — Public entrance by the covered flight of steps of the central door, every Tuesday, Thursday and Saturday from 12 to 4, and the first Sunday in the month from 9 to 12.

MUSÉE DUPUYTREN, 15, rue de l'Ecole-de-Médecine. — Open every day, excepting Sunday, from 11 to 4, only to students or doctors furnished with cards.

MUSÉE DE L'ANATOMIE COMPARÉE, 12, rue de l'Ecole-de-Médecine. — Open only to students and doctors, every day excepting Sundays from 11 to 4.

MUSEUM OF MUSICAL INSTRUMENTS, 15, rue du Faubourg-Poissonnière. — Open to the public Thursday 12 to 4, to foreigners Monday 12 to 4. (Catalogue 2 francs.) Many pianos, violins, violincellos, etc., having belonged to artistic celebrities, are to be seen here.

MUSÉE ET BIBLIOTHÈQUE DE L'OPÉRA. at the Opéra; open every day, excepting Sunday, from 11 to 4. Very interesting exhibition for lovers of music, comprising objects belonging to the dramatic and musical arts of all epochs.

MUSÉE ASTRONOMIQUE DE L'OBSERVATOIRE. — Very fine collection of astronomical instruments and objects. Open the first Saturday of each month. Permission to be obtained from the director.

MUSÉE DU MOBILIER NATIONAL, 103, quai d'Orsay. — Open Sundays, Thursdays and holidays from 10 to 4. May be visited other days, by permission from the Director.

MUSÉE DES ARTS DÉCORATIFS, at the Palais de l'Industrie. — This exhibition was first held in 1877, instituted by the Duc de Chaulnes, its first président. It is situated in the south east pavillion, entrance by the door N° 7, and is open to the public every day from 10 to 5. Entrance fee : week-days, 1 franc; Sundays, 50 centimes. Magnificent collection of specimens of interior decorative art.

MUSÉE DE SCULPTURE COMPARÉE, in the Trocadero Palace. — This exhibition occupies the two wings of the Palace. Open free to the public, every day, Mondays excepted, from 11 to 5 from May to Sept. and 11 to 4 the other months.

MUSÉE DES ANTIQUITÉS KHMERS, Palais du Trocadéro. — Admission as above.

This is an exhibition of curious sculptures of gigantic edifices erected by the Kmers, people of Gamboge. A staircase conducts you to a basement where there are also statues of men, animals, etc., from Gamboge. Collection very interesting to amateurs.

MUSÉE ETHNOGRAPHIQUE. — 1st floor of the Trocadéro Palace. — Admission Sundays and Thursdays, from 12 to 4, and other days at the same hours with cards from the Administrator. Contains upwards of 40,000 objects and costumes of different peoples, many of which are exhibited on statues modelled after nature.

MUSÉE PÉDAGOGIQUE, 41, rue Gay-Lussac. — Open from 10 to 5, excepting Sundays, to persons provided with a working card of admission, which can be obtained either at the Museum or on application to the Ministère de l'Instruction Publique.

MUSÉE GUIMET OR MUSEUM OF RELIGIONS, Place d'Iéna and rue de la Boissière (Avenue du Trocadéro). — This Museum contains the celebrated collection of M. Emile Guimet amassed during his voyages in the Orient, and comprises objects and authentic documents, etc. appertaining to the study of Oriental and ancient religions.

MUSÉE DES FRAUDEURS (Museum of Frauds) under the roof of the octroi building. Place de l'Hôtel-de-Ville. — In a low hall are to be seen a quantity of objects used in connection with frauds of all descriptions. Corsets and pettycoats in indiarubber, artificial faggots, belts, carriage boxes, cases, etc., used by fraudulent persons in passing goods through the customs.

This collection, containing every trick and device imaginable' is very curious, but it is difficult to obtain permission to visit it. A written application must be made to the Director of the Octroi.

MUSÉE DES COLLECTIONS ARTISTIQUES DE LA VILLE DE PARIS, 15, rue de la Fontaine, Auteuil. — Open every Sundays, from 12 to 4. Very good museum of works of Art.

MUSÉE VALENTIN HAMY, 14, rue Bertrand. — This museum of work executed by the blind, is named after the founder of the school for the blind. Open free every Tuesday from 11 to 4 or 5.

MUSÉE DE CAEN, at the Institute, 21, quai Conti, in the north-west Pavilion. — This is the museum founded by Madame de Caen, well-known in connection with the " Prix de Rome ". For permission to visit the museum, application must be [made to the Secretariat de l'Institut.

MUSÉE GALLIÉRA, avenue du Trocadéro. — This handsome building, of classical design contains the collection of oilpaintings presented to the state by the Duchess of Galliéra.

BIBLIOTHÈQUE NATIONALE (National Library), rue de Richelieu, facing the square Louvois.

Open. — The medal, geography and stamp Rooms and the librarie Mazarine are open to visitors Sundays and Fridays from 10 to 4.

The Reading Room (Salle de lecture), rue Colbert. — Is open every day including Sundays from 9 to 4, 5 or 6 according to the time of year.

From Passion Sunday to Easter Monday the whole building is closed.

A buffet exists facing the cloak room, a great convenience for visitors.

For permission to use the reading room application must be made to Monsieur l'Administrateur-Général.

Cabinet of antique gems and medals. — This splendid Museum, forming a dependency of the Bibliothèque Nationale is open every Tuesday and Friday. from half-past ten to half-past three. Entrance rue de Richelieu, near the rue des Petits-Champs. Ring at the small door near the Fire and Police Station. The vestibule contains the Chamber of the Kings of Karnac, a monument transported hither from Thebes, and consisting of a series of Egyptian bas-reliefs; fronting the entrance, the celebrated Zodiac of Denderah, and under it the porphyry bath in which Clovis was baptized. Ascending the staircase, the *Salle de Luynes*, contains the magnificent collection presented to the National Library by the late Duc de Luynes. It consist of a series of Greek and Etruscan vases, adorned with pictures, Greek armour and various ustensils, bronzes, statuettes, and valuable medals and signet-rings, the whole estimated at 1,400,000 fr. The room to the left, lit by seven windows, contains the subjoined collection, considered one of the richest in Europe. In 1789, all the antiques in the treasuries of the Sainte Chapelle and abbey of St.-Denis were added to this cabinet; it also includes the superb collection of the Comte de Caylus, and 90 antique bronzes and terra-cottas bequeathed by the late Vicomte de Janzé. Among the most remarkable relics here preserved are two large carved silver discs; the lesser, found in the Rhone near Avignon, is improperly called the shield of Scipio; the larger found in the Dauphiné, is called the sheld of Hannibal; there is also a large oval black marble carved with cuneiform characters, besides a vast number of cameos, seals, intaglios, abraxas, talismans, and oriental inscriptions. Some of the glass stands contain various curious objects found in the tomb of Childeric, and a large cameo representing the Apotheosis of Augustus; two Etruscan vases, found at Agylla, and presented by Prince Torlonia to Louis Philippe. A catalogue of this museum, comprising 144,000 medals, has been published.

ISLAND OF THE LAKE, BOIS DE BOULOGNE

This beautiful island is picturesquely situated in the centre of the *Lac Inferieur* of the Bois de Boulogne. Ferry boats convey visitors to and from the Island. (Return 10 c.) On it is a cafe in the form of a Swiss Chalet.

The Park, known as the Bois de Boulogne, has an area of 2,250 acres, and is a fragment of the ancient Rouvray forest, so well known as the resort of robbers, suicides and duellists.

The Bois is most frequented from 3 to 5 in the afternoon, and the handsomest carriages and most elegant toilettes are to be seen on the favourite routes leading from the Avenue de Bois de Boulogne to the Lakes. Near the entrance, by the Porte Dauphine, are the Chinese Pavillions from the 1878 Exhibition, now used as a café-restaurant and concert.

CHURCHES

The city of Paris boasts of numerous churches, remarkable more especially for their architecture and historical relics; we will mention the principal ones.

The Paris churches are open all day to the public. On Sundays grand mass is celebrated about 10 o'clock (musical). In some churches, notably those of Notre-Dame, Saint-Roch, the Madeleine and Saint-Eustache, on fête days grand mass is celebrated with solos by the principal artistes of Paris. (Chairs 5 and 10 centimes.)

NOTRE-DAME, place du Parvis (Cité). — This church is open all day from six o'clock in the morning.

The most interesting object in this cathedral is the treasury, which is visible all day from 10 till 4 in winter and 5 in summer.

Visitors should apply to the Suisse, to the right of the choir, inside the surrounding railings. A charge of 50 c. is made.

To see the towers (20 c.), the great bell and the Sebastopol bell (another 20 c.) apply outside the Cathedral, to the left of the principal entrance. From the towers a splendid view is to be had, well worth the visit.

Historical. — The cathedral of Notre-Dame de Paris owes its foundation to Childebert. It is a magnificent specimen of gothic art, and, fortunately, escaped the devastations of the commune. It fell into ruin and its restoration was undertaken by Bishop Maurice de Sully, under Louis VII. about 1163.

This gigantic enterprise lasted about 200 years, was completed during the reign of Charles VII. (15th century).

Since this time the Cathedral has undergone several changes which have served to somewhat alter its primitive character.

This church is built entirely on piles and is 133 metres in length, and 48 metres broad. The height of the nave is 35 metres and that of the towers 69 metres.

Formerly the principal entrance was up 13 steps, but on account of the continual rising of the ground it is now on a level with the street.

Facade. — The facade is composed of three, superposed stories; the gallery under the grand rosace contains, in its niches, 28 statues of kings of France, benefactors of the cathedral-church, from Childebert down to Philip-Augustus; those which were placed there during the 13th century were destroyed in 1793. Above those of the kings are statues of Adam and Eve and of the Virgin Mary, with saints worshipping.

At the middle floor opens a magnificent rosace, 11 metres in height and the facade is surmounted by two square towers.

This imposing facade has three grand porches, erected under the arches, the sculptured portal represents the last judgment.

The Towers. — The towers of Notre-Dame rank amongst the first curiosities of Paris. Mounting the 368 steps which conduct you to the platform, a magnificent panorama spreads itself out before you.

In the "Tour du Midi" is the largest bell in France, (2ᵐ60 in diameter); only rung on the most solemn occasions, weighing 16 1/4 tons. Its clapper alone weighs nearly half a ton. The bell was baptized in 1672, with Louis XIV. for godfather. The tower contains four other bells for the service of the cathedral. Near the towers is to be seen the vast forest of chesnut timbers supporting the lead covering of the edifice, which weighs upwards of 210 tons.

The Spire. — The ancient Spire of the church was destroyed in 1881 and has been rebuilt : It tapers up, behind the two towers, to a height of 45 metres, and is built of oak, covered with lead.

Interior. — The interior of Notre-Dame presents an imposing appearance, on account of the general harmony and the boldness of the arches, which are supported by 21 thick pillars. There are five naves. On the first floor, extending round the principal nave and choir, is a gallery ornamented by 108 little columns, each of which is formed out of a single stone. On the occasion of grand ceremonies, this gallery serves as a tribune.

The church is lighted by the three principal rosaces and 103 stained glass windows, and contains several tombs, mausoleums and marble plaques erected to the memory of departed celebrities, notably those of: marshal comte d'Harcourt, by *Pigalle*; and several archbishops of Paris, de Beaumont, de Juigné, de Noailles, de Quelen, Affre, Sibour, Morlot and Darboy.

A magnificent organ is placed above the principal entrance. Twenty-three chapels form a belt surrounding the nave and choir.

In the nave is an elegant pulpit, surmounted by a baldaquin with group of angels.

Organ. — This grand organ is the work of Cavaillé-Coll, and was inaugurated the 7th March 1868. It is one of the most powerful and complete organs in France, having 86 stops and 6000 pipes.

Hostage memorial plates. — In the central transept are two black marble slabs upon which are engraved, in gold letters, the names of the hostages assassinated at Paris the 24th, 25th, 26th and 27th May 1871, during the communist struggle. There are 75 of them. On the left slab is written Clergy (clergé) and on the right Laity (laïques). The first list commences with the name of Mgr. Darboy and the other with that of the first President Bonjean.

Remark, in the chapelle de Saint Georges, the fourth of the belt, a stone statue representing Saint George and the Dragon.

In this chapel are erected two mausoleums of Cardinal Morlot and Archbishop Darboy, assassinated by order of the commune 24th May 1871.

Choir. — The choir is separated from the nave and surrounded by a fine polished and gilded iron railing. It is decorated with some beautiful woodwork in sculptured oak, and a series of remarkable bas-reliefs, representing Jesus-Christ and the Virgin Mary, separated by piers with arabesques and the Passion instruments. In the surrounding chapels are statues of Mgrs Affre, Sibour, Morlot and Darboy.

The choir owes much to the generosity of Louis XIV. Behind the high altar, resplendant with gilding, inaugurated in 1872, are statues of Louis XIII. and Louis XIV., the former placing his crown under the protection of the Virgin. Between these statues, at the end of the choir, is a group, in white marble, by *Coustou*, representing the Virgin supporting on her knees the dead body of Christ and, around, six bronze angels on columns.

The Treasury. (Le Trésor). — In the chapter vestry, to the right of the choir, is a collection in solid and elegant cases, of precious objects known as the treasures of Notre-Dame which, happily, escaped the devastations of the commune in 1871. Rich reliquaries, sacred vases and cups, crosses, pyxas, relics, all the objects contained in the Archbishop's private chapel, the anointing mantle of Napoleon, the sumptuous ornaments presented by the Emperors, the kings, Marie-Antoinette, a silver statuette of the Virgin given to the cathedral by Charles X., busts, the portraits of the different Archbishops of Paris, Affre, Sibour, Morlot and Darboy, a collection of cameos representing the popes since St. Peter down to Pius IX, a reliquary forming a cross, gift of Mgr. Guibert, and a pix sent by Leo XIII, on the occasion of his jubilee.

Every Friday during Lent and during Easter week, magnificent reliquiries are to be seen containing the crown of thorns, one of the nails of the cross and a piece of the cross, brought from the Orient by St. Louis.

In the exterior pourtour are famous stone pictures with bas-reliefs representing subjects drawn from the New Testament.

Do not forget to ascend the towers after having visited the interior of the cathedral.

THE MADELAINE. — Next in importance after Notre-Dame, comes the Madelaine, facing the rue Royale and the place de la Concorde. Open every day from 1 to 4, excepting Sundays and fête days. When the large doors are closed, enter by those of the lateral facades.

This vast, majestic looking temple, built in the greek style, on the model of the temple of Jupiter, at Rome, has about the same proportions.

It is surrounded by 52 Corinthian Pillars 49 feet in height. 28 steps lead up to the entrance.

The front is ornamented with a magnificent sculpture representing the last judgment.

On the bronze gates, of vast proportions, are represented, in 8 compartments, the laws of Moses (Triquetti).

Under the porticoes are 34 niches, each one containing the statue of a Saint, from Saint-Gabriel to the right, to Saint-Michael to the left. In the two niches of the facade are Saint-Philippe and Saint-Louis.

The foundation stone of this monument was laid by Louis XV. the 3rd April 1764, and it was not finished until the time of Louis-Philippe in 1843. It was at first intended for a church, then, after the Revolution of 1789, Napoleon wished to convert it into a temple of Glory. But Louis XVIII. made it definitely into a church, under the name of the Sainte-Madelaine.

The interior of the church is covered by three cupolas and two demi-cupolas, and is resplendant with marbles and gilding. Light is admitted through skylights in the cupolas.

To the right, on entering, the first chapel contains a marble group, by *Pradier*, representing the wedding of the Virgin Mary. A marble group in the chapel of the Baptismal Fonts, to the left, represents the Baptism of our Saviour, and is the work of *Rude*. The two graceful holy water pots in white marble are by Moyne.

An organ-loft dominates the principal entrance. The nave has six chapels, dedicated to the parishes of the church. Each chapel contains a statue of the sainte to whom the chapel is dedicated. The paintings above represent scenes in the life of Mary Magdelen.

A marble slab on the central column of the nave is in memory of the abbé J.-C. Deguerry, curate of the Madelaine in 1871.

A magnificent group in white marble by Marochetti representing the Apothesis of Mary Magdelen, ornaments the high-altar, with statues of angels praying to the left and right.

The paintings of the cupola of the hemicycle of the choir are by Zeigler; they represent the propagation of Christianity, Mary Magdalen at the feet of Jesus and historical personages from Saint-Louis to Napoleon I.

The pulpit is in sculptured wood, Renaissance style.

Note. — The chapelle de la Compassion, under the western collonade contains the tomb and a statue in white marble of the abbé Deguerry, curate of the Madelaine, shot as a hostage the 24th May 1871. To get to this chapel, leave the nave by the small door, to the left of the choir.

CHURCH OF SAINT-AUGUSTIN, boulevard Malesherbes, at the end of the boulevard Haussmann. — This church is one of the finest of New Paris. Above the three entrance doors are the pretty pictures; Faith, Hope and Charity. Fine dome, 164 feet high, 80ft diameter. Handsome windows, in stained glass, to the chapel of the Virgin, by *Brisset.* There is an immense crypt under the Church.

CHURCH OF THE TRINITY, Rue Saint-Lazare, at the extremity of the rue de la Chaussée d'Antin. — This was inaugurated in 1867, and is the elegant work of the able architect *Ballu.* It is one of the principal monuments of Paris. The facade is composed of a large portico, surmounted by a second stage pierced by an elegant rosace and a very high belfry. The portal is sculptured in Florentine style of the 16th and 17th centuries and opens on to a garden-square having a superficial area of about 3600 sq. yards. Facing the garden are three ornamental fountains and above which are statues of Faith, Hope and Charity by *Lequesne.*

In the interior are two elegant holy-water vessels, surmounted by statues symbolical of Innocence and Purity.

There are statues against each pillar of the nave. On the second pillar to the right is a marble slab bearing the following inscription :

« The Trinity church was converted into an ambulance during the siège of Paris 1870-1871, and the noble victims of our heroic resistance, were carefully tended here by the faithful of the parish ».

The church has a curious-looking high-altar. Behind the choir is a charming and spacious chapel of the Virgin, ornamented with handsome stained-glass windows. There are some very fine pictures by well known artists.

A spacious crypt exists under the choir communicating with the right and left hand vestries.

NOTRE-DAME-DES-VICTOIRES, place des Petits-Pères, near the place des Victoires.

This church built in 1639, was founded by Louis XIII., who consecrated it to the Virgin to commemorate his victories over the protestants and the taking of La Rochelle. The choir is ornamented in carved wood, and contains seven pictures by Carle Vanloo. The most remarkable of these pictures are those in the centre representing the allegory of the taking of La Rochelle, the prophecy before the bishop of Hippone, and the death of Saint-Augustin. In the chapels, and at the end of the choir are some stained-glass windows producing a very fine effect, representing the crucifixion.

The high altar is in white marble richly ornamented. In the first chapel to the right is a bronze representing Saint Peter seated on the Pontificial throne, object of special veneration, on the right foot of which the devout come to bestow a pious kiss. The chapel dedicated to Notre-Dame-des-Victoires is one of the richest in Paris, and is well worth a visit.

NOTRE-DAME-DE-LORETTE, at the extremity of the rue Laffitte and in the rue Chateaudun. — From the heavy and severe appearance of the exterior of this church, one is somewhat unprepared for the lavish profusion and elegance of the interior decoration. The church has the form of a roman basilisk. It was commenced in 1824 and finished in 1836, from the plans and under the direction of the architect Lebas.

The pediment represents Jesus-Christ adored by the angels, sculptured by Nanteuil, and is surmounted by statues of the three theological virtues : Faith, Hope and Charity, by Foyatier, Laitié, and Lemaire.

Having hardly entered the church, one is dazzled by the brilliancy of the gilding and paintings; the choir, as well as the nave and the chapels, are decorated with pictures from the able brushes of the well-known artists Schnetz, Orsel, Drolleng, Blondel, Picot, Hesse, Perrin, Heim, Couder, Devéria, Decaisne, Coutand, Camenade, Monvoisin, etc. Above the portico is a handsome organ loft, and in front of the carvec wood pulpit is a statue of the Virgin. A fine stained-glass window representing the Assumption is to be seen in the vestry at the end of the church to the left.

SAINT-SULPICE, place Saint-Sulpice (left side of the Seine) near the Luxembourg Palace. — The church Saint-Sulpice, a beautiful edifice of magnificent proportions, and commenced in 1646, on the plans of Charles Gamard, was finished by the architect Servandoni in 1849. Queen Anne of Austria was present at the laying of the foundation stone.

The principal facade, the two porches and the towers are of three orders; ionic, doric, and co inthian. The two towers, 210 feet in height, are not of the same kind; the metropolis boasts of the only church with this irregularity in style. The south tower was constructed by Maclaurin in 1749: that to the north, by Chalgrin, dates from 1777.

The choir, of which the magnificent high altar advances towards the nave, is ornamented with statues of Jesus-Christ, the Virgin Mary, and Angels and Apostles, by Bouchardon. It is 27 mètres 50 in length and is surrounted, as well as the nave, with seven majestic arcades supported by corinthian pillars. Eighteen chapels surround the nave and choir ending in the Chapel of the Holy Virgin.

The group in white marble, of the Virgin holding the Infant Jesus stands out splendidly at the end of this elegant chapel; it is the work of Pigalle. In St-John's chapel is the mansoleum of l'abbé Languet de Géry, curé of St-Sulpice, and in the chapel of S -Maurice is a statue of that Saint.

A richly decorated cupola by Lemoine represents the Assumption.

Above the vestry, to the right, is a statue of Saint- Sulpice.

The wedding chapel, to the left of the high altar is surmounted by a statue of St. Peter. It contains also a fine stained-glass window representing the marriage of the Virgin.

The paintings in the transept to the left, representing the crucifixion, and Jesus betrayed and delivered by Judas Iscariot, are the work of Signol. Those in the transept to the right represent the Resurrection and Ascension.

Notice the pulpit, due to the munificence of the Marechal de Richelieu, the dome of which is surmounted by a gilded group representing Charity. Opposite, a magnificent Christ on the Cross.

The baptismal chapel, the fonts of which are the work of Chalgrin, is under the peristyle of the building ; entrance by the first chapel on the left.

Every chapel contains several beautiful paintings by the celebrated artists Lafon, Pujol, Delacroix, Hesse, etc.

The magnificent organs are amongst the finest in the world.

The immense shells containing holy-water were presented to Francis I. by the Venitian Republic. Notice on leaving the church an elegant fountain decorated with statues of Fenelon, Bossuet, Masillon and Fléchier, the famous preachers.

SAINT-VINCENT DE PAUL, situated in the place de Lafayette. — This beautiful church was consecrated on 21st October 1844. It is reached by mouting several terraces of steps from the roadway.

The peristyle supported by twelve ionic columns, is surmounted by a pediment sculptured by Lemaire representing St.-Vincent-de-Paul, cross in hand, between the figures of Faith and Charity.

Two square towers 54 mètres high, crown this church ; one contains the clock, the other the bells. On the gallery encircling the towers are statues of St. Matthieu, St. Mark, St. Luke and St. John.

The bronze figures on the door, by Farochon, represent Christ and the apostles.

In the interior, notice a magnificent colonnade ; the frieze, painted by Flandrin, and considered his very best work ; the cupola of the choir painted by Picot; the platforms of the naves in carved wood with gilded ornaments; and the chapels, with beautiful windows.

Also notice the high altar with a splendid bronze by Rude of the crucifixion, and on the exterior of the woodwork figures in relief representing the patron saints of the Princes of the Orleans family.

Behind the choir is the chapel of the Virgin; it is ornamented by a beautiful group representing the Virgin, seated holding the infant Jésus above her head who is blessing the world. This masterly work, by Carrier Belleuse, was presented to the church by the Emperor Napoleon III. The statues of St. Joseph and St. Anne on each side of the entry to the chapel, are by the same famous artist.

Notice the pulpit in beautiful carved wood and the bronze baptismal fonts.

VAL-DE-GRACE. — The foundation of this building situated in the **rue Saint-Jacques,** dates from 1645. The first stone was laid by Louis XIV, at seven years of age.

Notice the dome, a copy of that of St..Peter's at Rome, and the cupola painted by Mignard. The high altar constructed in 1870 is ornamented by a group in white marble representing the Nativity.

The Val-de-Grace was formerly a celebrated convent of Benedictins, but is today a military hospital. Cardinal Dubois was consecrated archbishop of Cambrai here. The hearts of the Princes

NOTRE-DAME, THE MORGUE AND THE ILE DE LA CITÉ

This engraving represents the Chevet of Nôtre Dame : in the foreground the Morgue, and the Ile de la Cité, the most ancient part of Paris Under the Frankish Monarcheis the Church established its headquarters here ; but the Cité has long ceased to be the centre of Parisian life. It posseeses, however, the two finest sacred edifices in Paris : Notre-Dame and the Saint-Chapelle, the latter the finest specimen of gothic architecture extant. On the Ile are also the Palais de Justice, Préfecture de Police, Tribunal de Commerce, Pont-Neuf, numerous ancient chapels and Churches and the Hospital Hôtel-Dieu.

and Princesses of the royal family of France, and the bodies of the Princes of Orleans were deposited here in a special vault.

Notice in the court to the left a statue of Larrey.

SAINT-SEVERIN. — This church in the rue of the same name, replaces an oratory of the time of Childebert (IV century) destroyed by the Normans.

The actual facade dates from the xiii. century. The portal of the ancient church of St. Pierre-aux-Bœufs was built into its occidental facade, after the demolition of that church in 1809. This facade is crowned by a statue of the Virgin.

Saint Severin contains some précious stained-glass windows dating from the xv. and xvi. centuries.

To the left of the vestry door notice, in the wall, a very curious tombstone (1547) ; behind the choir in the chapel of the Virgin, a glazed altar, containing relics of St. Lea, and in the third chapel, on the right, a reproduction of the statue of St. Peter at Rome. All these chapels contain pictures by famous artists.

SAINT-MERRI. — The church, situated in the **Rue Saint-Martin**, which was but a chapel in the viii. century, was reconstructed in 1530. The portal richly decorated was restored during the reign of Louis Philippe.

The elegantly decorated choir, reconstructed in 1866, contains a rich high altar in the byzantine style; it is surmounted by a life size figure of Christ on the cross, in white marble, the work of M. Dubois.

On each side of the entry to the choir is a picture by Vanloo; one representing the Virgin and the Infant Jesus, and the other Saint-Borromée at prayer. The church possesses other beautiful pictures by Amaury-Duval, Lehman, etc., as well as some admirable stained glass dating from the xvi. century.

SAINT THOMAS D'AQUIN. — In the privileged parish of the **faubourg Saint-Germain**, this church commenced in 1683 was finished in 1740.

Notice in the chapel of Saint-Louis several beautiful paintings; in the transepts, chapels of the Virgin Mary, and of St. Vincent-de-Paul; between the choir and the nave, and in the cupola, several paintings by Blondel.

THE SAINTE-CHAPELLE, Palais de Justice. — Open free every day, excepting Mondays and holidays; from 11 to 4, in winter and 11 to 5 in summer.

This most ancient and precious jewel, of gothic architecture was erected by order of the king Saint-Louis, from plans by Pierre de Montereau, to preserve the relics the former had bought from Baudoin II, emperor of Constantinople, in 1241, and which consisted of the crown of thorns, and a piece, the largest known existing of the cross upon which Christ was crucified. (These relics are at the present moment amongst the treasure of the cathedral of Notre-Dame).

Commenced in 1245, the chapel was consecrated the 25th April 1248.

It was closed during the Revolution (1789-1793) and was utilised later on as a Record Office. The Sainte-Chapelle is now, after thirty years work, completely restored.

The colored windows in this Chapel are the most beautiful in existance and have been restored with great ability and success. The eyes are dazzled by the collection of such a combination of rich tones and shades and from the vivacity of the coulours, of which the secret of manufacture has never been discovered. They represent the principal scenes from the Old Testament, and the conveyance of the relics to the Sainte-Chapelle by Saint-Louis.

The elegant rosace of the portal dates from the time of Charles VIII., the subjects are taken from the Apocrypha.

You are shown, to the right of the choir a sort of private oratory or loop-hole where the king Louis XI., used to hear mass celebrated and from whence he could see without being seen, also the two seats of Saint Louis and of Blanche of Castile.

SORBONNE. — In the **place de la Sorbonne** opposite the lycée Saint-Louis. It is necessary to obtain permission to visit it from the secretariat de l'Academy de Paris, to the left of the porch.

This church, built by order of Cardinal Richelieu in 1643, completed the establishment of Robert de Sorbon, chaplain to the king St.-Louis, for the education of poor young people destined for the church.

The portal is crowned by a pedimemt similar to that of the Pantheon at Rome.

In the interior one notices to the left on entering a large and beautiful painting representing Sorbon presenting his pupils to the king St.-Louis.

The dome, decorated with pictures de Philippe of Champaigne is surrounded by four medallions.

In the interior of th transept on the right is the marble tomb of Cardinal de Richelieu, whose head cut off in the tomb by the revolutionists of 1793, was reinterred in 1866. Notice two black marble plaques with gold lettering in honour and to the memory of the great Cardinal; also a beautiful picture représenting Theology on the walls of the transept, and to the right of the choir, in a chapel, the marble cenotaph of the Duc de Richelieu.

SAINT-JULIEN-LE-PAUVRE. — In the rue of the same name, behind the ancient Hotel-Dieu. This church has been used by the Greek catolics since 1889.

It was famous even so far back as the vi. century, under Saint Grégoire de Tours. Pillaged and burnt by the Normans it was rebuilt in the 17th century, and became the priory of the celebrated abbey of Long-Pont, but was given up to the Hotel-Dieu in 1655.

The interior of the church, in the ogival style, comprises à nave and two side aisles, containing chapels very artistically decorated.

Between the nave and the choir is a superp image 8 metres high, entirely carved in massive wood and covered with remarkable incrustations. Also notice : against the walls various tombstones : statues of St. Vincent de Paul, of Montyon and of St. Landry the founder of the Hotel-Dieu ; the stalls of the choir, and in a pillar, a miraculous fountain, now dry.

THE CHURCH DU SACRÉ-CŒUR

— This church, in construction on the Butte Montmartre, after the plans of the celebrated architect Abadie, was commenced in 1875, and when terminated will have cost over 30 millions of francs.

This grandiose edifice, in the byzantine style, is being erected by subscriptions organized by the French clergy, and owing to its magnificent situation, will doubtless become one of the sights of the capital.

From the terrace in front of the church, a splendid view of Paris and its monuments may be obtained, decidedly as beautiful as that from the Eiffel Tower, besides which the church is more central.

As this church is situated in a rather intricate quarter, we advise our readers to take a hackney carriage when in tending to visit it.

Arriving at the public entrance, n° 35. Rue de la Barre, pass through the work-buildings about the facade of the church. From thence regard the unique panorama which unrolls itself of the south of Paris, between the Mont Valérien, the terrace of St.-Germain, the heights of Palaiseau, Villeneuve, Villiers-sur-Marne, and the cemetery of Perc-Lachaise.

Then enter the church, which is entrely free. Notwithstanding the fact that the central dome is as yet unfinished, one gathers some idea of the grandiose aspect the monument will assume when terminated.

Visit the bélfry, where may be seen the enormous bell inaugurated with great ceremony in 1895 by Cardinal Richard, Archbishop of Paris, and known as the " Savoyard ".

On leaving the church, obtain a card (25 centimes) to the right of the porch, and visit the crypt, where the chapels, notably that of St. Peter, are very beautiful.

THE CHAPELLE EXPIATOIRE. — Situated in a square, between the **rue des Mathurins** and the **boulevard Haussmann**, is the Chapelle Expiatoire, which recalls a world of souvenirs.

For permission to visit the chapelle. apply to the care-taker.

This monument, erected to the memory of Louis XVI. and to the Queen Marie-Antoinette, was commenced in 1820 and finished in 1826.

Built in the form of a cross, it is surmounted by a cupola. It is reached by a small garden, on the site of the ancient cemetery of the Madeleine, where the mortal remains of the ill-fated King and Queen reposed for 71 years,

In the interior notice two groups in white marble by Bosio: that to the right representing Louis XVI. ascending to the sky ; on the pedestal, in gold letters is inscribed the King's will. To the left, the Queen supported by Religion. The Queen's letter to her sister-in-law, Madame Elizabeth, dated 16th October 1793, engraved on black marble, is attached to the King's will afore mentioned.

Four semi-circular staircases on the right and left lead to a crypt, where a black marble altar contains the chalk and earth found touching the royal bones on exhumation.

THE PANTHEON. — For description of this edifice see page.

There are numerous other churches, but as they are of secondary importance, we do not describe them in detail. They are, on the right side of the river, notably these of : **Saint-Eugène**, rue Sainte-Cécile ; **Saint-Nicolas-des Champs**, rue Saint-Martin ; **Saint-Leu**, rue Saint-Denis and boulevard Sébastopol ; **Saint-Paul**, rue Saint-Antoine, 122 ; **Saint-Philippe-du-Roule**, rue du faubourg-Saint-Honoré, 154 ; **Saint-Pierre de Montmartre**, rue Saint Eleuthère, on the butte

Montmartre; **Saint-Honoré**, at Passy; **Saint-Jean** and **Saint-François**, rue Charlot; **Saint-Bernard**, at La Chapelle; **Sainte-Marguerite**. rue Saint-Bernard; **Notre-Dame d'Auteuil**, rue and place d'Auteuil; **Notre-Dame-de-la-Croix**, rue de la Mare, 6; **Saint-Denis-du-Saint-Sacrement**, rue de Turenne, 68; **Saint-Jean-Baptiste**, rue de Belleville; **Saint-Pierre de Chaillot**, rue de Chaillot; **Saint-Ambroise**, boulevard Voltaire, 73; **Saint-Georges**, rue Bolivar, 114; **Church de l'Assomption**. rue Saint-Honoré, 263; **Sainte-Elisabeth**, rue du Temple, 195; **Saint-Louis-d'Antin**, rue Caumartin; **Notre-Dame-de-Bonne Nouvelle**, rue de la Lune; **Notre-Dame-des-Blancs-Manteaux**, rue des Blancs-Manteaux, 12, etc., etc.

On the island of Saint-Louis, is the church of **Saint-Louis-en-l'Ile**.

On the left side of the river are the churches of: **Notre-Dame-des-Champs**, boulevard Montparnasse; **des Lazaristes**. rue de Sèvres; **Saint-Joseph-des-Carmes**, rue de Vaugirard; **Saint-Jacques-du-Haut-Pas**, rue Saint-Jacques, at the angle of the rue de l'Abbé-de-l'Epée; **Saint-Nicolas-du-Chardonnet**. rue Saint-Victor, 30; **Saint-Pierre du Gros-Caillou**, rue Saint-Dominique, 192; **Saint-Médard**, rue Mouffetard, 141; **Saint-Pierre de Montrouge**, avenue d'Orléans, at the angle of the avenue du Maine; **Notre-Dame-de-l'Abbaye-au-Bois**, rue de Sèvres, 16; **Notre-Dame-des-Carmélites**, rue Denfert-Rochereau and du Val-de-Grâce; **Saint-François Xavier**, boulevard des Invalides, 39; the **Church des Missions-Etrangères**, rue du Bac (Museum of instruments of penitential torture); **Saint-Thomas-de-Villeneuve**, rue de Sèvres, at the convent of the same name, etc., etc.

FOUNTAINS

FONTAINE LOUVOIS, place and square Louvois and Rue Richelieu. — This graceful fountain, erected in 1830, is the work of the celebrated Visconti. La Seine, la Saone, la Loire and la Garonne (the four principal rivers of France) are represented there by four charming statues, supporting the largest basin.

FONTAINE MOLIÈRE, rues Richelieu and Molière. — Erected by national subscription to the memory of the great comedian, opposite the house in which he died. The following is inscribed on the fountain: To Molière, born at Paris the 15th January 1622, died at Paris the 15th February 1673.

FONTAINE DES INNOCENTS, rue Saint-Denis and near the Central Markets. — The work of Jean Goujon and constructed in 1550, on the plan of Pierre-Lescot, this fountain, which attracts the attention and admiration of strangers, originally stood in the centre of the fruit market, Transported, stone by stone, to the place des Innocents, it is treasured as one of the rarest and most precious of parisian monuments. To be especially remarked: the sculptures of Niads by Jean Goujon.

FONTAINE DE GRENELLE by Bouchardon, **57, rue de Grenelle, near the Rue du Bac**. It represents Paris assisted on a gallery; at her feet the rivers Seine and Marne, and, on the sides, niches ornamented with bas-reliefs of the four seasons and two ships, emblems of the city of Paris.

FONTAINE DU CHATELET, place du Châtelet. — Erected in 1807, on the site of the old Châtelet prison. It is composed of a basement with two basins and statues of: Fidelity, Might, the Law, and Vigilance. The water falls from figures of Sphynx, and the summit of the monument is ornamented with a statue of Victory holding crowns.

FONTAINE SAINT-MICHEL, boulevard Saint-Michel, opposite the bridge bearing same name (left side of the Seine).

This beautiful fountain, which dates from 1860, is surmounted by a large statue of St. Michael casting down Satan. At the base of the monument two winged dragons furiously vomit water.

Following the above-mentioned fountains in importance, those of the place de la Concorde, place Daumesnil, place de la Nation, of Cuvier at the Jardin des Plantes, of the Zodiaque (avenue de l'Observatoire) with its eight sea-horses, its turtles, and a group representing the four quarters of the world, by Carpeaux; of Médicis, of place du Théâtre-Français, etc., etc., are worth visiting.

STATUES

Paris, the birthplace of so many celebrities. possesses comparatively few statues. Those worth seeing, however, are: The colossal statue of the Republic, on the Place de la République, work of the brothers Morice, the pedestal of which is ornamented by a bronze lion defending the urn of universal suffrage and bas-reliefs representing the principal feats of the first, second and third republics, as well as statues of Liberty, Equality and Fraternity.

Also, on the Pont-Neuf, the equestrian statue of Henry IV., and statue of the Republic in white marble in front of the Institut; equestrian statue of Joan of Arc, place de Rivoli; equestrian statue of Louis XIV., place des Victoires; the equestrian statue of Louis XIII, place des Vosges, (formerly Place Royale); of Marshall Ney, near the Observatory, at the entrance of which he was shot the 7th December 1815; of Bichat, in the court of the School of Medecine; of Larrey, in the court of the School du Val-de-Grace; those of Voltaire in the rue Monge and on the Quay Malaquais; of Claude-Bernard and of Dante before the college of France, and of Budé in the court, rue Saint-Jacques; of Denis Papin and Nicolas Leblanc, at the Conservatoire des Arts and Métiers; of Louis-Blanc, place Monge; of d'Aguesseau at Auteuil; of General Moncey, place Clichy; of Pinel, place de la Salpetriere; of Charlemagne, place du Parvis-Notre-Dame; of Alexandre Dumas, place Malesherbes; Gambetta's monument, place du Carrousel; of Shakespeare, Boulevard Haussmann; the Lion of Belfort (bronze), place Denfert-Rochereau, etc., etc.

COLUMNS

COLONNE VENDOME, Place Vendôme. — This column, commenced in 1806, and composed of 1700 bronze cannon taken from the enemy, was erected in 1810 to the glory of the French army. The Vendome Column, made on a model of Trajan's Column at Rome, represents on its 274 bronze plates, the principal events of the campaign of 1805, from the camp at Boulogne to Austerlitz. It is surmounted by a statue of Napoleon in the costume of a Roman Emperor.

Historical. — In 1814, when the allied troops entered Paris, the imperial statue was sawn through at its base, and thrown to the ground, and broken into a thousand pieces, which served to compose the equestrian statue of Henry IV erected on the Pont-Neuf.

During the Restoration an enormous fleur de lys, surmounted by a white flag, replaced the statue. Louis Philippe restored to the column the bronze statue of Napoléon I. in its legendary costume. Napoleon III has this again replaced by Napoleon in the costume of a Roman Emperor. After the war of 1870, the communists demolished this souvenir of French glory, which was re-established to the general satisfaction by a vote of the National Assembly the 30th May 1873.

COLONNE DE JUILLET, place de la Bastille. — Opposite the station of the Vincennes railway.

Erected to celebrate the fall of the Bastille, this column, which is 141 feet in height, was raised in 1831, and inaugurated during the reign of Louis Philippe in 1840. It commemorates two memorable periods : 1789 and 1830. There are interred the victims of 1830 who feel in the cause of liberty. The names of these heros are inscribed in gold letters on the column. Permission is given to visit the vaults from 10 to 4 (Apply to the guardian).

THE OBELISK, Place de la Concorde. — This monolith, called " Cleopatra's Needle " covered with hieroglyphics, was a present from Mehemet-Ali, vice-roy of Egypt. It is formed of a single block of rose granite, and its erection was superintended by the architect Labas in 1834. It is 68 feet in height and weighs 250,000 kilos.

TRIUMPHAL ARCHES

THE ARC DE TRIOMPHE DE L'ETOILE, at the place de l'Etoile, avenue des Champs-Elysées, is justly at the head of the Parisian arches. Before the construction of the Eiffel Tower, it was the hihgest building in Paris. It was commenced in 1806, by order of Napoleon, erected to celebrate the glories of the French Armies, and was terminated in the reign of Louis-Philippe, at a cost of nine millions of francs (£ 360,000. about). It is decorated with some magnificent bas-reliefs and very fine specimens of sculpture, and is a witness of the glorious triumphs of the first empire. Each stone tells of a victory, every name engraved thereon recalls a hero.

Each of the supports represents on the exterior, an enormous sculptured group.

The one to the right, looking towards the Tuileries, represents departure (1792), by *Rude*. That to the left represents Triumph, by Cortot.

On the side of the arch facing Neuilly, the right-hand support bears a group representing Resistance (1814) by Etex.

And last of all the support on the left side represents Peace (1815), Etex.

The Arc de Triomphe is one of the monuments which suffered the most during the com-

BUTTES CHAUMONT

This favourite resort of Parisians is the work of the celebrated
engineers M. Alphand and M. Barillet gardener in chief of Paris.
It cost upwards of ƒ 140 000.
On the summit of these hills once rose the gibbet of Montfaucon,
where criminals were hanged during the middle ages. (For fuller
description see page 76).

mune. It received during three entire weeks an average of ninety projectiles per day, which amounts in all to the number of 7000 shells. Since then the monument has been entirely restored.

The mortal remains of Victor Hugo were solemnly exhibited under the Arc de Triomphe during the day and night of the 31st of May 1885.

The Arc de Triomphe may be ascended every day from 10 to 4. Apply to the guardien (small gratuity).

THE ARC DE TRIOMPHE DU CARROUSEL, place du Carrousel, faces the monument erected to the memory of Gambetta. This arch was raised by order of Napoléon I in 1809. It is a model of the Septine Severus at Rome, and is surmounted by a figure of Victory in a car drawn by four horses, the whole in bronze, copied from those brought by Napoleon from the Piazza of St. Mark at Venice.

THE TOUR SAINT JACQUES, rue de Rivoli, and Place du Châtelet. This tower is all that remains of the church of Saint-Jacques de la Boucherie, pulled down in 1789 : It was brought by the municipal authorities in 1836 for 250,000 francs, and its restoration has since cost upwards of a million of francs

This magnificent tower was originally surmounted by a spire 30 feet in height. It is a fine specimen of the style of architecture preceding the Renaissance. The tower now occupies the centre of a fine public garden. Under the lower arch is a statue of Pascal. It was here that he made his experiments to ascertain the weight of the atmosphere. The total height is 178 feet (gratuity).

PORTE SAINT-DENIS. boulevard Saint-Denis. — This monument was erected in 1672 by François Blondel to the glory of Louis XIV, represented crossing the Rhine. It bears the inscription : Ludovico Magno, and has been the object of important restorations.

PORTE SAINT-MARTIN, Boulevard of that name. — Erected in 1674 by Pierre Bullet to celebrate the conquest of Franche-Comté, and the defeat of the Germans by Louis XIV. The arch is ornamented by four very fine bas-reliefs.

SQUARES ✦ PLACES ✦ MONUMENTS

Paris contains many squares; well-kept and ornamented with statuary, flowers, fountains, lawns and trees. They are open to the public all day.

SQUARE DU TEMPLE. — The square du Temple, occupies the ancient site of the Temple Tower, so sadly celebrated as the place of captivity of Louis XVI and Marie Antoinette. It has a superficial area af 7,200 square metres. The plantations of evergreens are divided into sixteen plots by gravel paths, and in the centre a miniature cascade escaping from an artificial rock, feeds a small lake. A statue of Béranger, the celebrated and popular singer, is in the square.

SQUARE SAINT JACQUES. — The square Saint Jacques, in the middle of which stands the ancient Tour Saint Jacques, is one of the most frequented squares in Paris. To mount the tower (from 12 to 3 every day) permission must be obtained from the Direction des Travaux, at the Hotel de Ville.

SQUARE DES ARTS ET METIERS. — The Square des Arts et Metiers, situated between the rue Saint Martin and the boulevard de Sebastopol, occupies a superficial area of 4,650 metres. Planted with old trees in full vigour, and surrounded by an elegant stone balustrade, it completes, with its lawns, fountains and its splendid statue recalling the victories of Inkerman, Alma and Sebastopol, the monumental ensemble of the Conservatoire des Arts et Metiers.

SQUARE DES TUILERIES. — The Square des Tuileries, situated between the pavillions of Marsan and of Flora, occupies the ancient site of the Palais des Tuileries, burnt during the Commune in 1871. It is separated from the Jardin des Tuileries by the rue des Tuileries and dominated by the Arc de Triomphe du Carrousel and the monument erected to the memory of Gambetta.

SQUARE LOUVOIS. — The Square Louvois situated in the rue de Richelieu, opposite the National Library, occupies the site of the old Opera, at the main entrance of which the duc de Berry was assassinated the 13th February 1820. A graceful fountain, the charming work of Visconti, occupies the centre of this miniature garden.

SQUARE DES INNOCENTS. — The Square des Innocents, situated to the left of the new halls of the central markets, near the rue Saint-Denis, deserves a visit. The celebrated fountain of

Jean Goujon has been transferred to this Square. Nothing could be more graceful than the Niads sculptured on the sides of this fountain.

After these are to be seen : The Squares of Montholon, Monge, Saint-Pierre, Saint-Sulpice, la Trinité, Parmentier, la Chapelle expiatoire, la place Malesherbes, Saint-Clothilde, Vaugirard, Belleville, des Batignolles, Montrouge, Charonne, Bon Marché, Grenelle, la place d'Anvers, Lamartine, etc., etc.

PLACE DU CARROUSEL. — This space and some flower beds now extend over the whole of the old spacious Court of the Tuileries. It derives its name from the tournament held here by Louis XIV. in 1662.

In the Place du Carrousel is the celebrated Arc de Triomphe du Carrousel, erected by order of Napoleon in 1806 and the two allegorical statues representing Law and War. From this square may be seen the Tuileries Gardens, the Obelisk (fellow to Cleopatra's needle, now on the Thames embankment). Champs Elysées and the Arc de Triomphe of the Place de l'Etoile.

On the Place du Carrousel is the Monument erected by national subscription to Gambetta, inaugurated the 13th July 1888.

GAMBETTA'S MONUMENT, Place du Carrousel. — On this monument Gambetta is represented standing up, his head slightly bent back, the right arm held forward, as, with an energetic gesture he shows his fellow-citizens the path of duty and honour. At his feet the defenders of the country are protected by a figure of the Guardian angel of France who is collecting together and rallying her disorganized army. On the socle beneath are four bronze statues representing Truth, Strength, Liberty, and Equality.

On the slab are inscribed the words of the immortal tribune, his appeal to the National defense, the apothesis of Universal Suffrage and a fragment of the speech of Cherbourg. The summit of the monument is crowned by an allegorical Group, in bronze, representing the Democracy as a young woman, seated on a winged lion.

PARKS ÷ WOODS

PARK MONCEAUX. — The Monceaux park, made by order of Philippe d'Orleans, from plans by Carmontel, belonged, under the first Empire, to Cambacérès.

Later on it became State property, and this lovely park is now open to the public, and forms the centre of a magnificent quarter of Paris, from whence start many of the principal arteries, viz boulevards Malesherbes. Courcelles, etc.

Open all day free to the public, either in carriages or on foot, the Monceaux Park is, without doubt, one of the most delightful resorts of New Paris. At night, under the electric light, the effect is simply fairylike. It is open until about 11 o'clock.

It has a beautiful surrounding grating, brilliant with gilding, which serves to link the four monumental entrances, of exceptional magnificence, and contains a collonade to which the appearance of a half ruin has been given, surrounding a semi-circular basin of water, fed by a river, winding amongst the grassy slopes of the garden.

To your right, the Pyramid. and a miniature cascade, escaping from an artificial grotto, falls, its glittering water splashing on to the rocks beneath ; to the left is to be seen the beautiful rotunda, inhabited by the park-keepers. and the restored ruins of the Naumarchie. About the park are numerous statues, amongst which the Paradise Lost by J. Gautherin is remarkable.

THE BUTTES CHAUMONT. — Perhaps the most extraordinary of the works undertaken in the construction of New Paris is the transformation of the Chaumont heights. situated to the north of Paris, between Belleville and la Villette into a vast park, covering a superficial area of about 54 acres. Open free, day and night.

This park was formerly a large waste ground, cut with ravines and hills, on the summit of the highest of which was raised the famous Montfaucon Gibbet.

The park is bordered on the east by the rues de Belleville and de la Villette, and on the south by a new boulevard which now connects the latter street with the rue de Puebla. The whole ground, may be taken in at one glance from the elegant balustrade skirting a portion of the new boulevard, and affording a splendid view of the whole country around. To our right we see in a deep ravine the railway round Paris passing through the park, where it disappears into the tunnel. Before us we perceive the principal feature of the park : a lofty island cut out of the natural rock and surrounded by a fine sheet of water. The height of this solitary rock is upwards of 60 feet : it ends in a peak. crowned with a belvidere of tasteful architecture commanding an excellent view of a large portion of the metropolis, and called the Temple of the Sibyl. This island is accessible on one side by a stone bridge, and on another by a suspension-bridge supported by rustic piers. In the valley is a delightful grotto, the interior of which sparkles with stalactites and stalagmites. Further on to our left, is a carriage-road spanned by a fine wrought-iron suspension bridge, 63 metres in length giving access to the higher portions of the ground, which is intersected by gravelled paths, and planted with valuable trees and shrubs. Here, on the 27th of September, 1870, the ninth day of the siege, a petroleum depot caught fire; and much fighting took place between the Versailles troops and the Communists in the latter days of May, 1871.

BOIS DE VINCENNES (Vincennes Wood). — The Bois de Vincennes is, like the Bois de Boulogne, remarkable for its cascades, lawns and beautiful pieces of water.

It is less aristocratic than the Bois de Boulogne, but is, since its latest improvements, the most picturesque of the walks in the environs of Paris. It covers au area of 2162 acres and is a favourite place of resort and recreation to the inhabitants of the eastern quarters of Paris. It contains the beautiful artificial *Lac des Minimes*, covering a surface of 20 acres, extending to the pretty village of *Nogent-sur-Marne* (fine railway viaduct over the river Marne).

On the Paris side of the wood are the *Asile des Invalides Civils*, for convalescent workmen, and the new *Military Hospital*.

PARC DE MONTSOURIS (The Montsouris Parc). — This park is situated boulevard Jourdan, and is crossed by the Sceaux Railway. It is not far from the station of the Tramway de Montrouge — gare de l'Est.

A very pretty Park, ornamented by a lake and verdunt grassy slopes it forms an interesting visit for the stranger. It contains a monument of Col. Flatters and an Observatory know as the Bardo Observatory, which figured at the Exhibition of 1867. Open free, day and night.

LE RANELEYH — Is situated avenue Ingres, near the Passy Railway station. This magnificent, shady promenade, with statues and lawns, has replaced a pleasure resort founded here in 1774, for the nobility. Near here are the Hothouses of the town of Paris. (Serres de la ville de Paris) For admission apply for tickets at the Hotel de Ville.

GARDENS

JARDIN DES PLANTES. — The garden of plants, situated place Walhubert, facing the pont d'Austerlitz (near the gare d'Orléans) is open all day to the public, as a promenade, but the Menagerie and the Museum (the former perhaps the finest in Paris) are only visible certain days and hours.

There are four things to be seen at the « Jardin des Plantes », viz : The Garden, the Museum, the Menagerie and the Hothouses.

To visit the Museum, Menagerie or Hothouses on any other than those days reserved to the public, a demand must be made, in advance, in writing, to the Director of the Museum for a ticket.

Itinerary. — Enter the garden by the place Walhubert, and, leaving the school of drawing, take the path to the right leading to the Carnivorous animals section of the Menagerie.

The Menagerie is open to the public every Thursday from 1 to 4, when the animals are not exhibited outside, and on other days from 1 to 4, by ticket only. The menagerie proper is composed of 22 boxes, with iron-barred fronts, where lions, lionesses, tigers, bears, panthers, etc., etc., promenade nonchalantly.

The feeding of these wild animals is held every day, at 3 o'clock, and is a curious sight. Enter by the small door to the left of the Menagerie. The Monkey house is also at this side of the Menagerie.

The Monkey House. — A vast rotunda surrounded by large trellis works, in cages, jumping and gambolling, as no body knows how to do better, are the little monkeys.

Facing the Monkey house is the Grand Rotunda, the home of the elephants, hippopotami, dromedaries, etc., and near the Rotunda to the left, is the bears'pit, asylum of some magnificent specimens of Bruin, who assume plastic poses and stand upright etc at the word of command.

Leaving the pit of bears, return to the grand rotunda and visit the Pheasant House and Falcon House, situated in an avenue to the left, facing the entrance.

The Faisanderie. — In this house, as in the Pheasant House at the Jardin d'acclimitation, are exhibited a varied collection of pheasants, partridges, pheasants, pintadoes and song birds.

At the side of the Pheasant House, a little to the right, is :

La Fauconnerie (The falconry). — In this long enclosure are exhibited, in separate compartments, eagles, condors, vultures, etc., etc.

To the left of the falconry, separated by a pathway, is the splendid new pavillion devoted to reptiles.

Le Pavillon des reptiles. — This Pavillion is well worthy of a visit to see its installation and arrangement. It is open to the public every Thursday, from 1 to 4; and other days at the same hours, by ticket.

Thanks to the numerous mirrors, the inhabitants of this room may be seen, as they are almost always hidden away, eazily coiled under blankets.

In the interior, under the centre of the magnificent rotunda, is an immense basin, surrounded by rocks and aquatic plants for the caymans, crocodiles, tortoises, etc., to take their constitutionals in.

Turn your back to the reptile building, direct your steps to the right, and you will soon arrive at the galeries d'anatomie comparée.

Galerie d'anatomie comparée. — Open to the public Thursdays and Sundays from 11 to 3, and Tuesdays Fridays and Saturdays at the same hours, but by ticket. Before the entrance of the gallery there are two remarkable whale-bones.

On the ground-floor, to the right, on entering, skeletons of whales, cachalots and carnivorous fishes.

On the first-floor, you will find, in the different rooms, a rich collection of skeletons of all kinds of animals, also rooms devoted solely to the human anatomy, where are types of all the races of the earth compared.

Amateurs of phrenology will find a complete collection of plaster-moulded heads, notably those of the famous criminals Lacenaire, Papavoine, etc.

In the court surrounding the Galerie d'anatomie comparée, to the left, is the salle de Paléontologie, a very curious antedeluvian museum, visible every Tuesday from 1 to 4, with ticket.

Leaving the Galerie d'anatomie, bear to the right, and, after passing the phoques, direct your steps straight to the Grand Labyrinth, planted with evergreens and crowned with a charming kiosk, from whence a splendid panorama unfolds itself.

The famous ceder of Liban, which was brought there by M. de Jussieu, in his hat, and a granite column erected to the memory of the celebrated naturitist Daubenton, indicate the road to the Labyrinth.

Facing the grand labyrinth, to the right, are the Hothouses (Serres), open every Tuesday, Friday and Saturday, from 1 to 4; entrance by ticket. They contain exotic trees and tropical plants, a very rich and rare collection.

Leaving the Hot-houses, descend the grand avenue, direct your steps to the right, towards the natural history gallery, where to the right, a new and magnificent building rears itself, in which is installed the galleries of Zoology.

Galeries de Zoologie. — Open to the public the Thursdays and Sundays, from 11 to 3 (and the Tuesdays, Fridays and Saturdays, from 11 to 3, on presentation of a ticket).

The gallery of Natural History contains :

On the ground floor. — Hall : Large mammiferous animals and skeletons of whales.

The salle : lions. tigers, bears and monkeys.

Surrounding Gallery : Show-cases containing reptiles, etc., etc.

On the first floor : Bird room : Parrots, Doves, birds of paradise, humming-birds, etc., etc.

Surrounding Gallery : Cases containing birds, reptiles, fish, molluscs and zoophites.

Hall : European birds.

Second Floor : Hall: Insects, arachnides and crustaceous specimens.

Surrounding Gallery : Cases containing insects, butterflies, worms and grubs, shells.

Leaving the Zoological Gallery, make your way directly to the Minerology and Geology Museums.

Bibliothèque, Galeries de Minéralogie, de Géologie et de Botanique. — Open every Thursday and Sunday, from 11 to 3; and Tuesdays, Fridays and Saturdays from 11 to 3, by ticket. Rich collections of metals, precious stones and minerals. Remark specially samples of the earth composing the crust of the globe, and several grand scenes of the Polar regions, by *Biard*. In the centre of the museum, to the right, is the statue of Cuvier, by David d'Angers, and to the left, that of Haüy, by *Brion*. Farther on, is that of M. de Jussieu.

Having visited these three museums, return once again to the grand avenue, and leave the garden by the door leading to the Place Walhubert.

JARDIN DES TUILERIES.— The Tuileries Garden, designed by Le Notre, to order of Louis XIV. is 2256 feet in length, and 990 feet in width. To the north of the Garden was the ancient couvent des Feuillants, and the terrace now existing on its site is known as the Terrace des Feuillants.

Open to visitors from one o'clock (after morning service). Entrance by the side doors when the principal doors are closed. The high altar consists of a fine group by *Marochetti*, representing Mary Magdalene being borne into Paradise by two Angels. (For full description see page 68).

Near this spot was the manège (riding school) in which were held the sittings of the National Assembly. The Tuileries Garden is bisected throughout its entire length by a broad avenue extending from the site of the ancient palace to the Place de la Concorde. At each end is a large circular basin. These Gardens are open to the public throughout the year. They comprise two large enclosures laid out in flower-beds, with two groves of chesnut, elm, plane and lime trees, skirting the principal avenue down to the Porte du Pont Tournant. Flights of steps and inclined paths lead up to the terrace overlooking the Place de la Concord. There are many fine statues scattered about the Tuileries Gardens.

The panorama of the 19th century, by MM. Alfred Stevens and Henri Gervex, stands at the foot of the terrace near the orangery. Part of the Gardens skirting the road leading from the Pont Royal to the rue des Pyramides, occupies the site of the ancient Tuileries Palace which was burnt by the communists on the 23rd May 1871, and remained a mass of ruins until 1883, when the remains of the old palace were pulled down and the Gardens opened.

JARDIN DU PALAIS-ROYAL. — The Palais-Royal Garden, surrounded by arcades and splendid shops, occupies more than 4,000 mètres. About 3 o'clock in the winter, or towards 5 o'clock in the summer, when the concerts held here are taking place, it presents a very animated appearance. A cannon is fired here every day at twelve o'clock, correct French time.

JARDIN DU LUXEMBOURG. — The Luxembourg Garden occupying three sides of the palace of that name, is the work of Jacques de Brosse. The plan, composed of an octogonal basin with grass plots, is skirted by flower-beds, and flanked right and left with elevated balustrated terraces shaded with fine chesnut groves. Spacious flights of steps descend from the terraces into the central part, which is decorated with numerous marble statues representing the celebrated women of France. On the eastern side of the garden, its chief ornament is a fountain built by Catherine de Medicis, after the designs of Desbrosses; its niche is a lorned with a group representing Polyphemus discovering Acis and Galatœa. Behind it, facing the street, there is a bas-relief by Valois, representing, Jupiter and Leda. In the adjoining grass-plot stands a beautiful marble group, by Garrand, of Cain and his family after the death of Abel, Further north is a large orangery, in which gratuitous lectures on pruning and grafting are given in summer. There is also a collection of about 500 different kinds of vine, brought from foreign countries; likewise a model apiary, lectures being given here at stated seasons on the rearing of bees. The garden is 919 metres long by 570 in breadth; its area is 340,064 square metres. A recent addition to the statuary of the garden consists of the monument erected to Eugène Delacroix, whose bust, in bronze, stands on a marble pedestal. The composition is of spirited design, the fountain from which the monument springs being in white marble, of classic taste. The inscription upon the pedestal runs as follows: " A Eugène Delacroix, 1798-1863, ses Admirateurs ".

WALKS

THE CHAMPS-ELYSÉES. — Besides her Boulevards, Paris possesses numerous promenades, all of which have their special character and attractions.

The Champs Elysées is really the national continuation of the Boulevards, as you have simply to cross the rue Royale and the Place de la Concorde and you are in this magnificient avenue.

Perhaps it would be well before proceeding up the Champs Elysées, if we take a look at the Place de la Concorde. This square is said to be the finest in the world. It was formerly known under the name of Place de Louis XV and was, until that king ascended the throne of France, an irregular piece of waste ground,

In the centre of the square is the Obelisk of Luxor, a magnificent relic of ancient Egypt, one of the two obelisks that stood in front of the great temple of Thebes, erected there 1550 years before Christ by Rameses III, of the 18th Egyptian dynasty. The two obelisks were presented to the French Government by Mehemet Ali, Viceroy of Egypt, in consideration of the services rendered by France to Egypt during the construction of the arsenal and naval establishment at Alexandria, but only one of them was removed.

The obelisk weighs 500,000 lbs., is 72ft in height, 7ft 6 in. in width at the base and 5ft 4 at the top. The apex is still in the rough state in which it was when discovered in Egypt. It stands on a single block of grey granite, from the quarries of Laber, in Brittany.

On each side of this monument is a fountain, the one dedicated to Fluvial and the other to Maritime navigation.

They consist each of a circular basin of polished stone, 50 feet in diameter, out of which rise two other smaller basins. Six cast-iron figures nine feet in height are resting on the prows of vessels, and six dolphins, held by as many Tritons and Nereids, spout water into the basin above. These fountains now repaired, suffered considerably from the cannonade exchanged between the Communists, who held the Tuileries Garden, and the Versaillais, who, on the 22d of May, 1871, already occupied the whole part of the city west of it.

The Place de la Concorde joins the Tuileries gardens and the Champs-Elysées. On the North is to be seen the Madelaine and on the south the Chambre des Deputés, and beyond this the Dome of the Palais des Invalides.

The Place de la Concorde has been rendered famous by many events, which I will give in their chronological order :

MAY 30, 1770. — During the rejoicing in honour of the marriage of Louis XVI., a fatal accident was caused, after a discharge of fireworks, by a panic in consequence of carriages driving among the crowd, and rushing towards the rue Royale, where the ground had been broken up for building; 1,200 persons were trampled to death, and about 2,000 others seriously injured.

JULY 12, 1789. — A collision between Prince de Lambesc's regiment and the people became the signal for the destruction of the Bastille.

JAN. 21. 1793. — Louis XVI, suffered death on this Place, (1) where the following persons also subsequently perished by the guillotine : July 17. Charlotte Corday; Oct. 2, Brissot and 29 of his colleagues. Oct. 16, Marie Antoinette, consort of Louis XVI. ; Nov. 14. Louis Philippe Joseph Egalité, Duke of Orleans; March 24, 1794, the Hebertists, Maratists, and Orleanists; April 8, the Dantonists, including Danton, Camille Desmoulins, etc. April 16, the Atheists, composed of Chaumette, Anacharsis Clootz, the wives of Camille Desmoulins, of Hébert, etc. ; May 12, Elisabeth Marie Hélène of France, sister of Louis XVI. ; July 28. Robespierre and his brother, Dumas, St. Just, and Couthon, Members of the Committee of Public Safety, with several others : July 29. seventy members of the Commune de Paris; July 30, twelve other members. From Jan. 21. 1793, to May 3, 1795, more than 2800 persons were executed here.

APRIL 10. 1814. — The Russians, Prussians, and Austrians were reviewed and Te Deum was sung at an altar on this Place.

FEB. 23. 1848. — The first disturbances that ushered in the memorable revolution of that year took place here.

FED. 24. 1848. — Flight of Louis Philippe and his family by the western entrance of the Tuileries Garden.

Nov. 4. 1848. — The Constitution of the Republic was solemnly proclaimed here, in the presence of the Constituent Assembly.

SEPT. 4. 1870. — The downfall of Napoleon III. and the Third Republic proclaimed, after the disaster of Sedan.

MAY 22, 1871. — A desperate conflict between the Versailles troops and the Communists, the latter in their retreat setting fire to public and private buildings.

Now to proceed with the Champs-Elysées. This is different from the boulevards in that the Boulevards are borderded by houses and the Champs-Elysées, from the Place de la Concorde to the Arc de Triomphe, is bordered by Palaces. This superb avenue, of which the engraving, page 79, will convey some idea of its beauty, its a scene of the greatest animation, in all seasons of the year, swarming with pedestrians and equipages of all kinds. From about two to five o'clock every day it is a dazzling and ever-changing scene of continuous movement, caused by the passing of Parisian Society to and from the Bois de Boulogne (corresponding with Hyde Park, in London).

In the evening, quite a different aspect and a different public. Still the same rush of vehicles, cavaliers, lady equestrians, rich men and beautiful women thronging the Avenue, taking the fresh air after dinner; but the evening the pedestrians are in the majority. Then, during the summer, the café-concerts on either side open their doors to the public, presenting a most brilliant spectacle.

Leaving the Place de la Concorde, pass between the two « chevaux de Marly » (Marly horses) two remarkable groups by *Coustou*, and follow the grand avenue, dominated by the Arc de Triomphe.

To the left are the café-concert de l'Horloge, the Restaurant Ledoyen, and the Palais de l'Industrie, with its majestic front; farther on the Palais de Glace (real ice skating rink) the Jardin de Paris, and the Panorama of the Champs Elysées.

On the right the two café-concerts, the Ambassadeurs and the Alcazar, some pretty fountains, and, further on, the Folies-Marigny Theatre (a pretty little house, beautifully decorated, principally light comedy) and finally the cirque des Champs Elysées (Champs-Elysées circus).

On this side of the Avenue are to be found numerous representations of those great treats for the children of all countries, Punch and Judy shows and goat carts, etc., etc.

After passing these you come upon the rond-point, about the centre of the avenue, round which are arranged four splendid fountains, surrounded by large plots of flowers.

After leaving the Rond-Point, following the Champs-Elysées, straight on, you arrive at the Arc

---

(1) The scaffold for the execution of Louis XVI, was erected midway between the centre of the place and the horses of Marly; that for Marie Antoinette between the centre and the gate of the Tuileries.

RESTAURANT UNIVERSEL

9, boulevard des Italiens, 9

PARIS

The ROAST BAR keeps the joints at the temperature of issue from the oven and preserves the full delicacy of their flavour.

DEJEUNERS
and
DINNERS
at
2 *francs*
and
3 *francs*
per
head
including Wine

DEJEUNERS
and
DINNERS
at
2 *francs*
and
3 *francs*
per
head
including Wine

TELEPHONE — READING ROOM

English spoken — Man spricht Deutsch

DEJEUNER OR DINNER
at **2** francs

I HORS D'ŒUVRE OR SOUP
2 DISHES AT CHOICE
OF EITHER MEAT OR VEGETABLES

CHEESE — DESSERT

A DECANTER OF WHITE OR RED WINE,
CIDER, MILK OR TEAPOT OF TEA

DEJEUNER OR DINNER
at **3** francs

I HORS D'ŒUVRE OR SOUP
2 DISHES OF MEAT AT CHOICE
(OR ONE MEAT & ONE VEGETABLE)
ONE MEAT & VEGETABLE
OR SWEETS ENTREMET

CHEESE — DESSERT

A BOTTLE OF BORDEAUX OR 1/2 BOTTLE
OF SUPÉRIEUR
(OR CIDER, MILK, TEA, ETC.)

Proprietor : **M. BLOTTIER Jeune**

9, BOULEVARD DES ITALIENS, PARIS

RESTAURANT UNIVERSEL

9, boulevard des Italiens, 9

PARIS

The ROAST BAR keeps the joints at the temperature of issue from the oven and preserves the full delicacy of their flavour.

DEJEUNERS

and

DINNERS

at

2 *francs*

and

3 *francs*

per

head

including Wine

DEJEUNERS

and

DINNERS

at

2 *francs*

and

3 *francs*

per

head

including Wine

TELEPHONE — READING ROOM

English spoken — Man spricht Deutsch

DEJEUNER OR DINNER
at **2** francs

I HORS D'ŒUVRE OR SOUP
2 DISHES AT CHOICE
OF EITHER MEAT OR VEGETABLES

CHEESE — DESSERT

A DECANTER OF WHITE OR RED WINE,
CIDER, MILK OR TEAPOT OF TEA

DEJEUNER OR DINNER
at **3** francs

I HORS D'ŒUVRE OR SOUP
2 DISHES OF MEAT AT CHOICE
(OR ONE MEAT & ONE VEGETABLE)
ONE MEAT & VEGETABLE
OR SWEETS ENTREMET

CHEESE — DESSERT

A BOTTLE OF BORDEAUX OR 1/2 BOTTLE
OF SUPÉRIEUR
(OR CIDER, MILK, TEA, ETC.)

Proprietor : **M. BLOTTIER Jeune**

9, BOULEVARD DES ITALIENS, PARIS

de Triomphe, situated at the Place de l'Etoile, or Place of the star, the rays of which are formed by twelve fine boulevards, which commence at this spot.

Note. — Whilst here, visit the interior and summit of the Arch, from whence a superb panorama may be seen of Paris (Small gratuity to attendant).

THE BOIS DE BOULOGNE. — The fame of the celebrated Bois de Boulogne is world-wide. But this favoured spot is no longer, as formerly, the favourite resort of poets and of lovers on their honeymoons. Still however it retains its ancient reputation, it is a lovely wood, and is now, as much as ever, the favourite walk of strangers and holiday-makers.

Where can such a crowd be found, such a class of people, such toilettes ? Everyone would answer :

Go to the Bois, between 4 and 5 o'clock in the afternoon, or on a raceday, when the Avenue du Bois de Boulogne, preceding and leading to the Bois, is crowded with equipages, equestrians and foot passengers.

To go to the Bois de Boulogne, take, for preference, a hackney carriage. One can be obtained from your hotel or from a livery stable at from 3 francs per hour, or taken in the street, 2 place carriages : 2.50 the hour, 4 seats, 2.75 the hour. If you discharge your carriage outside the fortifications of Paris, an indemnity of 1 franc must be given to a cabman taken in the street or 2 francs if from a livery stable. If, however, you keep the carriage and return home in same the price remains at so much per hour.

Another way to get to the Bois de Boulogne is by Rail, from the gare St.-Lazare. Trains leave every 15 minutes. Book for Avenue du Bois de Boulogne.

If you are several persons together, the most economical way to visit the Bois is in a carriage and it is always the most agreeable.

The Bois de Boulogne, outside the Paris fortifications and comprising a surface of 873 hectares, bears the name of a neighbouring suburb. Before 1789 its trees were decaying with age. The Revolution in part cleared it ; whatever was then spared was felled in 1814, to make palissades against the approach of the allied armies. In July, 1815, after the capitulation, the English under Wellington encamped here. It had grown again into a thick and beautiful wood, when the disastrous siege of 1870 once more rendered its partial devastation necessary. The Bois, now the property of the City of Paris, was noted for the annual promenade de Longchamps, and is now the most fashionable place of resort for a drive or a walk, where the finest horses of the capital are displayed. The annexed map will be found very useful in directing the visitor to the most interesting spots.

The best way of visiting this delightful resort is to enter it by the *Avenue du Bois de Boulogne*, commencing from the Rond Point of the Arc de Triomphe de l'Etoile. Continuing along the road exactly opposite to this Avenue, a few slight turns to the left will bring the visitor at once to the borders of the lakes, the great attraction of the wood. The first of these lakes, which are fed by the Artesian well of Passy, is 3.600 feet in length and 750 broad, and encompasses two islands, connected by a rustic wooden bridge, and occupying together an extent of 2,400 feet. Here, art and taste have combined to charm the eye with the most picturesque scenery. At the southern extremity, opposite the islands, two charming cascades, one of which is now popularly called *La Source*, pour their waters, bounding from rock to rock, or gushing from crevices skilfully arranged, into the lake beneath winding paths, emerging from the cool fir-groves scattered around, intersect the rich turf which clothes the banks down to the water's edge.

The second lake is separated from the former by a neck of land, called *Carrefour des Cascades*. This second lake is much smaller, and less attractive than the other ; boating may be indulged in on the first.

JARDIN D'ACCLIMATATION. — The Zoological Gardens of the Bois-de-Boulogne are open to the public all day. Entrance fee : week-days, 1 franc ; sundays and holidays, 50 cent. ; for a carriage and servants, 3 francs.

This prosperous model establishment was founded by a Limited C°, and is, without doubt, the success of the day, being one of the most charming promenades of Paris.

During the summer, concerts are held here at 3 o'clock every Thursday and Sunday. No extra charge is made.

Itinerary. — Enter the garden by the " porte des Sablons " and take your coupon to the right on entering.

A wide and magnificent avenue opens before you at the entrance, to your right are the Offices, to the left, the winter garden.

Walk straight on, then direct your steps to the right, to the Salle d'Exposition Florale and the Museum of hunting and fishing, a collection of traps and objects used in the capture of animals. The Hothouse and Museum communicate with the galleries of the permanent exhibition, where are the produce of several great Parisian industries.

From the Exposition, visit the Monkey House, where are all kinds of monkeys, and leaving this take the road to the grand aviary (grande volière) before which you will notice, from the distance, a statue of Daubenton, in white marble; on the way, to the left, cranes, peacocks, etc.

The grand aviary is a marvel of light construction, and contains 21 comparments of the rarest birds, sultana-hens, flamingos, pheasants, blackbirds, etc.

Pigeonnier militaire (military pigeon cot). — This pigeon cot is facing the grand aviary, containing very rare specimens of pigeons and those which are the objects of special studies.

At the end of the grand aviary descend by a small path, near a tree which bars the passage; after the pheasants you come to the semicircular fowlhouses, forming 28 divisions. Interesting exhibition of fowls, pheasants and pigeons.

After the fowlhouses cross the stream and at your right are the kangaroos, in front, the stables.

In front of the stables you take the tickets for the elephant, dromedary and pony rides and for the ostrich races, etc.

Facing the stables is the large circular lawn where the exhibition of savage peoples are held.

In the stables, which are divided into boxes, are the ponies, zebras, elephants and farther on, in another building, the giraffes, ostriches and dromedaries, preceded by goats and cows.

Leaving the stables, pass between the porcupine enclosure and the antedeluvian World panorama (entrance 50 c.), and again follow, to the right, the grand circular avenue.

To the right, are the rein-deer, to the left, the alpagas and lamas (the latter I should not recommend you to coax on the nose) and behind, the goats Rochery. Near, the phoca pond.

Then again, to the right, the cow-houses, where you can have a bowl of real pure milk, fresh and warm from the cow, for 40 cts.

Further on, still to the right, is the Aquarium, where you can admire the denizens of the submarine world. Four basins are reserved to the fresh water fish.

Then the magnificent cafe-buffet where a halt should be made for a few minutes rest and refreshment.

To the left of the buffet is the kiosk in which the concerts are held during the summer.

After leaving the café, to the left you will notice the stags and hinds, then, the reading room, where photographs of the animals may be bought, and the kennels.

After this, near a very curious tree the Grande Serre (Grand Hot-house) at the entrance to which are the rare birds, parrots of all kinds, where you may promenade amongst the world of flowers, plants and vegetables, grouped together with perfect taste.

You are at the end of the gardens.

For the purchase, sale or exchange of animals, apply at the Administration.

There are many ways of getting to and from the Jardin d'Acclimatation, tramways, omnibuses, railways and by hackney or livery carriage.

Return from the Gardens. If you have a carriage, return by the avenue de la Porte-Dauphine, opening in front of the exit of the Garden, take the avenue du Bois-de-Boulogne, avenue Hoche, parc Monceau and boulevards Malesherbes, Madeleine and Capucines.

If you are on foot, return to the Porte-Maillot, from whence you can take the rail to the gare St-Lazare or return to the Palais-Royal by the omnibus Porte-Maillot-Hotel-de-Ville (15 cent. each outside or 30 cent. inside).

PROMENADES

PROMENADE ON THE CHAMPS DE MARS. — Ascent of, and dinner on the Eiffel Tower. The ascents do not take place in winter, that is to say from October to the month of April.

Set aside a whole day during clear weather to visit the Eiffel Tower and the Champ-de-Mars. He who has never seen Paris from the Eiffel Tower has seen nothing.

Note. — Take a cab at ten o'clock, and go to the Champ-de-Mars, or the tramway from the Louvre will answer the same purpose. Starting from the Louvre you will descend from the Pont d'Iéna.

Description. — Arriving at the Pont notice : to your right the Trocadero Palace, with its numerous museums, beautiful cascade and park; to your left the Eiffel Tower, constructed entirely of iron, which attains the unprecedented height of 300 mètres (it is the highest monument in the world); then the Champ-de-Mars, in a majestic frame the central dome with its magnificent statue

GAMBETTA'S MONUMENT

This monument, facing the Arc de Triomphe du Carrousel, consists of a lofty stone pyramid with a bronze in high relief (by Aubé) representing the famous patriot as organiser of the national defence.

At the sides are decorative statues representing Truth and strength, and, on the summit, Democracy, a maiden seated on a winged lion, also by Aubé.

The numerous inscriptions are passages from some of Gambetta's political speeches.

PONT AND PLACE DE LA CONCORDE

This fine bridge divides the Chamber of Deputies and the celebrated Place de la Concorde; the magnificent square which has been the scene of some of the most stirring events in the history of France.

In the centre stands the celebrated obelisk of Luxor on the side of which are two beautiful fountains.

On the west may be seen the Arc de Triomphe and Champs-Elysées, on the north the Madeleine and on the east the Tuileries Gardens and Louvre.

of Fame. On the left is the Palais des Beaux Arts, and to the right is the Palais des Arts Libéraux.

Note. — These three edifices are, with the gallery of machines, situated behind the central dome and the Eiffel Tower, all that remains of the marvellous constructions created on the Champ-de-Mars for the Exhibition of 1889.

Itinerary. — Cross the bridge and enter the Champ-de-Mars by passing beneath the Eiffe Tower.

Remark in the park the basins with their rocks and cascades, before you the central fountains and the magnificent monumental fountain of Coutan, surmounted by a statue of the Republic. From there visit the central dome, and returning by the vast buildings still used for permanent exhibitions, come to the Eiffel Tower. Ascend it and have dinner on the first stage.

EIFFEL TOWER. — Ascent of Tower. The tower may be ascended in two ways : either by the staircases or by the lifts, as far as the second stage, but by the lift only to the summit.

Price of the Ascents. — Week days : to the first stage 1 franc, from the first to the second 1 franc ; from the second to the third stage 2 francs. Sundays : 50 centimes to the first stage, 50 centimes from the first to the second, and from the second to the third 1 franc.

The tower is divided by platforms into three parts : the first is 57 mètres high ; the second 115, and the third 280 mètres. The whole is crowned by a cupola, above which is a light-house, from which a monster electric light is directed.

This vast quadrangular pyramid is sustained by four iron pillars, each having a sectional diameter of 15 mètres.

Imagine the immense chandeliers of four branches each 100 mètres apart, and making an arc of 70 mètres.

The first stage is an immense platform 70 mètres square, covering a surface of 4,200 metres. From the exterior gallery may be had the finest panoramic view of Paris.

Panorama. — To the north : at your feet the Seine and the Pont d'Iéna, then the park and the Trocadero Palace. Farther on to the right the Arc-de-Triomphe and the Fort of Mont-Valérien. To the west : on the right the Seine, the Ile-des-Cygnes, the railway and viaduct of Auteuil. To the south: The park of the Champ-de-Mars with its monumental fountain, the Palais des Beaux-Arts and the Arts Libéraux, the dome of the Palais Central surmounted by the statue of Fame, and finally the vast cupola of the Gallery of Machines. Farther on to the left the dome des Invalides and the Panthéon. To the east : the view from this side is majestic ; in front of you the Opéra, the Palais de l'Industrie and the Vendome Column ; to the right the dome des Invalides, the towers of Notre-Dame and the Panthéon, and, towering above, the Butte-Montmartre, with its Church of the Sacre-Cœur.

Of course it goes without saying that the views from the higher stages are even more wonderful.

The Manometer. — Since 1891 the tower has been furnished in its entire height with a mercurial manometer, the most powerful one that has yet been made. It is composed of a steel tube of 4.5 mm. interior diameter.

After having contemplated while dining the admirable panorama which unrolled itself before your eyes, descend the Tower and go out of the Champ-de-Mars, cross the Pont d'Iéna and return to the boulevards.

BOIS DE BOULOGNE. — From the Barrière de l'Étoile, a magnificent avenue bordered by palaces and gardens (the ancient avenue de l'Impératrice, now the avenue du Bois de Boulogne) conducts you direct to the Bois de Boulogne by the Porte Dauphine, where the fortifications begin.

By following this beautiful avenue, to the left called the Route de Suresnes, you arrive at the Lac Inférieur.

If you have an hour to spare, go in a boat to the Chalet des Iles, the most beautiful spot in the Bois. Having arrived at the extremity of the Lac Inférieur, turn off to the right, and leaving the Lac Supérieur, cross near to a little waterfall, the Rond des Cascades; then follow a ravishing avenue of trees which will conduct you directly to the Hippodrome de Longchamps. From there, turning to the right you will arrive in a few moments before the Grand Cascade, one of the curiosities of the Bois de Boulogne.

Panorama. — In front of you Suresnes ; to the left the racecourse of Longchamp, the Tribune and the Moulin de la Galette. To the right the tower of the ancient Abbey of Longchamp, dominated by Mont-Valérien, the highest of the ancient forts of Paris. Having finished your visit to the Cascade, return by the Avenue de Longchamps to the Jardin d'Acclimatation.

To your left Bagatelle and the Club des Patineurs, to your right the Pré Catelan, where is situated the farm of the Jardin d'Acclimatation, the Paris Zoological Gardens.

MANUFACTURIES

THE GOBELIN TAPESTRY MANUFACTORY (Les Gobelins), 42, Avenue des Gobelins. — This national tapestry manufactory is open Wednesdays and Saturdays from 1 to 3.

Historical. — The manufacture des Gobelins was established in 1603 by Henry IV in the buildings occupied by the dyer, Jean Gobelin, on the banks of the Bièvre, towards the end of the 15th century. In 1662 it was acquired by Louis XIV. who, at the suggestion of Colbert, established there the « Manufacture des meubles de la Couronne » (Crown furniture manufactory).

After the end of Louis the fourteenth's reign, the Gobelins factory was devoted exclusively to the manufacture of tapestries.

The 25th May 1871 part of the factory and show-rooms were burnt by the communists.

SÈVRES PORCELAIN MANUFACTORY, at Sèvres, near Paris. — The Ceramic exhibition is open every day from 12 to 4 or 5, according to the time of year. The work-rooms are only to be seen by special permission from the Administration.

MANUFACTURE DES TABACS, Quai d'Orsay (Tobacco Manufactory). — Open Thursdays, from 10 to 12 and 1 to 3. Special permission must be obtained, for which application should be made in writing to the director.

PASSAGES

The Paris passages are very numerous; they are intended to shorten journeys and also serve as places of shelter in wet weather.

The most frequented ones are : the passage des Panoramas, Jouffroy and Verdeau, boulevard and faubourg Montmartre; the passages des Princes and of the Opera, boulevard des Italiens; the passage Vivienne, rue Vivienne; the passage Véro-Dodat, rue du Bouloi; the passage Delorme, rue St.-Honoré; the passage Choiseul, rue de Choiseul; the passage du Saumon, rue Montmartre, and the galerie d'Orleans, at the Palais-Boyal.

Paris Hot-houses. — The Hot houses of Paris are situated 115, avenue Henri-Martin, near the parc de la Muette and the entrance to the Bois de Boulogne. They may be visited every day from 1 to 5, or 6 in summer, with tickets for which application should be made to the Service des Travaux à l'Hôtel de Ville.

These houses contain plants used to ornament the gardens and squares of Paris. They cover an area of 7000 metres; amongst them those containing the palms and camelias are upwards of 12 metres in height.

Note. — These houses are to be transferred to the bois de Vincennes.

ENVIRONS OF PARIS

ALFORT. — This village is celebrated for the veterinary school founded there by Bourgleat in 1764. It is about a quarter of an hour by rail from Paris. Departure from the Chemin de fer de Lyon, boulevard Diderot.

ARCUEIL-CACHAN. — This village, about 3 miles from Paris, has 6.070 inhabitants. and is composed of two localities separated by a superb aqueduct, constructed in 1624 by order of Marie de Medicis, to bring the water from Rungis and the environs of Paris to the Luxembourg.

In the garden of the collège des Dominicians is a chapel containing the tombs of the clergy massacred under the commune the 25th May 1871.

This village played an important role in the defence of Paris. It has a remarkable church in the 15th century style.

ARGENTEUIL AND ORGEMONT. — Situated about 7 1/2 miles from Paris, departure from the Gare Saint-Lazare.

Noted for its asparagus and strawberries. It was in the convent of Argenteuil that the unfortunate

Eloisa was educated, and she retired here in 1120 before her entrance to the Paraclese, prepared for her by Abelard.

The Seine regattas, both yachts and steamers, are held at Meulon, near here.

In the church of Argenteuil is preserved a precious relic, the seamless garment worn by Our Saviour, given to the ancient monastery of Argenteuil by Charlemagne. Annually, on ascension day, a procession is held in honour of the sacred tunic, and every day at one o'clock the bells of the church are rung in memory of the hour at which the sacred relic was left there by Charlemagne.

After visiting Argenteuil, strangers would do well to continue their journey to Orgemont, about 15 minutes from Argenteuil on foot. The Moulin d'Orgemont is situated on a platform at the summit of a mount about 450 feet in height, from which point a magnificent view may be had of Paris and the course of the Seine from Saint-Cloud to Saint-Germain. Entrance fee to the Mill 15 centimes.

ASNIÈRES. — This important centre of rowing and boating, celebrated for its gudgeon and fried-fish, is about 3 miles from Paris on the Saint-Germain Railway, and is a charming riverside resort.

The best time to get a real idea of Asnières is on a Sunday.

During the second siege of Paris in 1871 this village was one of the chief points of attack and was much damaged.

ANDRESY. — Departure from the Gare Saint-Lazare by Argenteuil.

Curious church, charming neighbourhood, and a very ancient merovingien cemetery, discovered during the construction of the railroad.

ARPAJON. — This village, surrounded by numerous and charming promenades, was called Châtres in 1871, which name was subsequently altered in favor of Louis, marquis of Arpajon.

BARBISON. — Known, in the Parisian world of artists, as the « paint box », is a charming and modest village on the border of the Forest of Fontainebleau.

Theodore Rousseau, Millet, and several other renowned artists, having acquired properties in the village, in order to be near their dear forest, died here.

The permanent exhibition of paintings is well worth a visit. The private collections belonging to the various hotels are equally interesting. To visit these collections is easy. It is simply necessary to order refreshment of some kind, then to ask for permission.

BAGNEUX, a hamlet on the Sceaux Railroad, was occupied by the Prussians in 1870. There is a church of the twelfth century.

BELLEVUE, a collection of country houses, derives its name from the bright aspect and picturesque panorama opening out around it.

Biew. — At your left is to be seen Bas-Meudon, with its numerous restaurants; further on Billancourt, Boulogne, and the Bois de Boulogne. To the right, the Point du Jour, Paris and her monuments. To the left, Saint-Cloud and Mont-Valérien, crowned by its redoubtable fortress.

BOUGIVAL. — Another favorite boating resort, in a very picturesque locality. Near here is La Grenouillère, the celebrated rendez-vous of artists, the Parisian bohemian, and boating parties ; quite a curiosity of its kind. Ball, buffet, etc.

The road from Bougival to La Grenouillère is a delightful promenade of about twenty minutes along the shady banks of the Seine.

BICÊTRE. — John Bishop of Winchester, built a castle here in 1306, named Chateau de Wincestre, from whence came Bicestre, Bicetre. It also boasts of a celebrated hospital, used as an Asylum for male lunatics, and indigent old men. Near by stands a fort, which played an important part during the siege of 1870. It was reoccupied by the French on September 23rd, and held until the capitulation, effectively keeping in check the Prussian works at Choisy-le-Roi, Thiais, Chevilly and l'Hay. After the 18th March, 1871, the forts of Bicêtre and Ivry unaccountably fell into the hands of the communists without firing a shot, and were not re-occupied until the 25th May, when the troops were already masters of Paris.

BOURG-LA-REINE. — About a quarter of an hour by rail from Paris on the Sceaux line. Louis XV received the Infanta of Spain here in 1722. About a mile from Bourg-la-Reine, are the villages of Hay and Chevilly, scenes of severe struggles during the siege of Paris.

It was here also that Condorcet, persecuted by the Convention, committed suicide by taking poison, in 1794. There is a house built by Henry IV for Gabrielle d'Estrées with fine park.

BUC. — A village about 13 miles from Paris, is remarkable for an aqueduct of 19 arches erected by Louis XIV, which conveys water to Versailles (nearly two miles distant).

BEAUVAIS. — Is a town of about 14,000 inhabitants, 2 1/2 hours from Paris on the Northern line. In ancient times it was the capital of the Bellovaci, who surrendered it to Cæsar without a blow B. C. 57. It was destroyed by the Normans in 850, and besieged by the British in 1443. Celebrated for its Government tapestry manufactory and magnificent old cathedral.

CHAMPIGNY. — May be reached by the Vincennes Railway. A monument has been erected here in commemoration of a battle fought on the 30th Nov. 1871, which ended favorably for the French, the Prussians being compelled to retreat from their lines, which they were unable to retake on the 1st of December following. But expected help being delayed from without, and a severe frost having set in, the French retreated voluntarily the day after.

CHANTILLY. — Is a town about an hour by rail from Paris, on the Northern line, and was once the residence of the illustrious Conde. That part of the mansion called the Grand Château was demolished in 1789, and the works of art, with the exception of those which had been moved and hidden, were destroyed. On the Restoration in 1814, the Petit Château was restored to the house of Condé, and many improvements were made by the last of that name, who frequently resided there. His melancholy death taking place in 1830, Chantilly descended to the Duc d'Aumale, 4th son of Louis Philippe, who commenced rebuilding the chateau de Chantilly, on the foundations of the ancient residence, in 1876. The building is one of the finest examples of the French Renaissance style, and is after the plans of M. Daumet, the celebrated architect. The spacious galleries contain the Duke's unique collection of paintings, statues, rare books, and other works of art. Under his will the Duc d'Aumale has bequeathed the French Institute in trust for the nation the whole of this magnificent property with its priceless art collections and library. The domain of Chantilly, will, therefore, on the Duke's death, become national property. On the site of the present chateau formerly stood not only the residence of the Condés, but also a celebrated fortress of the 14th century. The Petit Chateau now forms a wing of the modern building. The stables are considered the finest in Europe. Admission to the chateau, stables and grounds is obtained without difficulty. The forest, adjoing the park, contains 7.600 acres; in its midst is a circular area called the Table Ronde, from which twelve roads branch in different directions. The lakes of Commelle, about an hour's walk across the forest, are skirted by the village of Commelle and the chateau de la loge, said to have been built by Blanche de Castille, mother of St.-Louis. An English Protestant church has been erected here; also a Wesleyan Chapel.

The semi-annual races take place in May and October. At the May meeting the French Derby is run for.

CHARTRES. — Is a town of about 18,000 inhabitants ; celebrated for its splendid cathedral.

CHARENTON. — Was celebrated for the controversies which took place there between Catholics and Protestants under Henry IV, Louis XIII, and XIV. It is better known now for its lunatic asylum. The fort played an important role in the defence of Paris in 1870.

CHATILLON. — This village is situated at the foot of a lofty plateau, and was converted by the Prussians during the war of 1870-1, together with the Tour des Anglais close by, into a most formidable stronghold. Immediately after the 18th March 1871, it was occupied by the Communists until the 3rd of April. A monument erected to the memory of those who fell here commands some fine views of Paris and neighbourhood. From the front of the new fortress, on a clear day, the tower of Montlhéry may be perceived in the distance, and a splendid panorama unfolds itself of the picturesque valley of the Bièvre.

CHOISY-LE-ROI. — Situated about eight miles from Paris, a station on the Orleans Railway, derives its name from a castle built there by Louis XV, of which a few scattered ruins still remain. *Rouget-de-Lisle*, the composer of the Marseillaise, lived here, and died in this village in 1806. A statue has been erected to his memory. It was by a bridge over the Seine at Choisy-le-Roi that the German army obtained their provisions during the siege of Paris of 1870, and to protect this bridge the place was fortified very strongly.

COLOMBES. — An ancient village on the plain of Jean Vallier, the seat of the last great sortie against Buzenval and Montretout, on the 19th January 1871.

COMPIEGNE. — A town of about 15,000 inhabitants, about an hour and a half from Paris, Northern Railway, is celebrated for its numerous historical monuments, castle, and beautiful forest. It was during the defence of Compiègne that Sainte Joan of Arc fell into the hands of the English on the 25th May 1430.

The celebrated rue de Rivoli runs along the side of the Tuileries Gardens and the shops under the arcades of this street are the special delight of foreigners and searchers after antiquities and curiosities.

From the rue de Rivoli, opposite the place Jeanne-d'Arc, a gateway leads into the Tuileries Gardens, decorated with many beautiful groups and statues. In the centre an ornamental basin and fountain.

Leaving this behind you see before you the obelisk of Luxor, on the left the Panorama of the Century and a second basin and fountain and through the gateway on the right the Rue de Castiglione and : —

THE VENDOME COLUMN

This Column, 145 feet in height, was erected to the honour of the french armies.

Its sides are covered with illustrations in relief of the various scenes in the campaigns of Napoleon I.

It is surmounted by a statue of Napoleon as a Roman Emperor.

Passing the Place Vendome you arrive in a few minutes (following the Rue de la Paix, bordered by sumptuous shops) at the Place de l'Opéra.

In 1260 the palace of Compiègne was founded by Saint-Louis. Compiègne is mentioned as far back as the time of Gregory of Tours. The famous prelate mentions the city as having been a royal residence, much frequented by the Merovingien and Carlovingian monarchs who came here to hunt in the vast forests. Louis XVI first met Marie Antoinette in this palace, and Napoleon I held the first interview with Marie-Louise here. The wedding of King Léopold I of Belgium with Princess Louisa of Orléans, eldest daughter of Louis Philippe was celebrated in the palace chapel.

In Compiègne, the chapel of St.-Nicholas merits a visit on account of its magnificent altar piece in carved oak, and the fine wood-work of the choir.

The Hôtel de Ville is one of the most beautiful Gothic monuments in France. This graceful edifice is surmounted by a belfry 160 feet in height, and was constructed in the reign of Charles VI, at the commencement of the 16th century.

Under the spire of the belfry are three automatons, vulgarly known as the Picantins, which chime the divisions of the hours.

The Musée Vivenel, a magnificent collection of art objects presented to the town by one of its inhabitants M. Vivenel, is worthy of a visit. It is open free to the public every Thursday and Sunday from 2 to 5. On other days application should be made to the concierge at the Hotel de Ville, to whom a small gratuity should be given.

The entrance to this Museum is in the interior court yard of the Hotel de Ville, in the right wing.

The Palace. — It is situated on the *Place du Château*, a spacious square, surrounded with alleys of lime-trees. The *Grand Vestibule* leads by the *Escalier d'Honneur*, a fine double-branched staircase, flanked with marble statues of l'Hopital and d'Aguesseau, to the *Salle des Gardes*, a long Doric hall, adorned with splendid panoplies. The *Salon des Huissiers*, to the left, contains a hunting scene under Louis XV., painted by Oudry. The adjoining *Salle à Manger*, an Ionic hall, opening into the garden, and painted in grisaille by Sauvage, opens to the right into a suite of apartments formerly inhabited by Madame Adélaïde, sister to Louis Philippe. The suite consists of a *Salon d'Attente*, painted in grisaille, and adorned with a splendid rural scene, executed in Gobelins tapestry, a *Salon de Réception*, with three mythological subjects in Gobelins tapestry, and, lastly, a *Chambre à Coucher*, with beautiful arabesques painted in the panels. The *Salon des Aides-de-Camp* contains large maps, painted on canvas, of the forests of Compiègne, Fontainebleau, St. Germain, and Marly. Next follows the *Salon du Conseil*, a splendid room, with a Gobelins carpet and Beauvais furniture. The walls are adorned with three fine pieces of Gobelins tapestry, representing sacrifices to Pallas, Flora, and Ceres, from originals painted in 1787, by Suvée. We next enter the *Salon de Musique*, with four pieces executed in Gobelins tapestry, representing Chinese and other oriental subjects. Next follows a bed-chamber, the ceilings and panels of which, painted by Girodet, represent the Evening Star and the Seasons. This bed-chamber leads to a second *Salon de Réception* ; the ceiling and panels over the doors are painted by Girodet.

The next room is the *Salon des Fleurs*. The coves of the ceiling, by Girodet, represent Departure, War, Victory, and the Return. Descending a staircase we find the *Salle du Spectacle*, with three tiers of galleries, and capable of containing 800 persons. The *Galery de don Quichotte*, with 31 paintings by Coypel, father and son, represents the most striking scenes of Cervantes' masterpiece. From this we enter the *Grande Gallery des Batailles*, which is a gorgeous saloon, built by Napoleon I., the arched ceiling, supported by 20 Corinthian columns, illustrating in 12 allegorical compartments, by Girodet, the victories of Wagram, Austerlitz, etc. The *Galerie Neuve*, built in 1858, is adorned with a series of eight paintings by Natoire, completing the series of scenes from Don Quixote above described. The chapel is Doric and Ionic ; the window represents, in stained glass, the Creator, Faith, and Hope. This palace is visible every day, from 12 to 4.

A spacious terrace behind the palace, adorned with statues, slopes down into the *Garden*, laid out in the English style. The *Forest* is seen from the terrace, and is reached by an arbour of iron frame-work, 4800 feet long and 14 feet in breadth. To the left, the terrace ends in a fine avenue of lime trees, planted on part of the old ramparts of Compiègne. The forest of Compiègne contains 36,590 acres, 338 roads, forming a length of 220 leagues. All the finger-posts pointing to the town are painted red.

In front of the Hotel de Ville to the right, is a fine statue erected to the memory of Joan of Arc, n 1880. In the rue Saint Corneille, nᵒ 19, are the remains of the enormously wealthy Abbey of Saint Corneille, founded by Charles the Bald in 876, destroyed during the Revolution.

The church of Saint Antoine, rue du Portail Saint Antoine, is a historical monument of the 12th century.

The church of Saint Jacques is the most important, and the British church in the town. It contains some fine pictures copied from the great masters.

Before leaving the town, visit the Gymnase des Minimes, an ancient church, and la Porte Chapelle, erected in 1552 by Philibert Delorme, by order of the constable de Montmorency.

After leaving the palace, visit the beautiful parc, and, if time permits, make an excursion into the forest.

FONTAINEBLEAU. — The palace and town of Fontainebleau are distant from Paris about 2 hours by rail on the Lyons Railway. In the centre of the place Centrale, to the left of the Grande Vue, stands a bronze statue of General Damesme, who fell in the insurrection of 1848. The chief attractions of Fontainebleau, however, are its palace, unrivalled for magnificence, and its picturesque forest. The palace is open to the public every day from 11 to 4; and the garden and park are open all day.

Fontainebleau may be seen in one day, but in our opinion, not less than three days should be devoted to properly visiting the palace, park and forest.

Visit first of all the Hotel de Ville. From the square may be seen the gate of the palace. This gate leads to the Garden of Diana.

The chateau de Fontainebeau, that is to say the present building, to which the principal entrance is by the Cour du Cheval Blanc a little farther on, was erected by Francis I., and was the favourite residence of that monarch. It was enlarged, embellished or restored by all his successors down to and including Napoleon III., It appears, however, that Fontainebleau was a Royal residence as far back as the days of the first of the Capets. Robert the Devout built a castle there in the 11th century, which was finished by Louis VII., of which little remains excepting the buildings surrounding the Oval Court.

The palace covers a superficial area of 60,000 square metres.

Although rich with artistic marbles, this chateau is still richer in historic memories. We give, in their chronological order the principal : In 1539 the reception of Charles-Quint by Francis I. In 1601 the birth of Louis XIII. 1692 arrest of Marshal de Biron by order of Henry IV., charged with high treason. and he was afterwards removed to the Bastille, where he was beheaded. The 10th of November 1657 Monaldeschi, the secretary and favourite of Queen Christine the Suede, was assassinated here by her orders, 1685 Revocation of the Edict of Nantes by Louis XIV. A year after the great Prince of Condé died in the Palace. In 1765 the only son of Louis XV. died here. In 1804 the chateau was restored by order of Napoleon, and in 1809 he was divorced from Josephine. In 1812 Pius VII was imprisoned here. In 1814 Napoleon signed his abdication, and made his formal farewell to his Imperial Guard. Louis Philippe in 1831 restored it on a magnificent scale, everything being restored in its original style, and it was here, in the forest, that his assassination was attempted by Lecomte. The Palace is now used as a summer residence of the President of the Republic, and during the three months of his stays the palace regains the gay and attractive appearance of the old days.

The apartments and Chinese museum are open to the public every day from 11 to 4 from the 1st of October to the 31st of March, and from 10 till 5 from the 1st of April to the 30th September.

Entrance is obtained by the door which faces the Place aux Charbons.

We enter first Diana's Garden, so-called from a fountain ornamented with stags'heads, and surmounted by a statue of Diana, all in bronze, erected by Napoleon, in the middle of a beautiful white marble basin. This garden was called the box tree garden under Francis I., and later on, under Henry IV. the Aviary Garden, on account of the aviary he had installed there, and, in the time of Louis XIII., the Orangery Garden, on account of an Orangery which replaced the aviary.

Leaving the fountain, advance to the right towards the palace, take the avenue leading in the direction of the exist, and enter the Cour du Cheval Blanc, now known as the Cour des Adieux, which almost faces the grand monumental staircase called on account of its shape horseshoe. The Cour du Cheval Blanc. derives its name from an equestrian statue in plaster, a model of the statue of Marcus Aurelius at Rome, which was placed under a dome in the centre of this court by order of Marie de Médicis. It was here that Napoleon bade farewell to his National Guard at the foot of the grand staircase. On this account it is now known as the Cour des Adieux. The frontage of the chateau is composed of five pavillions, bearing the names of, 1, the *Pavillion des Aumôniers*, or *de l'Horloge*; 2, the *Pavillion des Ordres*; 3, the middle pavillion, called *des Peintures*, adorned with a bust of Francis I; 4, the *Gros Pavillion*; 5, the *Pavillion des Armes et des Poêles*, from German stoves erected there in the time of Francis I. In the centre is the *Escalier du fer à cheval*. Here, eleven months after his farewell, Napoleon reviewed the troops he was about to lead to Paris. The other two sides of the court are formed by an old wing of the time of Francis I., and a new one, of a different design, erected by Louis XV. on the site of the splendid *Galerie d'Ulysse*, thus destroying some of the best frescoes of Primaticcio.

Interior. — The order in which the visitor is led through the different apartments is usually 1, to the upper gallery of the *Chapelle de la Trinité*; 2, the staircase descending into it; 3, the *Galerie des Fresques*, or *des Assiettes*; 4, the rooms formerly occupied by the Duchess of Orleans; 5, to the Horseshoe staircase, and 6, to the *Galerie de François I*. The *Chapelle de la Trinité* was constructed by Francis I., on the site of one erected by St. Louis; a fragment of the latter, a Doric arch at the bottom of the nave, still remains. The arched ceiling is painted by Fréminet. The altar, of the time of Louis XIII., is by Bordoni; the altar-piece, the Descent from the Cross, was painted by Jean Dubois; the four bronze angels, and the statues of Charlemagne and St. Louis, are by Germain Pilon. The marriages of Louis XV. and of the late Duke of Orleans, as also the baptism of

Napoleon III., were celebrated here. The *Galerie des Fresques*; is remarkable for its panels, with paintings of Fame, Victory, Juno, Ceres, Flora, etc., by Ambroise Dubois. The wainscoting below is decorated with 128 beautiful plates of Sèvres porcelain, representing the principal residences of the French monarch. Returning to the vestibule, we enter the *Galerie de François I.*, a magnificent hall, 60 metres in length, with a ceiling divided into compartments beautifully gilt, and a maze of scroll-work, caryatides, and arabesques in alto-relief on the walls, encompassing frescoes by Rosso and Primaticcio. On the panels of the wainscoting are various devices, the letter " F, " and the Salamander, the emblem chosen by Francis I.

The apartments des Reines Mères derive their name from having formerly been the residence of the Dowager Queens. In 1812 they were inhabited by Pope Puis VII., and afterwards by the Duchesse d'Orléans. The two first contain curiosities brought from Siam in 1861 by an embassy from that country, and they are all remarkable for their splendid specimens of Gobelins tapestry. In the first, a press contains several well wrought bowls and other metal utensils, girdles and weapons set with jewels. Close to this press is a palanquin with spangled curtains, and a beautiful throne to be carried like a palanquin; accompanying this throne is a rich, portable canopy, which like the throne is studded with precious stones. In the second room, which was the Pope's salon de réception, there are some weapons of beautiful workmanship, and a saddle and bridle, also studded with jewels, and some very curious, richly embroidered banners. After this, comes the chambre a coucher d'Anne d'Autriche. This room was used as an oratory by Pope Pius VII. during the eighteen months he was an unwilling inmate of the palace. It was here that Napoleon tried to compel him to sign the concordat, by which he would have renounced his temporal power. The ceiling of this room is gorgeously carved and gilt. The next room was used by Puis VII. as a study, and now contains his portrait, although arranged as cabinet de toilette; then comes another toilet room, the next chamber to which was his bedroom. In the adjoining room is a beautifully carved press by Jean Goujon. The next is an ante-chambre, and contains portraits of Charles VI., Louis IX., Henry IV., and Louis XIV. by Horonois, besides paintings by Poussin, Mignard, Breughel, etc.

Returning to the vestibule, a private staircase leads to the private apartment of Napoleon I., which was also that of Louis Philippe and Napoleon III. These rooms are rich in Gobelin tapestry. In the ante-chambre is a fine portrait of Mᵐᵉ de Montespan. The paintings over the doors are by Boucher. The cabinet du secrétaire, and the salle des bains leads to the cabinet particulier in which Napoleon I. signed his abdication. The very table on which he signed still remains in this room, In the cabinet de travail is the Emperor's writing desk. The ceiling, representing law and force is by Regnault. The bedroom contains the very furniture used by the Emperor. The paintings are by Sauvage. Next comes the salle du conseil, the splendid ceiling and the panels of the walls of which were painted by Boucher. The salle du Trône comes after. It contains a portrait of Louis XIII. by Philippe de Champagne, and is richly decorated. Opposite this portrait is the throne. This room was begun by Charles IX. Adjoining this a *Boudoir*, successively occupied by Marie Antoinette and the Empress Eugenie. The window-fastenings, beautifully adorned with wreaths of wrought iron, were made by Louis XVI., who is known to have been an adept in the mechanical arts. In the centre of the flooring is the cypher of the unfortunate Marie Antoinette. Next comes the late Empress's Bedchamber; the curtains and furniture were a present of the City of Lyons to Queen Marie Antoinette; it was successively occupied by Marie Louise, and Marie Amelie, late Queen of the French. The following room was the *Salon de Réception de l'Impératrice*, with a fine table of Sèvres porcelain, with the four Seasons, painted by Georget. The panels are by Sauvage, and the ceiling by Barthélémy and Vincent. From the *Salon des Dames d'Honneur*, seven steps lead up to the *Galerie de Diane*, nearly 100 metres in length, of Doric architecture; it was partially repaired by Napoleon, and completed by Louis XVIII. The ceiling is painted by Blondel and Abel de Pujol with scenes from the mythology of Diana and Apollo. A recess at the further end, called the *Salon de Diane*, contains a beautiful vase of Sèvres porcelain, with bas reliefs, illustrative of the Arts and Sciences. This room has now become the *Library* of the Palace. Near one of the windows of the gallery we see the coat of mail worn by the unfortunate Monaldeschi when killed by order of Queen Christina of Sweden, on the 10th of November, 1657. In the centre of the gallery is a picture of Henry IV. on horseback.

On leaving this gallery, the visitor passes to the landing place of the *Escalier de l'Impératrice*, with paintings relating to the chase; the larger one, representing Louis XV. and his suite hunting, is by Parrocel, the other by Oudry and Desportes. This staircase leads to the *Appartements Particuliers*, consisting of seven rooms on the ground-floor, wich were inhabited by the Prince Imperial and his attendants. The furniture is simple, but elegant. Returning to the landing place, we now enter the *Appartements de Reception*, the first of which is the *Antichambre de la Reine*, ornamented with tapestries, the subjects taken from Don Quixote; next is the *Salon des Tapisseries*, remarkable for its ceiling and hangings of old Flanders tapestry. The *Salon de François I.* succeeds, with its fine old chimney-piece, and its new Gobelins tapestry, representing events in French history, after designs by Rouget. Over the chimney-piece is a medallion, representing Mars and Venus, painted by Primaticcio. Here also we see a small mirror, presented to Louis XIII, by the Republic of

Venice. The *Salon Louis XIII.* looks upon the *Cour Ovale*, This apartment contains the portrait of Louis XIII., who was born in it ; it is also adorned with paintings by Ambroise Dubois on the ceiling and panels, with subjects borrowed from the Greek romance of Theagenes and Monastery founded by Philip Augustus. Here was the famous Dripping Rock, which, however, no longer drips. Pilgrimages were made to this rock on account of the reputation it had of yielding water of sovereign virtue in the cure of certain maladies, but its superstitious associations have vanished long ago. The monastery was suppressed by Louis XIV, and it is now known on account of a fair which is held there every Whit-Tuesday.

In June and September, races are held at Fontainebleau in a vast amphitheatre surrounded by the Rocher St. Germain and the thickly-wooded heights of Casepôt, Chauvet and La Solle.

COURBEVOIE. — Lying outside Paris, just beyond Neuilly. was one of the chief centres of attack against the Commune by the Versailles troops. A monumental group by Barrias, the celebrated sculptor was erected there in 1883 to commemorate the defence of Paris.

DAMPIERRE. — A fine park open to visitors every Friday. This superb castle was a residence of the Cardinal of Lorraine and of the Dukes of Chevreuse. It is the property of the Duchess of Luynes. It is very difficult to obtain an authorization to visit this castle.

ENGHIEN-LES-BAINS. — Is a watering-place about half an hour by rail from Paris, on the Northern line. It is much frequented by Parisians during the summer, besides being the resort of invalides for its sulphur springs. which have been celebrated for over a century. The Princess Mathilde has a villa at St. Gratien near here. Horses, pony carriages etc. are always procurable for rides and drives in the neighbouring forest of Montmorency.

ERMENONVILLE. — About 30 miles from Paris is celebrated for its castle, in a dependency of which Jean Jacques Rousseau died on the 2nd July 1778. A monument was erected to his memory on an island in the great park, called the Ile des Peupliers, where he was buried.

ISSY. — This village contains two important charitable establishments : The Hospice des Ménages and the Hospice Devillas. The fort on the hill was nearly ruined by the fire from the German batteries. It was occupied by the communists, March 20th 1871, and was not retaken by the Government troops until the 9th of May following.

IVRY-SUR-SEINE. — A small village remarkable only for its fort, which played an important part in the defence of Paris during the war of 1870. After the siege it was occupied by the communists but was retaken by the Versailles troops on the 25th May 1871.

MALMAISON. — About 9 miles from Paris, near the Paris and St. Germain railway. It was the favourite residence of Napoleon and the Empress Josephine. The latter died here on the 29th May 1814 and was buried in the ancient church of Rueil. To the left is a small pavilion, which was the private Cabinet of the Emperor, and where he planned some of his greatest compaigns. Several partial engagements took place here during the Franco-German War.

MAINTENON. — A small town remarkable for its old castle, the seat of the Duc de Noailles, who has done much to beautify it. In 1674 it was acquired by Madame de Maintenon. There is a splendid park laid out by Jean Cottereau and Le Notre.

MAISONS-LAFFITTE. — About twelve miles from Paris. Celebrated for its chateau built in 1658 by Mansard. At Maisons-Lafitte is one of the finest race-courses in the neighbourhood of Paris. There are some very fine training stables here, and probably on this account it is the favourite residence of the numerous English jockeys, and trainers engaged on the Paris courses. There is a magnificent park surrounded by pretty villas and charming promenades.

MARLY-LE-ROI. — About twelve miles from Paris, a pretty little village situated on a wooded height, and celebrated for the pumping engine invented by a carpenter from Liége to raise water to the aqueduct of Marly. M. Sardou has a very fine residence here, and in 1693 Louis XIV had a castle erected here, which is now in ruins.

MEUDON. — Which can be reached either by. Rail or by pleasure steamer, is a favourite holiday resort of the Parisians. The chateau de Meudon was blown up during the war of 1870 by the explosion of a powder magazine installed within its walls by the Prussians. It has been lately restored and is now utilized as a scientific establishment. There is a fine astronomical observatory here, having an exceedingly high tower of recent construction.

MONT-VALERIEN. — Mont-Valerien is celebrated as having been the scene of some of the

CATHEDRAL AT SAINT-DENIS

The magnificent Basilique of Saint-Denis is celebrated as the burial-place of the kings of France. It is open the whole day. The Royal Tombs are shown to visitors on week-days, every half-hour, from 8.30 a. m. to 5.30. p. m. (excepting during service). Admission free to the interior of the Cathedral, but a charge of 50 centimes is made for admission to the treasury and crypt. The attendant also expects a small gratuity. The Abbey was founded A. D. 640 on the site of the chapel erected in A. D. 278, above the grave of Saint-Dionysius or Saint-Denis. The High Altar is an imitation of 13th century style. Behind it is the Altar to Saint-Denis and his fellow-martyrs.

fiercest struggles during the siege of Paris. The formidable fortress is constructed on the site of an ancient missionary convent at a cost of four and a half millions of francs and is one of the strongest forts connected with the defences of Paris.

MONTMORENCY. — Better known to Parisians on account of its famous English cherries than for its magnificent forest, is much frequented by Parisians who make their journey to Montmorency a pretext for eating cherries and taking traditional donkey rides. A fortress was erected here in the 11th century by Burchard le Barbu. Nothing, however, now remains of the old castle. The neighbourhood is extremely picturesque, and from the site of the chateau perched like an eyrie on the brow of the hill a fine panorama unfolds itself of Paris, the forest and of the Hermitage, where Jean Jacques Rousseau compiled some of the works which have since rendered his name famous. Visitors should not leave Montmorency without seeing the Place du Marché, the church, the Hotel de Ville, and the celebrated White Horse Hotel, where in 1792, as the story goes, the Baron de Gerard and the artist Isabey, both of them at that time richer in prospects than purse, each settled his hotel bill by painting a side of the sign-board, which remains to this day.

MEULAN. — On the western railway is the centre of the meetings of the Cercle de la Voile de Paris (Paris Yachting Club), who have constructed a fine pavillon on the right side of the Seine, and who hold regattas here every Sunday. Meulan is also a centre of numerous picturesque and charming walks on the banks of the river.

MANTES. — A town on the Seine and Oise surrounded by charming environs and possessing some very curious monuments. Remark the Hotel de Ville, restored in the 17th century style, the tower Saint-Maclou dating from 1340, all that remains of the ancient church built with the toll money taken from the boats, and destroyed during the revolution. A fine view of the neighbourhood is to be had from the summit. Application to visit same should be made to the concierge of the Mairie, to whom a gratuity should be given. The church of Notre Dame de Mantes is also worth a visit, dating from the 17th century. Before leaving Mantes excursion should be made to Lemay and to Gassicourt, interesting hamlets in the vicinity.

MELUN. — A town of about 13,000 inhabitants, 45 kilomètres from Paris. Worthy of note : the churches of Saint-Aspais, Notre Dame, the belfry of St. Barthélemy and the tower of the Hotel de Ville.

NOGENT-SUR-MARNE. — This town, situated in the valley of the Marne, is celebrated for the viaduct of the Belfort line which crosses the valley.

It is a favourite Parisian holiday resort; special fêtes and water tournaments being held here nearly every week throughout the summer.

The valley watered by the Marne, and the groups of smiling villas and country seats, picturesquely built on the sides of the hill, crowned by the above-mentioned viaduct, presents a superb view. The winding course of the river, upon which so many rude combats have been delivered, adds to the picturesque aspect of the scene.

If you happen to be in Paris on a fête day, go to Nogent, between which village and the adjoining Joinville-le-Pont, you will enjoy the charming and animated scene presented by this rendezvous of the Parisian Boating Clubs, and will be sure to spend an agreeable day.

PIERREFONDS. — About 9 miles from Compiègne, on the borders of the forest, possesses two principal attractions : its castle, restored by Viollet-le-Duc, and the thermal establishment, beautifully situated upon the borders of the lake; the former was built by Louis, Comte de Valois, in the 14th century, and was beseiged four times between the 15th century, and 17th centuries, to be afterwards partially demolished by order of Cardinal Richelieu.

Napoleon I. bought the ruins of this redoublable fortress, so long the asylum of brigandage and rebellion, for a small sum, but it was not until the time of Napoleon III. that this marvel of military architecture of the Middle Ages was restored to its primitive state.

Nothing could be more imposing than the exterior aspect of this magnificent feudal fortress, Rising on a barren rock flanked by its eight towers, and seeming to revive the memories of a past age.

Entering the castle by the Cour d'Honneur you find yourself in the courtyard, decorated with statues, and containing the large hexagonal tower, the principal staircase, and the chapel.

After visiting the chapel, making the tour of the buildings, you see a large exterior staircase leading to the ground floor of the castle, facing which and ornamented with four grotesque statues of animals, is an equestrian statue of the founder of the fortress : Louis, Comte Valois, who was assassinated by the emissaries of the Duc de Bourgogne in 1407.

You will enter the interior of the castle by a small staircase leading into the grand reception room, which is richly decorated in carved wood, and contains an ancient chimney-piece, in which a bullock could be roasted whole.

From this room you will visit the study, after which comes the bedroom, the latter richly decorated in panels of carved wood, above which all round the room are a series of paintings representing different episodes in the life of a feudal lord. The chimney-piece bears the motto of the Duc d'Orléans " Qui veult peut " (Where there's a will there's a way).

Leaving this room we next visit the hall of the knights of the Round Table, containing a curious chimney-piece, of which the mantel, sloping towards the ceiling, is decorated with a kind of genealogical tree, having for stoc King Arthur, and branches, the nine Knights of the Round Table, statues of whom also decorate the exterior of the castle towers.

Next comes the armoury, the treasures from which were removed during the war of 1870 to the Palais des Invalides.

This immense gallery is the most beautifully decorated hall in the castle.

Terminate the visit to the castle by la Salle des Gardes.

Before leaving Pierrefonds, visit the church and thermal establishment.

POISSY. — About an hour from Paris on the Western Railway, celebrated for the religious conferences held there in 1561, between the Catholics and Protestants, conferences which unfortunately had no other result than to render the religious quarrel between the two sects fiercer than ever.

Superb church of St. Louis, commenced by Philippe the Hardy in the 11th century.

The interior is composed of three naves and nine chapels.

Before quitting Poissy, see the prison, barracks, and the celebrated Pont de Poissy, built by Saint Louis.

If you have time, a charming walk may be taken to the village of Villennes, along the banks of the Seine, about 2 miles from Poissy.

RAMBOUILLET. — An hour by rail from Paris on the Brest line, possesses a remarkable Gothic church dating from the 11th century.

Celebrated for its castle, park and forest. The former was originally the property of the Counts de Montfort, after which it was acquired by the d'Angeunes family. Francis I. died there 15th. March 1547.

Napoleon I. used to stay here when hunting in the neighbourhood. and it was in this castle he slept for the last time, before taking refuge at Rochefort.

Charles X. signed his abdication here August 2nd. 1830.

The park is open to the public from 7 in the morning till an hour after sunset throughout the year.

After a promenade in the beautiful park, make your way to the church, which contains 2 pictures by well-known masters. From the church, visit the Hotel de Ville, and then the preparatory Military School.

The castle is open to the public from 10 till 5 in summer, and from 11 till 4 in winter. Enter by the iron gate to the Place d'Armes, and then by the small door to the right of the guard-house.

First Floor. — We first visit a large hall called the Salle de bal, of which the extremity previously formed a cabinet where Charles X. signed his abdication. On the right, up several steps, the Salle à Manger, with a small oratory on the left ; the Salle du Conseil of Charles X. with painted plan of the forest of Rambouillet, executed during the reign of Louis XVI. and annotated by him. The panels are sculptured ; those above the doors representing the attributes of Science. The Salon. the panels of which represent the four seasons, and which also contains four splendid Mirrors ; two small boudoirs and the study of Marie Antoinette.

A suite of corridors leads us to the Salle de Bains of Napoleon I., in which we see medallions of views of France and foreign countries, alternately decorated with trophies, then the Chambre a coucher of the great Emperor.

Second Floor. — This floor, closed to visitors, contains the apartments of the Duchesse de Berry and those of the Duchesse d'Angoulême.

Third Floor. — This is traversed by a long passage, on which open the rooms formerly occupied by the court officials and domestics. This passage ends in the Vieille Tour, in the room where Francis I. died.

Descending to the ground floor, we visit successively the Salle à manger des rendez-vous de chasse, the walls of which are inlaid with coloured marbles ; then the Salle d'Armes, the Salle à manger and the Salle de billard des gardes du corps under Charles X.

Then follows a Salle de bains constructed by the Comte de Toulouse, entirely inlaid with squares of enamelled Delft pottery.

Laiterie de la Reine. — About half a mile from the castle is the Laiterie de la Reine, a

Doric pavillon built for Marie Antoinette. Its ornaments were removed by Napoleon I. to Malmaison for the Empress Josephine.

The pavillion on the left contains the Salon de la Reine, decorated with four figures representing the Seasons, by Sauvage. The laiterie proper is a little to the right on entering.

In the interior one remarks a vast round table of white marble ; then comes a square chamber, at one end of which water escapes from the fissures of an artificial rock and falls in a rustic vasque in which a nymph is bathing sculptured by Beauvalet.

The laiterie terminated, you will be conducted by the English garden to la Chaumière.

ROBINSON. — A short distance from Paris, this village is a favourite rendez-vous of artists and pleasure seekers.

RUEIL. — A pretty little village, situated near Malmaison, the ancient residence of Napoleon and Josephine, on the road from Paris to St. Germain.

A collection of smiling villas picturesquely placed at the foot of a hill, this village is celebrated for its church which contains the tomb of the ex-Empress Josephine. It was founded in 1580 by Dom Antoine, King of Portugal, and was completely demolished by Napoleon III., to be afterwards reconstructed from plans by Lacroix, architect to the Emperor. The church contains a magnificently sculptured, painted and gilded organ loft, the gift of Napoleon III.

An inscription informs the visitor that this organ-loft is the work of the famous Florentine sculptor Bacchio D'Agnolo, executed in the 15th century for the church of Saint-Marie-Nouvelle of Florence.

To the right of the transept is Josephine's tomb, in white marble, by Gilet and Dubuc. The kneeling figure of the Empress is in Carrara marble by Cartellier.

The church contains also a monument in Carrara marble, erected by Napoleon III. in memory of his mother.

To visit the vaults, in the absence of the vestry clerk, apply 15 Place de l'Eglise.

About a quarter of an hour's walk from the church will bring you to the chateau of Malmaison, celebrated on account of the historical memories it evokes (see page 90).

SAINT-CLOUD. — A small town of about 5,000 inhabitants, picturesquely situated on the left bank of the Seine. On account of its proximity to Paris, Saint-Cloud has always been a great sufferer during the various wars. As early as 1346 the town was completely destroyed by fire by the British army, and again in 1411 by the Armagnacs. Later on Henry III. established his camp there to lay siege to the capital when he was assassinated by Clement.

On the 12th October 1870 the town was burnt by the Germans.

Rising again, however, like the Sphinx, from its cinders, the town is now. as in the past, the resort of Parisians and foreigners, who spend the summer season in this beautiful locality. one of the prettiest in the environs of Paris.

Visit the ancient college, facing the church, where the mortal remains of St. Cloud reposed for twelve hundred years.

After dinner, return to Paris by the Seine steamer ; fares: week days 20 c., Sundays 40 c. Trams also run between St. Cloud and the Louvre.

SAINT-DENIS. — This town can be reached either by tram from the rue Lafayette and Boulevard Haussmann, or by rail from the Gare du Nord. We recommend the visitor to take the latter route as being more praticable and agreeable. The journey takes but 15 minutes by rail; fares; 1st class 45 c.; 2nd 30 c.; 3rd 20 c. Trains every hour.

The town of St. Denis about 4 1/2 miles from Paris, is a manufacturing centre containing about 51,000 inhabitants.

Its chief attraction is the eglise canoniale ; a monument not only interesting for its architecture, but also remarkable as containing the tombs of the kings and queens of France, which make it quite a historical museum.

Leaving the station, an omnibus will conduct you for 10 c. to the cathedral ; the distance, however is so short that it is better to walk, in order to obtain a glimpse of the town.

Taking the rue du Port, and crossing the canal, the rue du Chemin de fer conducts us to the new parish church, completed in 1867, built in the XIII. century style, and very elegant. Opposite this church is the rue de la République, foltowing which we come to the Place d'Armes, in the centre of the town, where we find the antique basilisk of St. Denis.

Eglise Canoniale. — This church, which is open to the] public every day, is a splendid specimen of the pure French style of Gothic architecture.

Commenced by Suger, the celebrated Abbé of St. Denis, in 1137, on the site of the ancient church erected by Charlemagne, it was not finished till near the close of the XIII. century by Philippe the Hardy. Altered more or less during successive centuries, it was restored to its original state by order of Louis Philippe in 1845.

Built in the form of a latin cross, the exterior of the church has a grand effect.

The porch comprises three doors, which still retain vestiges of the original sculptures executed during the time of Suger. The figures in the centre represent scenes of the last judgment, and those to the right the Martyrdom of St. Denis. The bas-reliefs on the left door are modern.

The nave dates from the time of St. Louis and is 65 mètres in length by 12 mètres in breadth. The choir was consecrated as far back as 1144.

The tombs of the kings and queens of France, restored as before 1793 (in which year they were desecrated and partially destroyed by the revolutionary mob) are situated in the grand nave and side chapels, and constitute the principal curiosity of the church.

On entering remark in the chapel de la Trinité, to the left, the tomb of Charles de Valois, and of Marie d'Espagne, his wife, as well as that of Leon de Lusignan.

The reserved part of the building, containing the royal tombs, is open free to the public from half-part ten in the morning to 5 in winter and 6 in summer, but only under the conduct of a guide.

These visits take place every half hour. The guide charges nothing for his services, but expects a gratuity of 50 c.

To visit the vestry, the treasury and the crypt, the charge is 50 c. on week-days and 30 c. on Sundays; special cards are given at the vestry door ; these cards give the right to ascend the platform. Unfortunately the visits are too short to permit the tourist to examine the monuments at his leisure. Permission, however, for an extended visit, may be obtained by writing in advance to the Primicier.

Penetrating the reserved part, we traverse the 9th and 10th galleries of the second collateral.

These two galleries contain the tombs of Catherine de Courtenay; Louis de France, comte d'Evreux, and Marguerite d'Artois, his wife ; Clemence d'Hongrie : Blanche d'Evreux; Jeanne de France; Charles comte de Valois ; Charles d'Anjou: Louis and Philippe d'Alençon: Blanche de France, daughter of St. Louis ; Philippe, brother of St. Louis ; and Louis, son of St. Louis.

Against the pillar separating the two galleries is the magnificent statue of Marie de Bourbon, Abbess of Poissy.

We now arrive at the northern transept, in which to the left is the tomb of Louis XII. and Anne de Bretagne. a splendid monument of the 16th century. The magnificent bas-reliefs ornamenting the lower part of this tomb represent respectively : the entry of Louis XII. into Milan ; the passage of the Apennines ; the battle of Agnadel (gained over the Venetians): and the capitulation of Venice.

On the right : 2 beautiful columns; one erected to Cardinal de Bourbon, and the other to Henri III. Near these, the tombs of Robert II., the Pious, and of Constance d'Arles, of Henri I., and of Louis VI., le Gros, of Louis X., of Jean I. and of Jeanne de Navarre.

From this point, notice, to the right of the choir, the superb tomb of Dagobert I., the artistic marvel of the church. This monument, which no one (unless supplied with a special permit) is allowed to approach, is called with reason, one of the most remarkable curiosities of the Middle ages. It was erected by order of Saint-Louis.

Now remark, to the left, the tomb of Henri II. and Catherine de Médicis, a magnificent mauso- leum in white marble.

This monument is flanked by four beautiful statues representing the four cardinal virtues.

To the right : the tombs of Philippe le Jeune and of Constance de Castille, and of Carloman and Hermentrude, wife of Charles le Chauve.

We now climb a staircase, from whence we perceive on the right, the tombs of Clovis I. and of Childebert I., and, on the left, the mausoleums of Jean II. and of Philippe VI. of Valois ; Charles IV.; Jeanne d'Evreux; Philippe V., called the Long ; and Blanche of France.

Arriving at the top of the stairway, remark, on the right, the tomb of the comte de Dreux and of a princess of the royal french blood, whose identity, however, cannot be established. On the left, is a second monument to Henri II and Catherine de Médicis.

We now skirt the choir in order to reach the vestry on the opposite side. On passing, glance at the windows of the chapel at the end, which date from the time of Suger. Also notice, facing the vestry, the tomb of Frédegonde, dating from the VII. century.

The Vestry (Sacristie). — The first room on entering has rightly been termed a museum of religious art; it contains many paintings by famous french artists. Most of them being on sacred subjects, they carry such signatures as Landon, Barbier, Garnier, Guérin, Heim, Gros, Meisnier, Meujaud, etc., etc.

Note. — After having visited the vestry, the guide may conduct you to the Crypt, and then to the Treasury, which latter, however, forms part of the vestry.

THE THRONE ROOM AT FONTAINEBLEAU PALACE

Containing the throne of Napoleon I. It has a handsome
ceiling, contains also a chandelier in Rock Crystal, and
wainscoting executed during the reigns of Louis XII and
Louis XIV. For further information concerning Fontainebleau
see page 88.

The Treasury. — We now enter the Treasury, the immense riches of which were nearly all carried off by the mob in 1793. The manuscripts, which escaped the pillage, have been removed to the National Library.

The few objects of art saved from destruction in 1793, together with others given by the kings since that date, were still further reduced in 1882 by an audacious and successful burglary committed the 39th November of that year.

Amongst those now remaining are 2 curious altarpieces ; one, in silver, representing the Nativity and the Adoration of the wise men, is very elegant and dates from the time of Louis XIV.; its estimated value is 30,000 francs. The other, in engraved copper, dates from the XII. century, and represents Christ and the Apostles.

In a magnificent glass-cave, are some beautiful sacred vases, in gold and silver, two enamelled crosses of the time of Saint-Louis ; the crowns of Louis XIV. and Louis XV.; a very curious reliquary of the 12th century, etc., etc.

On leaving the sacristie; we descend a stairway on the left, then turn to the right in order to gain the entrance to the crypt.

The Crypt. — Descending a staircase we see to the right, in a passage, four colossal statues representing Religion, Force, France, and the City of Paris, designed for the tomb of the duc de Berry. son of Charles X., assassinated in 1820,

To the left, under the sanctuary, is the « Caveau des Bourbons » containing the coffins of Louis XVI. and Marie Antoinette; of Louis XVIII.; of Adelaïde and of Victorie of France ; of the duc de Berry and two of his children ; of Louis-Joseph and of Louis-Henri-Joseph de Condé, the last of the family, and of Louis VII. and of Louise de Lorraine, wife of Henri III.

This caveau is not open to the public, but one obtains a glimpse of the interior by the light of the guide's lantern through the grille.

All that remain of the works of art, portions of the royal sepulchres violated during the first revolution, have been repaired, and are found in the chapels of the crypt. Notice amongst others, the magnificent marble statues of Louis XIV. and Louis XVI., of Marie Leczinska and Marie Antoinette by Petitot, and the busts of Henri IV., of Marie Médicis and of Louis XVIII. by Valois : then medallions, bas-reliefs, a chapel dating from Dagobert's time, a grille in forged iron, and a statue of Charlemagne, as well as the caveau of Turenne, containing the bones of this great military genius.

On leaving the crypt, notice on the right the tombs of Pepin le Bref, his wife Berthe, of Louis III and Carloman.

To your left, at the side of the vestry : the tombs of Louis de Sancerre, of Charles V., of Jeanne de Bourbon, of Du Guesclin, of Charles VI. and of Isabelle de Bavière; the statue of Charles V., a masterpiece of the XIV. century; two bas-reliefs representing respectively the Battle of Bovines and the founding of the abbey of Royaumont ; then the tomb of Renée d'Orléans-Longueville and the statue of Beatrix de Bourbon.

To the right: the tombs of Isabel of Aragon ; of Philippe III., the Hardy ; of Philippe IV., the Bel, and of Clovis II. and Charles Martel. Notice, to the left of the choir, the tombs of Blanche and Jean, children of Saint-Louis.

To the left : the monument of François 1st and of Claude de France, with bas-reliefs representing the principal fait d'armes of the chevalier king.

An urn, dating from the Renaissance period, contains the heart of François 1st.

The tomb of Marguerite de Flandres, and Charles, Comte d'Etampes, remarkable work of the XIV. century ; the tombs of Louis d'Orléans and of Valentine de Milan, both exceedingly beautiful.

Now dismiss your guide, find your way by the previous route to the station, and return to Paris.

SAINT-GERMAIN. — Situated about 13 miles from Paris, this pretty town is celebrated for its castle, containing a museum of precious antiquities ; its terrace, from whence an enchanting view of the environs of Paris may be obtained ; and its magnificent forest.

Saint Germain is reached by the steam-tramway from the Arc de Triomphe, Fares : 1st class 1.65 ; 2nd class 1.15.

On leaving the station of St. Germain, the visitor finds himself at the Place du Chateau. To the left is the castle, and a little nearer the station, is the entrance to the park. To the right is the church of Saint Germain, and facing you a cab-stand, from whence, later on, we will hire a vehicle for a drive through the forest.

After having glanced at the imposing facade of the castle, lunch at one of the restaurants in the vicinity, and return to visit the museum.

The castle is open to the public : on Sundays from half past ten till 4, and on Tuesdays and Thursdays from half past eleven till 5 in summer and 4 in winter. On other days of the week (excepting

Mondays, when the galleries are completely closed) the museum is visible to visitors furnished with an authorization from the director. The park is open every day.

Before entering the castle visit the church, containing a beautiful pulpit, originally intended for the chapel at the palace of Versailles, and a mausoleum erected by order of Queen Victoria to James II of England. A statue of M. Thiers, a former President of the French Republic, stands opposite the park.

The castle. — The castle of St. Germain, built by Louis VI., was nearly completely destroyed during the wars with the English, with the exception of the magnificent chapel erected by Saint Louis. Repaired in 1367 by Charles V., who added to it a large square tower, it was completely restored by François 1st.

This castle, successively fortress, royal residence, asylum of James II of England, Military school, etc., etc., has now become a museum of national antiquities, extremely interesting to visit.

The Museum. — Our space being too limited to admit of our giving the details of museums outside Paris, we advise our readers to purchase a local guide, containing the fullest information, obtainable anywhere in the town price 1 fr. 50.

The Terrace. — The terrace of St. Germain, celebrated as much for its extent as for the beautiful view which it commands, is one of the most splendid promenades in Europe. It is 2400 mètres in length.

View. — From the terrace of St. Germain, straight in front, one sees an immense plain, dotted with villages To the right, the heights of Marly and of Louveciennes ; to the left, Montmorency ; and farther on, Mont Valérien, the summit of the Eiffel Tower and Montmartre.

Beyond the park du Vesinet, rises the belfry and cathedral of St. Denis.

The Pavilion Henri IV. — Situated at the commencement of the terrace, and now occupied by the hotel-restaurant where M. Thiers died in 1877, is all that remains of a royal castle commenced by Henri II., finished under Henri IV., and called the Chateau-Neuf.

This Chateau-Neuf, the favourite residence of Louis XIII., from whence he sadly comtemplated the necropolis of St. Denis, was at first greatly liked by Louis XIV., but being afterwards neglected by him and his successors for the splendours of Versailles, it was demolished by order of the Comte d'Artois, and there now rests only the chapel, to-day become one of the chambres of the restaurant.

The Forest. — The forest of Saint Germain, covering a superficial area of 4,400 hectares, the routes and walks of which are admirably kept up, is the rendez-vous of both stranger and Parisian. No one goes to St. Germain without visiting the forest,

Note. — Those having but a short time at their disposal, would do well to take a carriage from the place du Chateau. Tarif : week-days, per hour, 2 fr. 50 ; Sundays, 3 frcs.

Promenades. — The most remarkable, and therefore the most frequented, parts of the forest, are :

The Chateau de Val, at the extremity of the terrace, to the right (it may also be reached by the Avenue de la Muette).

The Pheasantry. — Reached by the Avenue de la Muette and turning, at the Etoile de Berry, by the third route to the left which we follow straight on.

The Pavilion de la Muette, reached by following the Avenue de la Muette and passing by the Etoile de Berry and l'Etoile du chêne Capitaine, and lastly an excursion which we recommend above all, should you go to St. Germain in the early part of September :

Les Loges, branch of the maison d'éducation for young ladies of the Legion of Honour at St. Denis. It is reached by a magnificent avenue 3 kilomètres in length, planted with 4 rows of trees. This avenue, binding the chateau de St. Germain with the Rond Point, is doubly celebrated by reason of the beautiful oak of Diane de Poitiers, and the famous.

Fete des Loges, which is held there every year, on the first Sunday in September, and continues for fifteen consecutive days. Nothing is more curious than this fair in the middle of the wood.

Having dined at St. Germain return to Paris by one of the evening trains, which leave every hour until 9.55. Last train starts at 11.20 on week-days and Sundays and fêtes at midnight.

SAINT-JEAN-AUX-BOIS. — Is a small village, not particularly interesting, which boasts of a church, formerly a dependency of a priory in the neighbourhood, and which contains some exquisitely carved wood, a curious gothic tomb, and fragments of beautiful windows.

SAINT-MANDE. — A small town of about 11,000 inhabitants, much frequented by Parisians for its pure air, and owing to its proximity to the Bois de Vincennes. Many charming walks in the vicinity.

SANNOIS. — This village is situated on a hill, the summit of which is occupied by the

THE CABINET IN THE PALACE AT FONTAINEBLEAU
IN WHICH NAPOLEON Ist SIGNED HIS ABDICATION

It was in this room that the great Emperor signed his abdication. The small round table, on which the act was executed, is still to be seen in the centre of the chamber.

Moulins de Sannois, from whence an unrivalled panorama of Paris and its environs spreads itself.

SCEAUX. — Was formerly the under-prefecture for the department of the Seine.

Built on the summit of a hill, it is justly celebrated for its salubrious air and charming environs, which attract a great number of visitors during the season.

Its streets, clean but badly paved, are lined with beautiful trees, but since the demolition of its park and castle, Sceaux has become merely a pleasant country resort.

The church, restored during the 17th century, is a small building in the gothic style, and contains the tombs of the Ducs de Maine and several princes and princesses of the Bourbon family. Notice a beautiful marble group, representing the Baptism of Jesus, executed by Tuby in 1681; also to the right and left of the choir, two handsome stained-glass windows, dating from the 16th century.

A few minutes walk from the church is the magnificent Lycée Lakanal opened in 1885.

Note. — That portion of the park still remaining forms a delightful promenade.

SÈVRES. — Celebrated almost as much for its charming environs as for its manufactory of porcelain, is a small town situated between the heights of Meudon and St. Cloud.

Lunch at one of the restaurants in the vicinity, and visit the manufactory.

Having but a limited space at our dispos-al, we do not go into particulars, but advise our readers to purchase one of the local guides, which are cheap and give full details and information.

SURESNES. — This town, agreeably situated on the banks of the Seine, is a favourite with Parisians as well as with strangers. Formerly a manorship, Suresnes was given to the Abbot of St. Germain des Prés by Charles the Simple.

It was here the celebrated religious conferences were held in 1593 which bound Henri IV. to the catholic faith. It was also the birth place of the celebrated engineer Perronet.

TAVERNY. — This village commands a magnificent view, being situated on the slope and at the foot of a hill adjoining the forest of Montmorency.

The Church dates from the 13th century and is one of the finest in the environs of Paris, and contains a handsome stone high-altar in Renaissance style, and wood carvings of the same period representing the martyrdom of St. Bartholomew. Above the southern porch is a fine window in the flamboyant style.

TRAPPES. — Ruins of the ancient Abbey of Port Royal; a favourite retreat before the destruction of the convent of men of learning and religion, around whom clustered such illustrious men as Racine and Pascal.

TROUVILLE. — Is now the most fashionable watering-place on the coast of Normandy. It is pleasantly situated at the mouth of the Touques. The season lasts from June to October. The Casino is a large handsome structure, with concert and ball rooms, and a fine terrace on the shore. Excellent beach.

VERSAILLES. — About 40 minutes by rail from Paris, departure from the Montparnasse Station, or by tramway starting from the Quai du Louvre, the journey occupies an hour and three quaters. A thoroughly appointed English four-in hand leaves the offices of the Daily Messenger, 167, rue St. Honoré, every morning at 10 o'clock, Sundays included, during the summer.

The town of Versailles was founded by Louis XIV.

The site of Versailles was hardly favourable for a town, and still less so for a park, as the water for its ornamental ponds had to be conveyed to it from a great distance at a vast expense. The town was called by Voltaire " *l'abime des dépenses* ", its palace and park having cost the treasury of Louis XIV. the enormous sum of 1000 million fr., while its annual maintenance also involved heavy expenditure. The accounts handed down to us regarding the erection of this sumptuous palace and the laying-out of its grounds almost border on the fabulous. Thus no fewer than 36,000 men and 6000 horses are said to have been employed at one time in forming the terraces of the garden, levelling the park, and constructing a road to it from Paris and an aqueduct from Maintenon, a distance of 31 m. from Versailles. This aqueduct was intended to bring the water of the Eure to Versailles, but was discontinued owing to the great mortality among the soldiers employed; and the breaking out of the war in 1688 prevented the resumption of the works. The waterworks of Marly were afterwards constructed, and a farther supply of water obtained from the ponds on the plateau between Versailles and Rambouillet.

After the year 1682 Versailles became the permanent headquarters of the court, and is therefore intimately associated with the history of that period. It witnessed the zenith and the decadence of the prosperity of Louis XIV.; and under his successor the magnificent palace of the " grand monarque " became the scene of the disreputable Pompadour and Du Barry domination. It was at the meeting of the Estates held here in 1789 that the " Tiers Etat " took the memorable step, — the first on the way to the Revolution, — of forming itself into a separate body, the Assemblée Nationale. A few months later the unfortunate Louis XVI. saw the palace of Versailles sacked by a Parisian mob, which included many thousands of women ("les dames de la halle"), and since that period it has remained uninhabited. During the Revolution it narrowly escaped being sold. Napoleon neglected it owing to the great expense which its repair would have entailed; and the Bourbons on their restoration merely prevented it from falling to decay and erected the pavilion on the south side. Louis Philippe at length restored the building, and converted part of it into an historical picture-gallery.

From 19th Sept., 1870, to 6th March, 1871, the palace was the head-quarters of the King of Prussia, and a great part of the edifice was then used as a military hospital, the pictures having been carefully covered to protect them from injury. An impressive scene took place here on 18th Jan., 1871, when the Prussian monarch, with the unanimous consent of the German states, was saluted as Emperor of Germany. To describe minutely all the events which occurred at Versailles during the above period would be to write a history of the Franco-Prussian war. The house No. 1, boulevard du Roi was the scene of the negociations between Prince Bismarck and Jules Favre on 23rd-24th Jan. and 26th-28th Jan., which decided the terms for the capitulation of Paris and the preliminaries of peace. After the departure of the German troops (12th Mar., 1871), Versailles became the seat of the French government, and it was from here that Marshal Macmahon directed the struggle against the outbreak of the Commune. It was not till 1879 that the government and the chambers transferred their headquarters to Paris.

The Church of Notre-Dame contains a monument of the Comte de Vergennes, minister of Louis XVI.

For full details of the Palace, as well as the Grand and Petit Trianon, see local guides, by vendors of which the traveller is assailed, on approaching the Palace.

VILLE D'AVRAY. — A pretty spot on the Versailles railway. Interesting church, and chateau dating from the 18th century. Near the railway is the Villa des Jardies, the scene of Gambetta's death, and once occupied by Balzac. Near the end of the rue de Versailles on the left are some picturesque ponds.

VINCENNES. — Can be reached either by tramway from the Louvre, from the Bastille, or by the Vincennes Railway.

It is interesing as one of the fortresses of the outskirts of Paris. In the Cour Marigny is a statue of General Daumesnil.

The chateau de Vincennes was commenced in the twelfth century, and has since been gradually enlarged. Used as a royal residence until 1740, Louis XV. then converted it into a porcelain manufactury. In 1751, the works being removed to Sèvres, the chateau de Vincennes became first a military school, and six years afterwards. a weapon manufactury.

Louis Philippe fortified the chateau and transformed it into an extensive artillery depôt, with an " Ecole de Tir ". It is now seldom shown to foreigners.

The chateau was used as a *State Prison* from the days of Louis XI. (1461-83) onwards. Among many illustrious persons who have been confined within its walls, may be mentioned the King of Navarre (1574), the Grand Condé (1650), Cardinal de Retz (1652), Fouquet (1661), Count Mirabeau (1777). the Duc d'Enghien (1804), the ministers of Charles X. (1830), and the conspirators against the National Assembly (15th May, 1848).

A melancholy interest attaches to the fortress from its having been the scene of the execution of the unfortunate Duc d'Enghien, the last scion of the illustrious Condé family. On the suspicion tha he was implicated in a conspiracy against the emperor, he was arrested by order of Napoleon on 14th March, 1804, on German territory, conveyed to Vincennes, and there condemned to death by a court-martial. The sentence was executed on 20th March, and the body of the duke interred in the fosse where he was shot. In 1816 Louis XVIII. caused his remains to be removed to the chapel, where he erected a monument to his memory.

In May, 1871, the chateau was one of the last places occupied by the insurgents. They evacuated it on the approach of the Versailles troops, leaving one of their number concealed in a casemate, with instructions to set fire to the powder-magazine when the troops had entered. As, however, almost certain death awaited him in any case, the unfortunate man preferred suicide to the execution of his murderous commission.

The **Chapel** with its tasteful Gothic front, begun in 1379 under Charles V., and completed in 1552 in the reign of Henri II., has recently been restored. The lofty vaulting and the stained glass by *Cousin* are worthy of notice. The monument of the Duc d'Enghien. now in the old sacristy, a poor work by *Deseine*, consists of four figures in marbre : the duke supported by religion, France bewailing his loss, and a figure emblematic of Vengeance.

The **Salle d'Armes**, or Armoury, fitted up in 1819, is said to contain weapons sufficient to aquip 120,000 men. The artillery stores occupy the ground-floor, and the other arms the floor above.

The **Donjon**, or Keep, in which state-prisoners were formerly confined, is a massive square tower of five stories, 170 ft. in height. with four smaller towers at the corners. The walls are 10 ft. thick, The platform, to which 237 steps ascend, commands a fine view of the surrounding district.

To the east of the chateau is the Fort de Vincennes, beyond which begins the

Bois de Vincennes, a beautiful park, much less frequented than the Bois de Boulogne, but of scarcely inferior attraction, though unfortunately disfigured by the plain in the centre.

The park was once a forest, where Louis IX. (d. 1270) used to hunt and to administer justice ; but it was entirely replanted by Louis XV. in 1731. Since that period considerable encroachments on its extent have been made by the railway and the fortifications, but it still covers an area of about 2250 acres, including the Champ de Manœuvres (1/2 m. wide) in the middle, and the artillery " Polygone ". It 1857-58 it was successfully transformed into a public park by *Vicaire* and *Bassompierre*. It is more natural than the Bois de Boulogne, and contains fewer exotics.

PRESIDENCE OF THE FRENCH REPUBLIC
(ELYSEE-PALACE)

MONSIEUR FELIX FAURE
Président of the Republic
General Secretarial Department and Military Household.

* Mr. Tournier, O. ✳, Brigadier General, General secretary of the Presidence ; Head of the military Household (Officer of the order of the Legion of Honour).
* Mr. Paul Germinet, O. ✳, Naval Captain (Officer of the order of the Legion of Honour).
* Mr. Ménétrez, ✳, Lieutenant Colonel of Infantry (Knight of the Legion of Honour).
* Mr. L. M. Bourgeois, ✳, Chief of squadron of Artillery (Knight of the Legion of Honour).
* Mr. Moreau, ✳, Chief of Batallion of Engineers (Knight of the Legion of Honour).
* Mr. Lombard, Chief of Batallion Marine Infantry.
* Mr. George de Lagarenne, Chief of squadron of Cavalry.
* Mr. F. Meaux Saint-Marc, Chief of Batallion of territorial Infantry.

Mr. Le Gall O. ✳, Inspector of Administrative Services of Marine and Director of the Cabinet of the President of the Republic (Officer of the Legion of Honour).
Mr. Blondel, ✳, Chief of Private Secretarial Department (Knight of the Legion of Honour).
Mr. de la Motte, ✳, Captain of « Chasseurs à pied « (Knight of the Legion of Honour).

DIPLOMATIC CORPS
Section I. — AMBASSADORS

ENGLISH EMBASSY .... }
ENGLISH CONSULATE .... } 39, rue du Faubourg Saint-Honoré
Open from 11 A. M. to 3 P. M.

GREAT BRITAIN AND IRELAND, 39, rue du Faubourg Saint-Honoré
Sir Edward Monson, Ambassador extraordinary and Plenipot.
Mr. Henry Howard, Minister Plenipotentiary, 51, avenue Friedland.
Mr. H. Austin Lee, First Secretary, 14 bis, avenue du Trocadéro.
The Hon. Charles Harding, Second Secretary, 12, rue Pierre-Charron.
Mr. Walter Fownley, Second Secretary, 23, rue de Marignan.
Mr. D. M. Harford, Second Secretary, 4, avenue d'Antin.
Mr. R. D. Norton, Third Secretary.
Mr. Roland Graham. Third Secretary.
Mr. J. M. C. Chœtham, Third Secretary, 8, avenue Percier.
The Hon. Francis Egerton, Honorary Attaché.
Lieut. Colonel Douglas Dawson, Military Attaché, 8, avenue Percier.
Cap. Lewis E. Winty R. N. Naval Attaché.
Sir Joseph A. Crowe Commercial Attaché, 28, avenue du Trocadéro.

* Ordnance Officers to the President of the Republic.

AMERICAN LEGATION, 59, rue de Galilée
AMERICAN CONSULATE, 36 *bis*, avenue de l'Opéra
Open from 10 A. M. to 3 P. M.

UNITED STATES OF AMERICA; 24, avenue Kleber
Chancellerie : 59, rue Galilée
His Exc. James B. Eustis, Embassador Extraordinary and Plenip. (May 1893).
Mr. Henry Vignaud First Secretary, 39, rue Galilée.
Mr. Newton, B. Eustis Second Secretary.
Major Sanford C. Kellogg, Military Attaché.
Lieut. Commander Raymond P. Rodgers, Naval Attaché, 6, rue Christophe-Colomb.

AUSTRO-HUNGARIAN EMPIRE, 37, rue de Varenne
His Exc. Count Molkenstein-Trotsburg, Ambassador Extraordinary and Plenip. (1ᵉʳ Feb. 1895).
Count Henri Lutzoü, Counsellor, 9, rue de Marignan.
Count Esterhazuf First Secretary, 19, rue Marbeuf.
Count L. de Berchtold, Second Secretary, 11, rue Jean-Goujon.
Count Nicholas Revertèra, Attaché, 102, rue de l'Université.
Mr. G. L. Wagner, Attaché.
Colonel Schneider. Military Attaché, 51, avenue Henri-Martin.
Baron Vesque de Püttlingen, 83, rue de Chaillot.

SPAIN, 34, boulevard de Courcelles
His Exc. the Duke de Mandas, Ambassador Extraordinary and Plenip (13 July 1895).
The Marquis de Novallas, First Secretary.
Count de Sorrelpalma, Second Secretary, 10, rue Pierre Charron.
Mr. E. Ferraz y Alcala Galiano Third Secretary, 7, rue de Rome.
The Marquis de San Carlos de Pedroso Third Secretary, 30, avenue Kléber.
Comte de Pradère, Third Secretary, 4, rue Paul-Baudry.
Commandant Marquis de Valcarlos, Military Attaché, 90, avenue d'Iéna.
Captain Eschagüe y Santago, Military Attaché, 20, avenue ue Villiers.
M. R. del Rio, Consulate Attaché.

GERMAN EMPIRE
His Exc. Count Munster, Ambassador Extraordinary and Plenip. (5 Nov. 1885).
M. de Schœn, Counsellor, 41, rue Dumont-d'Urville.
M. Wedel, Second Secretary.
Count de Bèlora-Schlatau. Third Secretary, 14 bis, avenue du Trocadéro.
M. de Brüning, Secretary.
Lieut.-Colonel de Schwartz-Koppen, Military Attaché, 86, rue de Lille.
Cap. Siegel, Naval Attaché, 4, rue Léo-Delibes.

ITALY, 73, rue de Grenelle
Chancellerie : 11, rue de Penthièvre
His Exc. Count Soruilli Brusatit di Vergano, Ambassador Extraordinary and Plenipotentiary (18 Feb.
1895).
M. Antonio Quarto di Belgioioso, count del Vaglio, Secretary.
The marquis Paulucci di Calboli, Secretary, 73, rue de Grenelle.
M. Carignani, Secretary.
The marquis de Torre-Alfina, Attaché, rue de Villersexel.
M. Romato Avezzana, Attaché.
Lieutenant-colonel Alexandre Panizzardi, Military Attaché, 52, rue du Colisée.

RUSSIA, 79, rue de Grenelle-Saint-Germain.
His Exc. Baron de Mohrenheim, Ambassador Extraordinary and Plenipotentiary (19 april 1884).
M. de Giers, 12, rue Marbeuf.
M. C. Nariskhine, First Secretary, 107, rue de Grenelle.
M. Alex. Swelctikins, Second Secretary, 25, rue Bassano.
Baron M. Korff, Second Secretary, 28, avenue Marceau.
M. Zographo, Attaché.
M. Adolphe de Franckenstein, Attaché, 46, avenue Gabriel.
Colonel Pee Tronbelskoy, Attaché, 6, rue d'Argenson.
Prince Alexis Orloff, Attaché, 45, rue Saint-Dominique.
General baron de Freederickz, Military Attaché, 65, avenue Marceau.
Lieutenant Martinof, Naval Attaché.

CASCADE OF SAINT-CLOUD

The Grand Cascade in the park at Saint-Cloud, divided by an avenue into the Haute and the Bass Cascade, was designed by Lepautre and Mansart, and adorned with allegorical statues of the Seine and the Marne by Adam. The fountains play in summer on the second Sunday of each month from 4 to 5 o'clock, as well as during the fête of Saint-Cloud on the last three Sundays of September. The largest jet rises to a height of 136 feet.

TURKEY, 10, rue de Presbourg

His Exc. Zia Pacha, Ambassador Extraordinary and Plenipotentiary (6 novembre 1894).
H. Missak Effendi, 24, rue Murillo.
Djemal Bey, First Secretary.
Resmi Bey. Second Secretary.
Muhieddin Bey, Third Secretary.
Osman Cheriff Bey, Attaché.
Alaeddin Bey, Attaché.
Colonel Tewfik Bey, Military Attaché.

VATICAN, 58, rue de Varenne

His Exc. Mgr Ferrata Archbishop of Thessaloniça, Nuncio of the Holy See (21st July 1891).
Mgr J. Celli, Auditor to the Nunciature.
Mgr A. Peri-Morosini, Secretary.

SECTION II

ENVOYÉS EXTRAORDINARY & MINISTERS PLENIPOTENTIARY

ARGENTINE REPUBLIC, 122, Champs-Elysées

N... Envoyé Extraordinary and Minister Plenipotentiaire.
M. G. Martinez Campos, First Secretary chargé d'affaires.
M. E. Garcia Mansilla, Second Secretary.
M. Angel M. Mendez, Hon. Secretary, 5, rue d'Antin.
Captain E. O. Connor, Naval Attaché, rue Bosquet, 53.

BELGIQUE, 38, rue du Colisée

Baron d'Anethan, Envoyé Extraordinary and Minister Plenipotentiary (13 november 1894).
Baron Eugène Beyens, 6, rue Bizet.
Prince Pierre de Caraman-Chimay, Secretary, 41, quai d'Orsay.
Baron Albéric Grenier, Secretary, 26, avenue de l'Alma.
M. Emmanuel Havenith, Secretary, 10, rue Cambacérès.
M. Maurice Rooman, Secretary, 3, rue de Castellane.
Prince A. de Caraman-Chimay, Attaché, 8, rue d'Astorg.
M. E.-L. Bastin, Chancelor to the Légation.

BOLIVIA, 66, rue Pierre-Charron
Chancellerie : 74, rue François-Ier

M. Manuel de Argandona, Envoyé Extraordinary and Minister Plenipotentiary (10 april 1891).
M. G.-M. Paz, First Secretary.
M. Maxenio de Argandona, Attaché.
M. Gosé, N. Rodrigue, Attaché, 3, avenue Kleber.

BRAZIL, 3, place Malesherbes
Chancellerie : 17, rue de Téhéran

M. G. de Pisa, Envoyé Extraordinary Minister Plenipotentiary (12 oc. 1890).
M. Alberto Fialbo, First Secretary, 10, rue de la Néva.
M. A. N. de Feitosa, Second Secretary, 11, rue Legendre.
M. de Barros-Moreira, Second Secretary, 21, rue Beauphu.

CHILI, 53, avenue Montaigne
Chancellerie : 25, rue Marbeuf.

M. Augusti Malte, Envoyé Extraordinary Minister Plenipotentiary (20 novembre 1891).
M. Domingo Vega, First Secretary, 2, rue Meissonier.
M. M. Saldias-Rors, Second Secretary.
M. F. Rivas Vienna, Second Secretary.
M. Luis de Cazotté, Attaché.
Capt. Luis A. Goni, Naval Attaché.
Colonel Patricio Larrain, Military Attaché.

CHINA, 7, place Victor-Hugo.

Prince Yang, Envoyé Extraordinary and Minister Plen.
Isching-Ichang, First Secretary, Chargé d'affaires.
Hien Yuong, Attaché.
Ou Isung-Lien, Attaché.
Pang Icheng-Lié, Attaché.
Icha-Ichi-Ouien, Attaché.

COLUMBIA

M.   , Envoyé Extraordinary and Minister Plenipotentiary.
M. G. Mallarino, Secretary, Chargé d'Affaires, 26, avenue Marceau.
M. M. Getting, Attaché, 148, boulevard Haussmann.
M. Ricardo Samper, Attaché, 152, avenue des Champs-Elysées.

COSTA RICA, 14, rue Le Peletier.

M. Manuel de Peralta, Envoyé Extraordinary, Minister Plenipotentiary (Mar 7th 1887)
M. Anselmo Votio, First Secretary.
M. A. Lanuza, Attaché.
M. G. A. Aguilar, Secretary.

DENMARK, 29, rue de Courcelles.

Count de Molthe-Hvitfeld, Envoyé Extraordinary and Minister Plenipotentiary (April 9th 1860).
Baron C. de Lowenshiold, Secretary, 29, rue Cambon.

EQUATOR, 10, rue d'Offemont.

M. Antonio Flores, Envoyé Extraordinary and Minister Plenipotentiary (29 octobre 1892).
M. Dorn and de Alsua Secretary, 80, rue de Moncey.
M. M. Daviles, Attaché.

GREECE, 27, rue Marbeuf
Chancellerie : 3, rue Desbrousses

M. N-P. Delyanni, Envoyé Extraordinary and Minister Plenipotentiary (1er fév. 1886).
M. Constantin-A-Criesis, First Secretary, 42, rue de Lubeck.
M. Chr. Christidis, Second Secretary, 18, rue Clement-Marot.

GUATEMALA, rue de Chateaubriand, 27.

M. Fernando Cruz, Envoyé Extraordinary and Minister Plenipotentiary (May 10, 1892).
M. Domingo Etrada, First Secretary.
Dr Louis Leval, Attaché.

HAYTI, 63, rue Pierre-Charron.
Chancellerie: rue Montaigne, 9.

M. Alfred Box, Envoyé Extraordinary and Minister Plenipotentiary (Sept. 25, 1890).
M. Murville-Férère, First Secretary, 7, rue Vézelay.

JAPAN, avenue Marceau, 75.

M. A. Soné, Envoyé Extraordinary and Minister Plenipotentiary (10 Sept. 93).
M. T. Kato, Secretary, avenue de la Grande-Armée, 10 bis.
M. Ochii, Secretary, 32, rue de Lubeck.
Captain Mr. S. Upin, Naval Attaché.

MEXICO, 14, rue Daru.
Chancellerie : rue Alf. de Vigny, 7.

M. Antonio de Mier, Envoyé Extraordinary and Minister Plenipotentiary (23 Nov. 94).
M. Gustavo Boz, First Secretary, 16, avenue Carnot.
M. Henrique Olarté, Second Secretary, 125, Champs-Elysées.
M. Eduardo A. Esteva, Thrid Secretary.
Dr Ramon Macias, Attaché.
M. E. de Eséandon, Attaché, avenue Victor-Hugo, 30.
M. R: Gallardo, Attaché.
M. Fernandez de Arteagua, Attaché, 9, rue Gounod.
M. Garcia Torres, Attaché, 80, rue Lauriston.

MONACO, 25, rue de l'Arcade.

Baron F. du Charmel, Envoyé Extraordinary and Minister Plenipotentiary (10 Oct. 1889).
M. Depelley, Counsellor, 2, rue Jean-Goujon.

CHATEAU OF SAINT-GERMAIN

This Chateau was formerly known as the Vieux Chateau, to distinguish it from the Chateau Neuf, of which the Pavillion Henri IV, remains the sole relic. During the early middle ages the French Kings possessed a fortress here commanding the Seine. The chapel, still in existance, was built by Louis the Pious. During the wars with England the castle was destroyed. Restored by Charles V. the present building was erected by Francis I., who celebrated his nuptials here with Claudia, daughter of Louis XII.

NETHERLANDS

Chev. de Stuers, Envoyé extraordinary and Minister Plenipotentiary (20 Oct. 85).
M. de Weede, Counsellor, avenue Victor-Hugo, 137.

NORWAY-SWEDEN, 56, rue d'Iéna.
Chancellerie : 12, rue Bassano.

M. Due. Env. ext. and Min. plen. (july 5, 1890).
Count Wrangel, First Secretary, 5, rue Copernic.
Count Wachtmeister, Attaché, 9, rue des Écuries-d'Artois.
Count Ehrensinard, Attaché, 40, avenue Marceau.
Captain Hedengren, Military Attaché.

PERU, 7, rue de Castiglione.
Chancellerie : 8, avenue Hoche.

M. José F. Canevaro, Envoyé Extraordinary and Minister Plenipotentiary (7 April 93).
M. G. de La Fuente, First Secretary, rue Wasington, 45.
M. F. Cauevaro, Second Secretary.
M. V. A. Olano y Ville, Attaché.
Colonel Enrique Lara, Military attaché, 24, boulevard Maillot (Neuilly).
Captain Delboy, Naval attaché, rond-point des Champs-Elysées, 12.

PERSIA, Place d'Iéna, 1.

General Nazare, Aga, Yemin es Saltane, Envoyé Extraordinary and Minister Plenipotentiary
(August 18, 73).
Youssef Khan, Nazare, Aga, Attaché.
Ardachir Khan, Nazare, Aga, Attaché.
Mirza Abdulla Khan, Attaché.

PORTUGAL, 32, rue de Lubeck (Téléphone).

M. de Sonza Roza, Envoyé Extrardinary and Minister Plenipotentiary (August 30, 94).
M. Bartholomin Pereira, First Secretary, 18, rue Boccador.
M. Q. de Sampayo, Second secretary, 5, rue Fresnel.
M. A. de Sonza, Hon. Attaché, 3, rue de Sontay.

ROUMANIA, 50, avenue Marceau.
Chancellerie : 33, avenue Montaigne.

M. O. N Lahovary, Envoyé Extraordinary and Minister Plenipotentiary (May 25, 93).
Prince Nicolas O. Gluka First Secretary, 11, rue du Colisée.
M. Spiridou Bibeses, second Secretary.
M. Alexander Pizostuy, Attaché.
M. N. Lahovary, Attaché.
Comm. Demetre Vallaus, Military Attaché, 1, rue Godet-de-Mauroy.

SALVADOR, 4, rue de La Bourdonnais.

Mr. Crisanto Medina, Env. ext. and Min. plen. (dec. 20, 1894).

SERVIA, 9, rue Freycinet.

M. Milontine Garachanine, Env. ext. and Min. plen (july 28, 1894).
M. Voislan Markovitch, Secretary.
M. Dragomir, M. Jancovitch, Attaché.

SIAM, 14, rue Pierre-Charron.

Prince Vadhana, Env. ext. and Min. plen. (jan. 26, 1890).
Phra Suriya, Chargé d'affaires.
Luang Visait, First Secretary.
Luang Visuth, Attaché.
Luang Bhardi, Attaché.

SOUTH AFRICAN REPUBLIC, 226, rue de Rivoli.

M. Beelaerts von Blokland, Envoyé Extraordinary and Minister Plenipotentiary (12 April 90).

SWITZERLAND, 15 bis, rue de Marignan.

M. Lardy, Envoyé Extraordinary and Minister Plenipotentiary (March 1, 1883).
M. Duplan, counsellor, 19, rue Montaigne.
M. Gustave Boissier, Second Secretary, 27, rue Montaigne.
M. Lucien Cramer, Attaché, place Delaborde, 14.

URUGUAY, 30, rue de Lubeck.
Chancellerie : 20, rue de l'Opéra.
M. Juan Zorilla de San Martin, Env. ext. and Min. plen. (dec. 8, 1894).
M. Alejandro Heropa, First Secretary, Chargé d'affaires, 3 *bis*, rue Jardin.
M. V. S. Martinez, Hon Secretary.
M. A. Sieura, Attaché.
M. T. Rivara, Attaché.

SECTION III. — CHARGÉS D'AFFAIRES

BAVARIA, 72, rue de Bellechasse
Baron de Tucher (3nd April'89).

LIBERIA
Chancellerie : rue Boursault, 59.
Baron de Stein (28 May 1895).

LUXEMBOURG, rue Bizet, 6.
M. Vannerus (2nd December 1896).

SAINT-MARTIN, avenue du Bois-de-Boulogne.
Baron Jean Roissard de Bellet (24th May 1890).

SECTION IV. — CONSULATES

GREAT BRITAIN AND IRELAND
Mr. A. P. Inglis, Consul, 39, faubourg Saint-Honoré.
Mr. G. G. Falconer Atlee, Vice-consul (11 to 3).

UNITED STATES
Mr. S. E. Morss, Consul général, 36, avenue de l'Opéra.
Mr. Clyde Shripsline, Vice-consul général.
Mr. E. P. Mac-Lean, Consul général Delegate.
Mr. C. F. Hubbard-Smith.
Mr. D. T. S. Fuller, Attaché.
Mr. Augustus, Biesel.

ARGENTINE REPUBLIC
M. Dupenty, Consul général, rue Chateaudun, 28.
M. Jules Hollande, Vice-consul.

AUSTRIA-HUNGARY
Baron Gustave de Rothschild, Consul général, rue Laffitte, 21.
Chev. G. Oesterreicher, Consul général adjoint.
Baron E. Jacdos de Haulstein, Consul.
M. Louis E. Popper, Chancellor.

BELGIUM
M. E. L. Bastin, rue Bizet, 6.

BOLIVIA
M. J. Caso, Consul général, boulevard Haussmann, 154.

BRAZIL
M. J.-B. Leoni, Consul général, rue des Mathurins, 23.

CANADA
M. Hector Fabre, O, ✳, C. M. G. Commissioner general, rue de Rome, 10.
M. Paul Fabre, Secretary.

CHILI
M. J.-N. Irarrazaval, rue Meissonier, 4.

BIRD'S EYE VIEW OF VERSAILLES

Versailles, with a population of about 50,000, the capital of the Seine-et-Oise department, owes its origin to Louis XIV., who built the palace and resided there during the latter part of his reign.

The celebrated fountains (grandes eaux) in the gardens of the palace, play on the first Sunday in every month from May to October, when visitors arrive in vast crowds to view this beautiful spectacle. They play between 4 and 5 o'clock, and every display costs nearly £400.

COLOMBIA
M. Bernardo de la Torre, Consul général, Cité Rougemont, 6.

COSTA RICA
M. Ch. Goguel, Consul général, rue Le Peletier, 14.
M. Em. Goguel, consul.

DENMARK
M. Paul Calon ✳, Consul général, 53, rue d'Hauteville.

DOMINICAN REPUBLIC
Chancellerie : rue du Louvre, 42.
Baron E. Oppenheim, avenue du Bois-de-Boulogne, 64.

EQUATOR
M. Dorn y de Alsua, ✳, 80, rue de Monceau.

SPAIN
M. C. Florez, ✠✠, Consul, 6, rue Bizet (12, to 4).
M. Enrique Gaspar, Vice-consul.
M. Trigueros y Lete, ✳, Chancellor.

GERMANY
M. A. de Faber du Fau, 78, rue de Lille (1 to 4).

GUATEMALA
M. Domingo Estrada, 27, rue de Châteaubriand.

HAYTI
M. A. Gluck, avenue de Messine, 6.

HAWAI
M. Alfred Houlé, rue Nouvelle, 5.

HONDURAS
M. Louis Gaubast, Consul général, rue de Compiègne, 2.
M. Paul Mandiets, Consul, rue Desmarquay, 6.

LIBERIA
M. J. Chaves, rue de Maubeuge, 47.

LUXEMBURG
M. Eugène Bastin, O. ✳, Consul général, rue Bizet, 6.

MEXICO
M. Aurelio Melgarejo, Consul général, rue Bourdaloue, 5.
M. F. de Pasalagua, Vice-consul.

MONTENEGRO
M. Paul Melon, Consul général, place Malesherbes, 24.

NICARAGUA
M. Désiré Pector, Consul général, rue Rossini, 3.
M. F. Hirtz, Consul.

NETHERLANDS
M. Van Lies, O. ✠, Consul général, rue de Lubect, 35 (1 to 4).

NORWAY-SWEDEN
M. G. Brostrœm, C. Consul général, boulevard Malesherbes, 28.
M. G. Nordling, Vice-consul, 14, rue d'Athènes.

ORANGE FREE STATE
M. Ch. de Nosenthal, rue Labruyère, 3.

PERSIA

M. Eugène Pereire, Consul général, 6, rue Auber.
M. A. Hermann, Vice-consul, rue de l'Echiquier, 25.

PERU

M. E. Agulo, Consul général, rue de la Pépinière, 7.

PORTUGAL

Chancellerie : 35, rue de Berri.

M. D'Eça de Queiroz, Consul général, 35, rue de Berri.
M. C. Dominingues Secy, rue Bailly, 11.

ROUMANIA

M. Pierre Aubry, Consul général, 19, rue de l Opéra.

RUSSIA

M. A. de Kartzow, C. ✳, Consul général, 79, rue de Grenelle.
M. Zarine, Vice-consul, 38, rue Boissiers.

SALVADOR

M. Enrique G. Carrillo, 49, rue de Rivoli.

SAN MARINO

M. Emile Reaux, G. O. ✠ Consul général, 5, rue Gounod.

SERVIA

Count M. de Camondo, G. ✳, Consul général, 66, rue de la Chaussée-d'Antin.

SIAM

M. Albert Gréhan, Consul général, 3, rue Pierre-le-Grand.

TURKEY

M. Elie Léon, Consul général, avenue du Bois-de-Boulogne, 30 *bis*.
M. J. Noguès-Effendi, Consul, 85, rue Richelieu.

VENEZUELA

M. J.-R. Nunez, Consul général, 9, rue Freycinet.
Baron F. de Corvain, Vice-consul, 5, rue d'Antin.

CHATEAU OF VERSAILLES

This magnificent palace, was erected by Louis XIV, owing to his having conceived a dislike to St-Germain as it commanded a view of the tower of St-Denis, the royal burying place. It has been uninhabited since the first Revolution.

During the siege of Paris 1870-71 the king of Prussia established his headquarters here, and it was here he was proclaimed Emperor of Germany January 18th 1871. After the departure of the German troops Versailles became the seat of the French Government, and it was not until 1879 that they transferred their headquarters to Paris. (For fuller details consult the official catalogues).

INDICATEUR

DES

SALONS RUSSES

Anglais & Américains

A

Abbema, Miss Louise, 47, rue Laffitte.
Abbott, S. N., 131, boulevard Montparnasse.
Abercrombie, Miss (Artist), 5, rue Léopold-Robert (Chestnut Hill, Pa. U. S. A.).
Ablett, W. J., 157, avenue de Wagram.
Abrams, L. Hôtel Cassette, rue Cassette.
Acly, Miss, Saint Margaret's American Church School, 50, avenue d'Iéna.
Adalsward (Bon and Bness.), 65, boul. de Courcelles.
Adam, Mme (Nouvelle Revue), 190, boul. Malesherbes.
Adams, Miss Lilian, 18, r. Magenta (Asnières), (G.B.).
Adams, The Revd. Dr. W. J. (L. L. D.). Chaplain of Christ Church, Neuilly, Résidence, 51, boulevard Bineau, Neuilly.
Adams, Miss (Grand Opéra), 1, r. Louis-le-Grand.
Adams, Miss Vicary, 187, rue de la Pompe.
Adamson, David Combra, 15, rue Hégésippe-Moreau.
Adhemai, Mlle d', 7, rue Boccador.
Adiny (Grand Opéra), 2, rue Saint-Didier (Sundays).
Adler, Dr. H., 16, avenue de l'Opéra.
Adler, A. d', ambassade de la Russie, r. de Grenelle.
Adler, Mr., 24, rue d'Amsterdam.
Aderberg, Comtesse d', hôtel de Calais.
Aginar, Mme, 105, r. de la Pompe. (G. B.). Saturday.
Ahier, Mme, 133, boulevard Haussmann.
Albertini, Mr. and Mrs. Diaz, 25, avenue du Bois-de-Boulogne, Paris.
Alexander, Charles, 37, boulevard Magenta.
Alexander, H. E. American Notary, 24, boulevard des Capucines.
Alexander, Mr. Hy. Addison, 19, rue Scribe, Paris.
Alexander, Mr. and Mrs. John White, (née Elisabeth Alexander), 31, boulevard Berthier, Paris.
Alger, Mr. and Mrs., rue d'Edimbourg.
Alkland, Thomas, 30, rue de Provence.
Allcock, 83, avenue du Bois-de-Boulogne.
Almirall, R., 29, rue Cassette.
Altmann, A., 13, rue Leverrier.
Amant, Jean (H. C.), 15, quai Bourbon.
Amy, Mr. G. J., 19 bis, boulevard du Port-Royal.
Anderson, A. A., 59, avenue de Saxe.
Anderson, Capt. J. H., 34, rue Marbeuf.
Anderson, Mr. and Mrs., 41, avenue Marceau.
Anderson, W. W., 25, boulevard Haussmann.
Anderson, The Revd., S. H., av. de la Grande-Armée.
Anderson, Dr. D. E. M. D., and Mrs., 5, r. du Bois-de-Boulogne (Friday).
Anderson, J. Esq., 1 bis, avenue Carnot.
Anderson, Miss and Miss Harriet Agnes, care Morgan Harjes and Co, Paris.

Anderson, Mr. Larz, secretary to the United States Embassy, Rome.
Anderson, Miss Stella, care of Mrs Walden Pell, 1, avenue Montaigne, Paris.
Anderson, George, 18, rue de l'Université.
Anderson, Miss Sarah Clemence, 187, r. de la Pompe.
Andreus, Mr. James, Reform Club, London.
André, St. M., 9, boulevard Malesherbes.
Andrew, 6. rue Boissonnade.
Andrews, Mrs. Clarence, 29, rue Boissière.
Andrews, Miss, 6, route Albis, Rambuteau.
Anglemont, Vicomte and Vicomtesse d' (née Thomas), 12. rue Lincoln (Thursday).
Apletchcef, Mme d', 45, rue de Courcelles.
Aramon, Count and Countess J. (née Marie Fisher), 111, rue de l'Université, Paris.
Archdeacon, Edmond, Mr. and Mrs., 15, avenue des Champs-Elysées.
Archdeacon, Mr., 121, avenue Wagram.
Archdeacon, Mr. P., 36, rue des Ecuries-d'Artois.
Archdeacon, J., 56, avenue Montaigne.
Archer, Mr. George Mortimer, 64, rue de Vaugirard.
Aristarchi, Bey, 15, rue Treilhard.
Arnaux, Miss Elisabeth d', 187, rue de la Pompe.
Arnaux, Miss Marie, 187, rue de la Pompe.
Arnold, Sydney (President Brit. Cham. Com.), 40, avenue de la Grande-Armée.
Arnold, The Misses Charlotte Bruce, care of J. Munroc, and Co Paris.
Arrington, Miss, (Artist), 4, rue de Chevreuse.
Arthur, Mr. and Mrs. John, 19, rue Marbeuf.
Arthur, Mr. Paul, 4, rue Troyon.
Arthur, Miss E., 7, rue de Berry.
Astor, Mr. Wm. Waldorf, 18, Carlton House-Terrace, London.
Atlee, Mr. and Mrs. G., Falconer, 3, avenue de Messine (Librarian and Vice-Consul H. B. M's. Embassy.
Atterbury, Mr. and Mrs. Charles, 7, East, 33, Street, New-York, and care of Morgan, Harjes and Co, Paris.
Atterbury, Mr. Grosvenor, 7, East, 33, Street, New-York, and care of Messrs. Morgan, Hajes and Co, Paris.
Auffm-Ordt, Mrs. William (née Harbeck), 10, rue Marignan, Paris.
Auffm-Ordt, Mr. Clement, 10, rue Royale.
Auffm-Ordt, Mr. and Mrs. W., 10, rue Marignan (Thursday).
Aulan, Marquis and Marquise (née Christmas) de Saurez, 40, rue Villejust.
Aulors, A., 35, rue des Capucines.
Aunay, Comte and Comtesse d', 29, rue Marbeuf.
Austin, Dr. C. K. (M. D.), 29, rue Cambon.

Avenel, Vicomte and Vicomtesse George d', 23, rue Galilée (Saturday).
Ayer, F., Hôtel Continental.
Ayer, Mrs. J. C. (née Josephine Southwick), 19, rue Constantine, Paris.
Aylmer, John, 4. square Lamartine.
Azevedo de Silva, Comte and Comtesse d'), 105, boulevard Haussmann.

B

Backhouse, Mrs. and Mrs., 112, boul. de Courcelles.
Bacon, Henry and Mrs. (Artist), 14, av. de l'Alma.
Bacon, Miss Lucy (Artist), Eragny par Gisors, Eure, France.
Baçon, Mrs. Ellen Kendall, 7, rue Lemaitre, Puteaux (U.-S.).
Bagshawe, W. H. W., 51, av. de Villiers.
Bail, Joseph, 11, quai Bourbon.
Bain, Miss Harriett (Artist), 13, rue Boissonade, Kenosha, Wisconsin.
Bainbridge, G., 155, av. des Champs-Elysées.
Baker, Mrs. Ellen, 7, r. Lemaître, Puteaux (U.-S.).
Bakewell, Mr. John Junr (Artist), 205, boulevard Raspail, Oakland, bal. (U.-S.A.).
Ballard-Smith, Mr. and Mrs. (née Butterfild, London repve. of the New-York World, 16, Herbert Crescent, Hans, place S. W., London.
Baltazzi, Mrs., 67, av. Marceau.
Bancroft, Miss Ellen (Actress), 36, Woburn, Place Russell square, London.
Banks, Mrs., 11, rue de l'Arc-de-Triomphe.
Banuelos, Count and Countess de (née Thorndyke), 19 bis, rue Constantine, Paris.
Barber, Mr. Donn, 133, boulevard Raspail, Paris.
Barbery, Mrs. (née Rœderer), 7 and 7 bis, avenue Bosquet (Tuesday. Friday), villa and Saint-Maurice-du-Lac, Enghien.
Barbet de Jouy, 27, r. de l'Université, (Monday).
Barbey, M. (Music.), 16, rue Halévy.
Barbey, Mr. and Mrs., 45, avenue Marceau.
Barclay, Lady (née Belzim), 11, rue]François Ier.
Barclay, Capt. Edward, 11, rue François Ier.
Barclay, Cecil, 11, rue François I.
Barclay, Thomas, L. L. B., 17, rue Pasquier.
Barclay, Mr. and Mrs. George (née Beatrix Chapman), Rome, Italy.
Barker, H. L., 5, rue Delambre.
Barker, Frederic, P. G., 114, r. St-Denis, Courbevoie.
Barker, Edward, 11 bis, r. des Couronnes, Courbevoie.
Barker, Mr., 45, rue de Douay.
Barker, Mr. Donn, 133, boulevard Raspail.
Barkley, Dr. F. T., 5. rue de la Paix.
Barkworth, Mrs., 5, rue Léo-Delibes.
Barlett, 3. rue Dutot.
Barley, Mr., 45, avenue Marceau.
Barlow, M., 22, rue Delambre.
Barnard, Dr., 362, rue Saint-Honoré.
Barnard, Mr. and Mrs. (née Santruschee), C. Inmann, 12, rue Goudot-de-Maurol (Tuesday).
Barnhorn, Clément, J., 27, rue Campagne-Première (U. S.).
Barraclough, Mr. William, 85, avenue Kléber (New-York, U. S. A.).
Barret, Dr. and Mrs., 14, rue de l'Hôtel-de-Ville, Neuilly (Wesdesnay).
Barret, Mr., 17, avenue de l'Opéra.
Barrett, Mrs. O. D. (Sappho), 29, rue Contambert.
Bartelo, Miss Lilian, 4, rue Robert-Estienne.
Bartels, Mrs. (of Chicago, U. S. A.), 4, rue Robert-Estienne.
Bartels, Miss Florence, 4, rue Robert Estienne.
Bartholdi, M. (Sculptor), 82, rue d'Assas.

Bartlett, Mr. and Mrs. Paul W. (Sculptor), 47, rue Doctor-Blanche.
Barwley, Mrs. Violet, same address.
Baskerville-Glegg, Mrz, 23. av. du Bois-de-Boulogne.
Bassano, Marquis and Marquise (née Symes), 9, rue Dumont-d'Urville and 3, Marlbourough Gate Hyde Park.
Basset, Mr. and Mrs. A., 90. rue d'Amsterdam.
Basset, Colonel, 12, rue de Penthièvre.
Bastien, Lepage-Emile, 39 bis, rue des Chezy, Neuilly (Seine).
Batchelor, Gordon, 147, boul. Malesherbes (U. S.).
Batemann, Mrs., 48, avenue Marceau.
Battaille, Mrs. O'Hagan, 15, rue du Bel-Respiro.
Baume, Mr. and Mrs., 17, rue de Rivoli.
Baxter, Mq. and Mrs. F., 41, rue de Chaillot.
Bayan, Mr. and Mrs., 40, rue de Maubeuge.
Bayley, Mr., 5, rue de La Peyrouse (Monday).
Bayly, Mrs. and Miss Lancelo-Saunderson, 37, avenue de la Grande-Armée (Thursday).
Beamish, G. C., 84, rue d'Amsterdam.
Beaton, Rev., Patrick and Mrs. (Church of Scotland), 21. rue Presbourg.
Beau, Henry, 22. avenue de Saint-Ouen (Canada).
Béchet, Mr. C. Claudius, 77, r. Saint-Lazare, Paris.
Beer, Frédéric (Sculptor), 147, avenue de Villiers.
Behenna, Mrs. K. Arthur (Artist), 50, avenue d'Iéna, (New-York, U. S. A.).
Belden, Miss M., 15, rue Lord Byron.
Belfrage, Miss, 179, rue de Courcelles.
Belhard, Mr. and Mrs., 20, avenue de l'Alma.
Bélichou, Mme Gustave, 13, rue Boissonade.
Beljame, A., 29, rue Condé.
Bell, Mrs., 3, avenue Montaigne.
Bellet, Baronne de, 44, avenue du Bois-de-Boulogne.
Bellot, Mme Louis (née Carol), 24, rue Boccanor (Tuesday).
Bemberg, Harman (Composer), 30, avenue de Messine.
Benchhardt, Mr., 12. avenue de l'Alma.
Benham, Henry J. N. D., 15, rue Boileau.
Benhy, Jacques (Composer), 34. rue Ponthieu.
Bennett, Mrs., 14, boulevard Malesherbes.
Bennett, W. A., 18, rue Chauveau-Lagarde.
Bennett, James Gordon, 120, av. des Champs-Elysées.
Benson, W. N., 13, rue Boissonade.
Berard, Mr. et Mrs. (née Dana), 37, avenue Hoche.
Berckheim, Baron and Baronness de (née Pourtalès), 22, rue du Berri.
Beresford, J. C, 203. boulevard Raspail.
Bernhardt, Mme Sarah, 56, boulevard Perière.
Bert, Mme Paul (née Clayton), 12, avenue Carnot.
Berwick, Baron de, 29, rue Fortuny.
Beylard, Mr. and Mrs. E. Duplessis (née Julia Poëtt Howard), château de Rudobauges, par Pudanges, Orne, France.
Bicknell, E. M., rue Léopold-Robert.
Bideleux, Mr., 37. rue Lafayette.
Biesel, M. and Mrs Augustus, 55, av. Victor-Hugo.
Bigelow, Ch. Bowen, 23, rue Boissonade.
Billcroche, A. G., 100, rue d'Amsterdam (G. B.).
Binder, Mr. and Mrs. Henry, 49, rue Ampère and at Maisons-Laffitte.
Binder, Mr. George, 6. avenue de Mac-Mahon.
Bing, Mr. and Mrs. Charles, 58, rue de Monceau.
Bing, Ferdinand, 42, rue du Général-Foy.
Bing, S., 9, rue Vezelay.
Binneh, Miss, 21. rue de l'Arc-de-Triomphe.
Binney, Mr. and Mrs. Horace, 28. av. du Trocadéro.
Binney, Mr. and Mrs. Horace (née Sorchan), 28, avenue du Trocadéro, Paris.
Birchby, Mr., 144, rue Saint-Denis.
Bisbing, H. S., 22, rue des Martyrs (U. S.).
Bischoffheim, Mr. and Mrs. Ferdinand (née Paine), 140, avenue des Champs-Elysées.
Bishop, Winfred, 21, rue de Naples.
Bispham, Mrs. Henry (Artist), 5, avenue de la Grande-Armée (New-York).

B | **B**

Bispham, Mrs., 6, avenue de la Grande-Armée.
Blackington, Miss, care of Morgan, Harjes and Co, Paris.
Blackinton, Mr., 42, avenue des Champs-Elysées.
Blackith, Huggons, 6, rue Richepanse.
Blackstone, Mrs., 10, rue Laurent-Pichat.
Blackstone, Mrs. Sarah, 5 bis, rue Jadin (U. S.).
Blackwell, Mrs. C. Augusta, care of J. Munroe and Co, Bankers, rue Scribe, Paris.
Blackwood, Lord Terence (Secretary H. B. M.'s Embassy), 3, avenue Montaigne.
Blaker, Hugh, 22, rue Delambre.
Blair, Mr. and Mrs. Watson, F. (née Alice R. Keep), care of Morgan, Harjes and Co, Paris.
Blanchard, Col Bailly, 2, rue de La Pérousse.
Blashfield, Mr. and Mrs. E. H., 4, rue de Courcelles (Tuesday).
Blirs, Mr. and Mrs. George (née Anaïs, C. Casey), 13, Piazza del Independenza, Rome.
Blount, Henry and Mme, 59, rue de Courcelles.
Blount, Sir Edward, K. C. B. and Lady (née Jerningham), 59, rue de Courcelles and Imberhorne Manor, E. Grinstead.
Blowitz, O. de (" Times " Correspondent), 2, rue Greuze. Business address, 35, boul. des Capucines.
Blumenschein, E. H., 9, rue des Fournaux.
Bodington, Oliver, E. and Mrs., 14, r. Pierre-Charron.
Bœler, Mrs. and Miss, 6, rue de Commailles (New-York, U. S. A.).
Boggs, Franck Myers, 31, boul. Haussmann (U. S.).
Bogoluboff, M. de, 21, boulevard des Batignolles.
Bogue, Dr., 75, boulevard Haussmann.
Boissevain, Mr. Daniel, 8, Wilton, Place Belgrave square, London.
Boland, Major, 1, rue d'Aguesseau.
Boldini, Jean (Painter), 41, boulevard Berthier.
Bolles, Mr. Randolph (Arhitect), 5, rue de Commailles (New-York, U. S. A.).
Bond, the Misses, 3, rue du Colisée.
Bondy, A., 16, place Vendôme.
Bonguerman, W., 75, r. Notre-Dame-des-Champs.
Bonheur, Mlle Rosa (Painter), 7, rue Gay-Lussac and Château de By, Thomery (Seine-et-Marne).
Bonn, Dr. J. V., 25, rue Bergère.
Bonnat, L., 48, rue Bassano.
Bonvallot, Mrs., 15, rue Boissy-d'Anglas.
Booth-Clibborn, Mr. and Mrs., A. S., 3, rue Auber.
Borissovsky, M., 29, rue Maubeuge.
Bors, Mr. et Mrs. Christian, 1, avenue Montaigne.
Bosdet, Henry de C., 25, boulevard Haussmann.
Bosman, Mme (Grand Opéra), 35, rue des Aubépines and Colombes.
Bostwick, A., 131, boulevard Montparnasse.
Bougereau, William C. (Painter), and Mrs., 75, rue Notre-Dame-des-Champs.
Bourgeoise, L., 131, boulevard Montparnasse.
Bourget, Paul (Man of letters), and Mme (née Daird), 20, rue Barbet de Jouy.
Bouiwman. Miss, 28, avenue d'Iéna.
Bouring, Mr. and Mrs. Thomas B. (née Annie H. Howd), 7, palace Gate, Kensington, W., London.
Boutoille. Miss L. E., 17, rue Montaigne.
Bowden, J. F. D., 25, avenue Marigny.
Bowen, M. James Alison and Mrs., 6, av. Montaigne.
Bowen, Mr. and Mrs. Herbert, W. (née Augusta Floyd), United States Consulate, Barcelona, Spain.
Bowes, Mr. and Mrs. Hely, 7, rue Bassano.
Bowler, Mrs. George Pendleton (née May Williamson), care of J. Munroe and Co, Paris.
Bowler, Mr. Robert Pendleton, Union-Club, New-York and care of J. Munroe and Co, Paris.
Box, Mr. Alfred (Minister Plenipotentiary of Haiti), 63, rue Pierre-Charron.
Boyd, Arthur, 39, rue Marbeuf.
Boyden, D. F., 2, rue Aumont.
Boyer, Mlle Rachel (Comédie Française), 19, boulevard Inkerman. Neuilly.
Boyland, Dr. Halsted, 15, rue Vernet.

Boyle, Abbé, 5, rue des Irlandais.
Bradby, Mr. and Mrs., 4, avenue Hoche and Beggearnhuish, England.
Bradford, Mr., 22, rue Bouchet.
Bradford the Revd. E. E. (Curate of Saint-George's Jubilee Church), 7, rue Auguste-Vacquerie.
Bradford, Miss Blanche, 69, avenue d'Antin.
Bradhurst, Mr. and Mrs. A. Maursell (née Evangeline Page-Wood), Pebmarsh, Essex.
Brailles, Baron and Baronne Chandon de (née Garison), 81, avenue Marceau, Paris.
Braine, Dr., 8, avenue Victor-Hugo.
Brandés, Mlle (Comédie Française), 95, rue Jouffroy.
Braunecker, Mme de, 10, rue Copernic.
Bremner, Mr. and Mrs., villa Strathmore, 151, avenue de Genevilliers, Colombes.
Bremner, Mr. and Mrs., H. M., villa Strathmore, 151, avenue de Genevilliers, Colombes.
Bremont, Mr. and Mrs., 95, boulevard Montmorency, Auteuil (Saturday).
Brewster, Mrs. Geory, 10, rue de la Paix (New-York, U. S. A).
Bridgman, Mr. and Mrs. Henri H. (née Alice Bradford Eldridge), Aldine Club, New-York and San-Remo, Italy, and care of Broun, Shipley and Co, London.
Bridgman, F. A. and Mme, 48, rue Jouffroy (U. S.) and 146, boulevard Malesherbes.
Bright, John, Irwin, 3, rue Bonaparte.
Brigstocke, Mr., 9, avenue Malakoff.
Brin, Baron and Baroness (née Ledoux), 4, rue du Bel-Respiro and Château du Beau-Soleil, Lachapelle, Basse-Mer (Loire-Inférieure).
Bristed, Mrs. Astor (née Grace Sedgwick), villa Felseck, Innsbruck, Austrian-Tyrol.
Brockwell, Miss, 3, place Rivoli.
Brodhurst, Mrs. (Surgeon and Physician), 6, rue du Mont-Thabor.
Brodie, A. Kenneth, 34, rue Notre-Dame-des-Champs.
Broen, Miss de (Foundress of the Belleville-Mission), 3, rue Clavel, Belleville.
Brolemann, Mr. and Mrs. Auguste (née Ellie Stewari), 6, avenue d'Iéna, Paris.
Bronson, Miss Edith Millicent (late Arthur), married June 26 th. 1895, Rucellai Ct Comiso. Venice.
Bronson, Mrs. Arthur (née Katharine Dekay), Rucellai Ct Comiso, Venice.
Brooker, Mr. and Mrs., 7, avenue Kléber.
Brooker, Mr. and Mrs., 135, boulevard Haussmann.
Brooks, Thomas, E., 48, rue du Bac and villa de la Garde, Dinard.
Brooks, Mr. Thomas, 6, rue Solférino, Paris.
Brown, Miss Edith (Artist), 65, boulevard Arago (Boston, Mass, U. S. A.), Auteuil.
Brown, Miss Paudy (Artist), 21, rue Valette.
Brown, Mr. and the Misses, 33, boulevard de Versailles, Montretout, Saint-Cloud.
Brown, H., 11, 6, rue Boissonade.
Brown, B. C., 163 bis, rue de Vaugirard.
Brown, W., 15, rue Richepanse.
Brown, Mr. and Mrs., 69, avenue d'Antin.
Brown, W. J., 1, rue Caumartin.
Brown, Rev. Stephen, R., 48, rue Pergolèse.
Brownall, Miss Matilda (Artist), 4, rue de l'Oratoire.
Bruck, Mlle Rosa (Comédie Française), 20, rue Euler.
Brugière, Mr. and Mrs. Jules E. (née Sarah Van Buren), Down Town Club, New-York and care of J. Munroe and Co, Paris.
Brulatour, Mr. E. J., rue Léo-Delibes (U. S.).
Brumide, Laurent S., 59, avenue de Saxe (U. S.).
Brunnow (Prof.) and Mrs. Rudolph E. (née Marguerite Beckwith), châlet Beauval, Vevey, Switzerland.
Brush, G. D., 65, boulevard Arago.
Bryant, Miss, 39, rue Galilée, Paris.
Bryant, Mr., 39, rue Galilée.
Bryant, Mrs., 39, rue Galilée.
Bryant, Mr. K., 12, cité Bergère.

Bryant, W., 12, cité Bergère.
Bryant, Wallace, 6, rue Boissonade.
Brydon, Mme L. A., 8, rue de Presbourg and villa Sainte-Catherine, Dinard.
Buchanan, Mrs. and Mrs. P. R , 34, avenue Kléber.
Buckland, Arthur Herbert, 3, rue Vercingétorix.
Buell, Mme Madeleine Polk (U. S. A.), 25, av. Wagram.
Bulfield, Joseph, 7, impasse Marie Blanche (G. B.).
Bull, Dr. G. J., 4, rue de la Paix.
Bull, Dr. George J. (U. S. A.), 4, rue de la Paix.
Bullet, Miss Emma, 31, rue de Tocqueville (Correspondent of The Brooklyn Eagle)
Bullivant, Mrs., 10, rue Poncelet.
Bumpas, Miss Josephine, 187, rue de la Pompe.
Bunneli, Miss Julia (Sculptor), 105 bis, boulevard Montparnasse.
Bunny, Rupert C. W., 18 bis, impasse du Maine.
Burckhardt, Mr. and Mrs. Ed., 12, avenue de l'Alma, Paris ; 105, boulevard Haussmann, Paris.
Burggraff, G. L. F. de, cité Gaillard (G. B.).
Burgy, Henri V., 229, rue Saint-Honoré.
Burnett, Mme Alice (G. B.), 21, rue Montenotte.
Burn-Murdoch, Miss M., 10, r. de la Grande-Chaumière.
Burns, Walter H. and Mrs., 43, rue du Faubourg Saint-Honoré.
Burton, C., 68, rue des Marais.
Burton, Mme Charles, 6, avenue de Messine.
Bussh, Countess Hun de (G. C.), 55, r. du Cherche-Midi.
Bussin, George (Artist, H. C.), boulevard de Courcelles and 233, faubourg Saint-Honoré.
Bussot, Mrs. Louisa, 82, rue d'Hauteville (G. B.).
Butler, Miss (G. B.), 21, rue Montenotte (Trasday).
Butler, Miss Clarence, La Verne, 99, rue de Vaugirard (U. S.).
Butler, Mr., 79, rue Notre-Dame-des-Champs.
Butterwoth, Mrs. A. J., 7, rue de La Trémoille.

C

Cachard, Mme, 101, avenue des Champs-Elysées.
Cachard, Mr. Henry, same address.
Cachard, Mrs. Edward (née Caroline Chazournes). 91, avenue des Champs-Elysées, Paris.
Cachard, Mr. Henry, 91, av. des Champs-Elysées, Paris.
Cachard, Mr. Edward B., 91, avenue des Champs-Elysées, Paris.
Cagwin, L. F., 203, boulevard Raspail.
Calder, Mr. Sterling (Sculptor), 9, r. des Fourneaux
Calhoun, R., 66, boulevard du Port-Royal.
Campbell, Mme, 44, rue Bassano (U. S. A.).
Candler, Mr. D., rue Saint-Simon.
Canfield, B. King, 11, impasse Rousieu (U. S.).
Capro-Smith, Mrs. L., 3, rue Yvon-Villarceau.
Caraman-Chimay, Princess de (née Ward), 15, rue de Berri.
Caraman-Chimay, Prince Pierre de (Secretary of the Belgian Legation), 41, quai d'Orsay.
Cardozo, Mrs., 5, rue Daru.
Cardwell the Rev. James, 13, avenue Victor-Hugo.
Cargill, Mrs., 47, avenue Henri-Martin.
Carlier, E. J. (Sculptor atelier), 6, rue du Regard.
Carmicheal, Mr., R. S., 4, rue Saint-Florentin.
Carmicheal, Mrs., 44, rue Cambon.
Carne, the Misses, 4, avenue Carnot, Paris.
Carnot, Mme Sadi, 19, avenue de l'Alma and Château de Presles, La Ferté-Alais (Seine-et-Oise).
Carolus Duran (Artist), 125, avenue des Champs-Elysées and 11, passage Stanislas and villa Carolus, Montgeron (Seine-et-Oise).
Carter, Miss, 4, villa Michon.
Carter, Mr. John Ridgeley, 15, rue Pierre-Charron, Paris and 15, Chesham Street, London.
Carter, Mrs., 5, rue Léo-Delibes.

Carvalho, Léon (Director of the Opera-Comique, 8), boulevard des Batignolles.
Casa-Argudin, Marquis and Marquess de (née Maria C. De Valle), Madrid.
Casa-Miranda, Count snd Countess de (née Christine Nilsson), 3, rue Clément-Marot.
Case, Mrs. A. N., 6, Léopold-Robert (U. S.)
Case, Mrs. J. P., av. des Champs-Elysées, Paris.
Casella, Mrs. Ella, 217, boul. Saint-Germain (G. B.).
Casella, Nelia, 217, boul. Saint-Germain (G. B.).
Casey, Mr. and Mrs., Wm. Chandler (née Flora-Mac D. Wooddock, 27, Waverley Place New-York and United States, Embassy, Berlin.
Casimir-Périer, Jean, château de Pont-sur-Seine (Aube).
Castellane, Comte and Comtesse Boniface de (née Anna-Gould), Champs-Elysées, Paris.
Castellane, Marquis and Marquise (née de Juigné) 1, boulevard de la Tour and château de Roche, cotte-Saint-Patrice (Indre-et-Loire).
Castle, M., 203, boulevard Raspail.
Castries, Count Henry and Countess (née de la Moricière), 75, rue de Grenelle.
Cauffmann, S. J., 21, rue de Trévise (U. S.).
Cauldwell, M. W., 131, boulevard Montparnasse.
Cavé, J. C. (Painter) H. C., 36, rue Notre-Dame-des-Champs.
Cayley, Violet, 39, avenue d'Eylau.
Chabrol, Count Roger de, 81, rue de Lille.
Chase, Mr. John, 79, rue Notre-Dame-des-Champs (Boston Mass)
Chatfault, Countess de, 5, avenue d'Eylau.
Chamberlain, Miss Elisabeth, care of Morgan, Harjes and Co, Bankers, Paris.
Chambers, Mrs. Ada C., 18, rue de Milan.
Chandon de Briailles, Baron and Baroness G. (née Garridon), 18, rue Caumartin, Paris.
Chanler, Mr. and Mrs. Robert Winthrop, 125, avenue des Champs-Elysées.
Chapman, Mrs. John Jay (née Minna Fimmins) at Rome and care of J. S. Morgan and Co, London.
Chapman, Mr., 31, avenue de l'Opéra.
Chapman, Mrs., 6 ter, avenue Mac-Mahon.
Chapman, Miss (Artist), 30, rue Boissonade.
Charette, Baron le Général de, and Mme (née Polk), Basse-Motte.
Charlton, Miss, 53, rue d'Amsterdam.
Charpentier, F. M. (Sculptor), 17, rue Campagne-Première.
Charpentier, Georges (Editor), 11, rue de Grenelle.
Chartland, Mrs. L. J. (née Louise G. Macomb), 32, East 26, th. St. New-York and at Biarritz, Basses-Pyrénées.
Chartres, Mgr., Duke and the Duchess de, 27, rue Jean-Goujon, château de Saint-Firmin, Chantilly and villa des Fayères, Cannes.
Choiseul, Marquis and Marchioness de (née Claire Coudert), 12, Pierre-Charon, Paris.
Chrounchioti, M., 28, avenue d'Antin.
Church, Mr. Willard, 51, Irving Place New-York and care of Munroe and Co, Paris.
Churchiel, Mrs. A. (née Churchiell), J. Munroe and Co, Paris.
Churchward, Captain A., 6, rue des Cérisoles.
Clark, Miss, 4, rue Léopold-Robert.
Clark, Miss Ladie, 4, rue Léopold-Robert (Providence R. J. U. S. A.).
Clark, Miss, 6, villa Michon.
Clark, F. B., 203, boulevard Raspail.
Clark, Mr. and Mrs., Chas. Gordon-Sp., 11, rue Lincoln, Paris.
Clarke, T. M., 10, place de la Bourse.
Clarke Campbell ("Daily-Telegraph" Correspondent) and Mrs., 116, avenue des Champs-Elysées. Mondays.
Clarke, Mr. and Mrs. C. Gordon, 11, rue Lincoln.
Clarke, Dr. Alexander, S., 2, rue Cambacrès.
Clarke, S. P., 35, rue Delambre.

C	**C-D**

Cumming, Dr., 12, rue Royale.
Cumming. Mrs. ,15, rue du Louvre.
Cumming William, 9, avenue Sainte-Foy, Neuilly.
Curier. C. B., 131. boulevard Montparnasse.
Clarkson, Dr., rue de Belzunce.
Clausen. George, 24. boul. des Capucines (G. B.).
Cleland-Ponsonby, Mr. and Mrs. (née Horwitz), villa Acadie, Pau.
Cleland, Miss, 52, avenue Victor-Hugo.
Clement, Miss Fanny, 187, rue de la Pompe.
Clement, Miss Ethel, 187, rue de la Pompe.
Cleveland. Mrs. Augustus, 75, av. des Champs-Elysées.
Clifford, Mr. and Miss, 8, avenue Carnot.
Clinch, Mr., 35, rue Châteaubriand.
Clurland, Mrs., 75, avenue des Champs-Elysées.
Cohen, Miss Ellen G., 9, rue Campagne-Première.
Cole, Miss, 110, boulevard Malesherbes.
Colgate, Mrs. Sallie, 17, avenue Victor-Hugo, Paris.
Collier, Ma., 177 bis, rue des Aubépines. Colombes.
Collins, Miss, 20, avenue Victor-Hugo.
Collins, Mr., George, 8, rue du Dôme.
Collins, R.. 152, rue de Vaugirard.
Collis, F. M., 28, avenue d'Iéna.
Colson, J. C., 66, rue Caumartin.
Comman, Mr. H., 10, r. des Champerons, Colombes.
Comman, Mrs., 3., rue de Penthièvre.
Compton, Nr., 123, avenue du Bois-de-Boulogne.
Conner, E., 13, rue de Belzunce.
Conrath, Dr., 16. place Vendôme.
Constant. Benjamin, 15, impasse Hélène.
Constant. Benjamin, 27, rue de Pigalle.
Cook, Miss. 15, rue Chaptal.
Cooke, Mrs. Williams (Artist),175,r. Vaugirard, Chicago.
Cooke, Very Rev. Osmund, 50, avenue Hoche.
Cooke, Miss (Artist), 131, rue du Cherche-Midi.
Cope, Mr. and Mrs. Walter, 13, rue Perdonnet.
Corbett, Rev. Sidney and Mrs., Hôtel Byron, rue Laffite (Philadelphia U. S. A.).
Corbin, Mr., 7, avenue Kléber.
Corbin, Mr. and Mrs. Richard E., 7, avenue Kléber.
Corbin, Mr. and Mrs. Richard W. (née Rhoades), 7, avenue Kléber. Paris.
Cormon, 13, rue d'Aumale.
Cornet, Counte and Countess, L.,126, boul. Haussmann Sundays.
Cornwall, Miss Mary, 27, rue Fresne.
Corttoyo. Counters, 36, avenue du Bois-de-Boulogne (U. S. A.).
Coubertin, Baron and Baroness Pierre de, 20, rue Oudinot. Mondays.
Coule, W. J., 7, rue Delambre.
Courmont, Mme M de' 17, rue Freillard.
Court, John, 211, boulevard Raspail.
Courval. Vicomtesse de (née Ray), 6. r. Paul-Baudry.
Coussino, Mme de, boulevard Haudrin (U. S. A.).
Cowen, J., 9. Bradford avenue, London.
Cowie. Mrs , 5, avenue Montaigne.
Cox, Mrs. Wheeler, 32, rue de Lubeck.
Coxe, V. H. C. (New-York Herald), 34, rue Penthièvre.
Crane, Mr. Frédéric, 68, rue de Rennes (Setanket, N. Y. U. S. A.).
Crane. E. A., 15, rue de la Paix.
Crane, J. W., 41, boulevard des Capucines.
Crane, Mr. and Mrs., 14, rue François Ier.
Crawford, Robert ("Daily-News" Correspondent), 60, boulevard de Courcelles.
Crawford, Mrs. Emily, 60. boulevard de Courcelles.
Crawshaw, L. T., 35, rue Delambre.
Cree, Dr. and Mrs., 8, rue d'Assas.
Creed, Henry, 19, avenue Neil.
Cressonière, Mme de (Matron of the American Girl's Club), 4, rue Chevreuse.
Crowe, Miss, 42, rue de Bruxelles.
Crowe, E. B., 28, avenue du Trocadéro.
Crowe, Sir Joseph A. and Lady (Commercial Attaché to H. B. M's Embassy), 28, avenue du Trocadéro.

Crowen. Ferdinand de, 203, boulevard Raspail.
Cryder, Mr. and Mrs. Duncan (née Ogden), Biarritz, France.
Cuceul. E. A., 9, rue Campagne-Première.
Curtis, Miss, 84, rue Bonaparte (Studio), 150, rue de Vaugirard.
Curtis, Mr. and Mrs. Atherton (née Louise C. Burleigh). Paris.
Curtis, Mrs. Louise (Burleigh Artist),5, r. Boissonade.
Curtois, Miss, 84, rue Bonaparte.
Cushing, Mr. and Mrs. F. W., rur Chalgrin.
Cussack, Mrs. Edith E., 18, rue de Milan.
Custing. Mr. and Mrs., Hôtel Liverpool.
Cutter, Mr. and Mrs., 4, rue Marbeuf.
Cutting, Mrs. H., 33, rue Marbeuf.
Cutting. Mrs. Robert L. (née Moale), Paris.
Cuyler, Mrs. James Wayne, Paris.
Cuyler. Sir Philip and Lady Graz Egerton (née Cuyler), avenue du Bois-de-Boulogne, Paris.
Czetwertynski, Prince Boris Swiatopolski, 34 bis, avenue du Bois-de-Boulogne.

D

Daboll, Dr. and Mrs., 14, avenue de l'Opéra.
Dampierre, Vicomte and Vicomtesse de (née Corbin), 4, rue Galliera.
Dana, C. G.. 235. faubourg Saint-Honoré.
Dana. L. W., 12, rue de Presbourg.
Dannat. William, T., 45, avenue de Villiers.
Darmesteter. Mrs. (née Hartog), 3, rue Bara (G. B.).
Darmesteter, Mrs., 18, boul. de la Tour-Maubourg.
Darrax, Marquis and Marchioness de (née de Bois-Guibert), 23, rue Bugeaud.
Dashwood, J., 346. rue Saint-Honoré.
Dashwood, Mrs., 346, rue Saint-Honoré.
Davenport, Dr. Isaac, 30, avenue de l'Opéra.
Davenport, William, S., 30, avenue de l'Opéra.
Davenpont-Wheeler, Mr. and Mrs., 2, rue Marbeuf, and Redclyffe, Newhaven.
Davidson, 154. avenue de l'Opéra.
Davies, Miss Isabella Sarah, 129, boul. Péreire.
Davies, Mr., 3, rue Saint-Georges.
Davis, 48, boul. Sébastopol.
Davis, A., 3, rue Meyerbeer.
Davis, J., 34, rue d'Hauteville.
Davis, L. M., 131, boul. Montparnasse.
Davis, Miss H Anna, care of Morgan, Harjes and Co, Bankers, Paris.
Davis, Mr. C. Belmont, United states Consul. Florence, Italy.
Davis, S., 5, rue Rude.
Davis Warren, 5, rue Rude.
Dawson, Miss., 8, rue Daru.
Dawson, Rebecca, 6, square Croissac (New-York).
Day, Robert, S., 11, impasse Roussin (U. S.).
Day Robt (Contractor), 141, boul. Montparnasse (San Francisco).
Deacon, Allan, 9, rue Bara (G. R.).
De Broen, Miss, 3, rue Clavel.
Decazes, Duc and Duchesse (née Singer), 12, rue de Lubeck, Paris.
Decazes et de Glucksberg, Duc and Duchesse (née Singer), 22, aven. du Bois-de-Boulogne, and La Grave, Saint-Denis-de-Piles (Gironde).
Deering, Dr., 3, rue Godot-de-Mauroi.
De Grey, Lord and Lady, 161, av. des Champs-Elysées.
Deivonne, Comte and Comtesse, L. Forest de (née Andenrich). 15, avenue Bosquet.
Delanay, H. P., 32, rue des Dames.
Delano, Mr. and Mrs., W. H., 4, rue Creveux.
Deligny d'Alosno, Count and Countess Eugène, 64, rue François Ier.

D

Delmue, M. M., 106, boul. Montmartre.
Déloye, Mme (née Fox), 15, rue Mansart.
Delpit, Mrs. C. (née Molyneux), 19, rue Mont-Rosier, Neuilly.
Dennis, W. H., 19, rue Roquépine.
Deschamps, Pierre, 2, rue de Ponthieu.
Des Escarts, Miss, 108, rue du Bac.
Dessar, Louis, G., 15, rue Le Verrier (U. S.).
Desvarren.
De Varreux, Miss, 12, rue Greffulhe.
Dewhon, Mrs., 8, avenue d'Eylau.
Dewhurst, A. S., 203, boul. Raspail.
Dey, H. E., 13, rue Campagne-Première.
Dickinson, Mr. and Mrs., Howard, C. (née Agnes, D., Wagstaff), J. Munroe and Co, Paris.
Dickson. Miss Estelle (Painter). 13, rue Mansart.
Didsbury, Dr., 3, rue Meyerbeer.
Dielison, Mr. and Mrs., 58, boul. Clichy. (Friday).
Dijievanoska, Miss Hedwige, 187, rue de la Pompe.
Dillon, H. Patrice, 84, boul. Rochechouart.
Dillon, Miss, 41, avenue Montaigne.
Dino, Duchesse de, 21, place Vendôme, and Château de Montmorency (Seine-et-Oise).
Dinsmore, Mr. and Mrs. Clarence Gray [(née Kate Jerome), 76, aven. Marceau, Paris.
Dion. Comtesse de, 5. rue Planche.
Divonne, Comte and Comtesse (née Audenried), 52 bis, rue de Varenne.
Dodge, O. B., 5, rue Saint-Ducor.
Dodge, William, 3, rue d'Alençon (U. S.).
Dodson, The Hon. John., Honorary Attaché to H. B. M's Embassy, 86, faub. Saint-Honoré.
Dorey, Mr. and Mrs., 85, rue Lubeck.
Dorey, W. H., 83, boulevard Pereire.
Dortic, Mr. and Mrs Henry, 138, Champs-Elysées.
Dortic, Mr and Mrs., H. F. (née Rogers), 138, Champs-Elysées, Paris.
Doucet, L., 64, rue de la Rochefoucauld.
Dougherty, Mrs., 18, rue Marbeuf (G. B.).
Douglas, Mr. and Mrs., 5, rue Alfred Stevens.
Drake, Henry, 43 et 45 aven. du Bois-de-Boulogue.
Drake, J. E. (Artist), 13, boul. de Courcelles.
Drake, Mr. and Mrs., 43, aven. du Bois-de-Boulogne (Tuesday)
Drake (Prof.), 13, boul. de Courcelles.
Draper, G. H., 39, rue Galilée.
Draper, Miss Emily, H., 128, boulevard Montparnasse (G. B.).
Draper. Mr., George H.-Vy. 39, rue Galilée, Paris.
Dresser, Miss Edith Stuyvesant, same address.
Dresser, Miss Nathalie Bayard, care of Morgan, Harjes and Co, Paris.
Dresser, Miss Suzan Le Roy, same address.
Drexel, A. J., 31, boul. Haussmann.
Droin, Miss Clara, care of J. Munroe Co, Bankers, Paris.
Dube, Mr., Mattie, 70 bis, rue Notre-Dame-des-Champs.
Du Bellet, 1, rue des Brousses, quai de Billy.
Dubois, P., Ecole des Beaux-Arts.
Du Bos. Mme (née Johnston), 47, avenue Henri-Martin.
Duchamps, Albert (New York Herald), 5, rue Laugier.
Duleep Singh. Prince, Maharanee, 40, rue Fortuny (Telephone).
Dumas, Madame Alexandre, 11, rue Ampère, and chateau de Champfleur, Marly (Seine-et-Oise).
Dumas, Madame Ernest, J. B. (née Milne-Edwards), 57, rue Cuvier.
Du Mond, Fred. Melville, 93, avenue Henri-Martin. (U.S.)
Duncan, Mr. and Mrs., 197, avenue Daumesnil.
Duncan, The Misses, 12, rue Boccador.
Dunn, Dr., 15. rue des Pyramides
Dunn, Dr. and Mrs., B. Sherwood, 15, rue des Pyramides.

Dunn, the Rvd. Cuthbert, 50, avenue Hoche (G. B.).
Dupuy, Dr. and Mrs., Eugène, 53, av. Montaigne.
Durand, Mr., Ernest, 92, rue Maubeuge.
Du Villard, Marquis and Marquess, Raymond de la Four (née Julia J. Chapin), 2, r. Cambacérès, Paris

E

East, Mr., 4, place d'Iéna.
Eaton Mrs. 67, aven. des Champs-Elysées.
Eddy, Christopher. 13 rue d'Amsterdam.
Eddy Clarence and Mrs. (of Chicago U.S.A.) Hôtel de Calais.
Eddy, Mr., 20, r. de Rome. and Eddystone, Nanterre.
Edmonds, Miss Lilian, 10, r. de la Grande-Chaumière.
Edmonson, W. J., rue Delambre.
Edwards, Mr., 7, rue du Bois-de-Boulogne.
Edwards, Mr., 25, rue Marbeuf.
Edwards, Mrs. Charles, 51, rue Saint-Georges, and Château de la Cour-du-Bois, Mamers, Sarthe.
Edwards-Pilliet, Mrs., Dr., 4, rue Richepanse.
Edwind, Lord., W., 128, avenue de Wagram.
Egerton, Capt. Geo., Naval attaché to H. B. M's Embassy, 39, rue du faubourg Saint-Honoré.
Eggleston, Mr. and Mrs., George Cary (née Marion Craggs), hôtel de l'Athénée, Paris.
Egleston, Miss (Illustrator), 131. rue du Cherche-Midi.
Elder, Ch. A., 7, rue du Sabot.
Elisseeff, M., Grand-Hôtel.
Elisseeff, Mlle, 85, avenue Kléber.
Elkins, Miss May, 187, rue de la Pompe.
Ellatz, Miss, 15, avenue de la Grande-Armée.
Ellicott, H. T., 23, avenue du Bois-de-Boulogne.
Elliot, the Misses, 72, rue Lauriston.
Elwell, Frank, William, 9, rue Campagne-Première (G. B.).
Elwell, Mrs., 223, av. de Paris, plaine Saint-Denis.
Elwell, Mr. and Mrs. F. Edwin (née Molina, M. Hildresth), 7, rue Scribe, Paris.
Emdem, Louis, and Mme (née Van der Heym), 11 bis, rue Boissy-d'Anglas.
Emmett, John, 5 bis, rue Martel.
Emory, Commander and Mrs. William, 11, avenue Malakoff, Paris.
Emoven, Mme, 11, avenue Malakoff (U. S. A.).
Emslem. Mr. Charles, 32, avenue de Courcelles.
Enderolt, Miss, 16, rue Siam.
England, Mrs., 15, rue Leo Delibes.
England, Mr. and Mrs., 15, rue Leo Delibes.
Ensley, Miss (Artist), 1, rue Leopold Robert (Providence, R. J. U.S.A.).
Eram, Dr. L., 15, rue de la Paix.
Erlanger, Baron and Baroness (née Slidell), 76, avenue Kléber, and Villa Louisiane, Deauville, Calvados, and 6, Hamilton Place, Piccadilly, London.
Eschmann, M. d', 99, avenue de Villiers.
Erskine, Miss, Hôtel de Wagram, rue de Rivoli.
Este, Miss Florence, 53, rue Notre-Dame-des-Champs (U. S.).
Esté, Miss Florence (Artist), 75, r N.-Dame-d.-Champs
Estrella, Baron et Baroness d', 28, rue de Lubeck.
Etheridge, Mr. and Mrs., R. Mordaunt, Villa Eveline, Bois-Colombes.
Eu (H. R. H. Gaston d'Orléans, Count d') (and Countess née Princess Imp. de Brésil), 9, av. Kléber and 7, boul. de Boulogne, Boulogne-sur-Seine.
Eustace, Henry, 66, rue Basse-du-Rempart.
Eustis, James B., Ambassador and Plenipotentiary of U. S. (20 Jan. 93), 24, avenue Kléber.
Eustis Newton, B., Secretary to U. S. Embassy, 24, avenue Kleber.
Eustis, Mr., W. E., United States Embassy, 24, aven. Kléber, Paris.

Eustis, Miss., United States Embassy, 24, avenue Kléber, Paris.
Evans, Dr. John, 19, avenue de l'Opera.
Evans, Dr. Thomas, W. and Mrs., 42, avenue du Bois-de-Boulogne.
Evans, John, 19, avenue de l'Opéra.
Evans, Miss (Effie) Mackensie Hôtel de Calais.
Evans, Thomas W., 15, rue de la Paix.
Evans, Miss Adelina (Painter), 4, r. de Chevreuse.
Exelby, Mr. and Mrs., 70, av. de la Grande-Armée.
Eyre-Powell, Mrs. Anna, 22, rue Brunel (Saturday).

F

Fabre, Hector, C. M. G. (Commissionner-General of Canada), and Mme, 35, rue Marbeuf.
Fabre, Paul, 35, rue Marbeuf.
Fahnestock, Mr. and Mrs. Gibson (née Andrews), Florence, Italy.
Fairchild, Miss. 39, rue Galilée, Paris.
Fairfax, Miss Maud Christian, 187, rue de la Pompe.
Falguière, Alexandre (Statuaire, Membre de l'Institut), 68, rue d'Assas.
Fallonsbee, Mrs., 25, rue des Mathurins.
Farman, T. F. F., Editor of the " Standard ", 53, rue Lafayette.
Farmer, Miss Laura, 187, rue de la Pompe.
Farmer, Miss Fanny, 187, rue de la Pompe.
Farrar, Mrs., rue Brémontier.
Farrett, Edward, 6, avenue Mac-Mahon (G. B.).
Farrett, Miss, 6, avenue Mac-Mahon (G. B.).
Faure-Miller, Dr., 28, rue Matignon.
Faure-Miller, Dr. (Physician to Sir Richard Wallace Hospital), and Mrs., 28, rue Matignon.
Faure-Miller, Dr. Roland, and Mrs., 8, rue de Miromesnil.
Faure-Miller, Dr. Harold, 28, rue Matignon, and 17, boulevard du Cannet at Cannes.
Fawcett, Mrs., 92, rue de la Boëtie.
Fay, Miss Adèle (Artist), 9, r. Campagne-Première.
Faye, C. de, 117, rue Saint-Lazare.
Febe de Faur, Mrs., 4, avenue d'Eyleau.
Felloes, F., rue Delambre.
Fenwick, Mr. and Mrs., 5, square du Roule.
Fenwick, Chas., 21, rue Martel.
Fenwick, F., 24, rue Martel.
Fenwick, Mr. and Mrs. F., 5, square du Roule.
Fereboschi, Mr. and Mrs., 56, avenue Kléber.
Ferguson, Mr. Thomas, B., Union Club New-York, and United States Legation, Stockholm.
Ferguson, Miss E. G., United States Legation, Stockholm.
Ferguson, Mrs. J. du B., United states Legation, Stockholm.
Ferguson, Mrs., 5, rue Berryer.
Ferrabochi, Mr. and Mrs., 56, avenue Kléber, Paris.
Ferrari, Henri (Director of « La Revue Bleue »), 146, boulevard Raspail.
Ferrari, François (Editor to the Gaulois), and Mrs (née Colombari de Montègre), 63, av. Kléber.
Ferrata (His Excellency Monseigneur D.), 58, rue de Varenne.
Ferrier, G., 62, rue Saint-Didier.
Ferrière, Mr. and Mrs. James L. (née Benson), 52, rue d'Anjou.
Ferrière, James, 42, rue d'Anjou.
Fetridge, W. Pembroke, 13, av. du Bois-de-Boulogne.
Fetridge, H. Pembroke, 13, av. du Bois-de-Boulogne.
Fetridge, Misses, 13, avenue du Bois-de-Boulogne (Sunday).
Feydeau, Georges, and Mrs. (née Carolus-Duran), 75, rue de Chaillot.
Feyen, Eugène (Painter), 11, boul. de Clichy.

Ffarmer, Mrs. (Matron, Victoria Home), 22, rue Borghèse, parc de Neuilly.
Field, Mr. and Mrs., 157, rue du faubourg Saint-Honoré.
Field, Hickson, Mrs., 3, rue du Cirque.
Field, Mrs. Marshall (of Chicago), Hôtel de Hollande, 20, rue de la Paix.
Fiërens-Peters, Mrs. (Grand-Opéra), 18, rue Baudin.
Finaly, Mr. Hugo, 12, rue Pierre-Charron.
Fischoff, Eugène, and Mrs. (née Sedelmeyer), 7, avenue de Coq and Château d'Ambleville, Bray-et-Lû (Seine-et-Oise).
Fischoff, G, rue de la Rochefoucauld.
Fitch, Mr. and Mrs., Harold, 11, rue Delaborde (Mondays), Château de Pradine, Gramnois (Vaucluse) and avenue Fitch, au Prado, Marseilles.
Fitch, Mrs and the Misses, Square Croisic, 12, boulevard Montparnasse.
Fitch, Douglas (Same addresses as above).
Fitz-James, Count and Countess de (née de Gontaut-Biron), 105, rue de Longchamps and Château de Benais, par Bourgueil (Indre-et-Loire).
Fitz-James, Duke de, 22, rue Fabert.
Fitz-James, Count Robert de, and Countess (née de Gutmann), 41, rue des Ecuries-d'Artois (Friday).
Flack, Mr.. " Hôtel Victoria ", rue Castiglione.
Flameng, Leopold (Artist-Engraver), 25, boulevard Montparnasse, and at Courgent, par Septeuil (Seine-et-Oise).
Flameng, François (Artist-Painter), and Mrs., 18, rue d'Armaillé.
Flammarion, Camille (Astronomer), 16, rue Cassini and at the Observatory of Juvisy.
Fleming, H., 44, rue de Villejust.
Fleming, Mr. Chas., W., 7, rue Meyerbeer.
Fleming, Miss, 154, boul. Haussmann.
Fletcher, H. J., 7, rue Scribe.
Flint, Mr. and Mrs., 22, rue Truffault.
Flower, Miss, 121 bis, rue de Grenelle.
Fogarasi, Victor, 8, rue des Capucines.
Foley, Mr. Arold. 4, rue Leopold-Robert (Hackensack New-Jersey (U. S. A.).
Follansbee, Mrs., 25, rue des Mathurins.
Forain, Jean Louis, and Mme (née J. Bose) (Artist-Painter), 1 bis, boulevard Gouvion-Saint-Cyr.
Foras, Comte et Comtesse de (née Marie D. Meredith Read, Sofia, Bulgaria.
Forbes, H., Courcy, 53, avenue de l'Alma.
Forbes, Mr. and Mrs. Francis, B., 57, rue Pierre Charron.
Forbes, the Misses Pauline and Florence, 53, avenue de l'Alma, Paris.
Forbes, Mr. and Mrs., Francis B., 57, rue Pierre-Charron.
Forbes, Mr., 35, rue de Seine.
Forbes, Charles, Stuart, 53, avenue de l'Alm.
Forbes, Mr., 20, rue de Ponthieu.
Forbes, the Rev. Father James (S. J.), 35, r. de Sèvres.
Forbes, Mr. and Mrs. Villiers, Dinard (Ille-et-Vilaine)
Forda, Harry., S., 85, r, Notre-Dame-des-Champs.
Fordyce, Arnold, 36, rue de Provence.
Forest, Miss Katherine de (Harper's Magazine), 9, rue de Freycinet, rue Pierre-Charron.
Forrest, A. C., 7, rue Laffitte.
Foster, Mr. Chester, 19 bis, rue Clément-Marot.
Foster, Miss (Studio), 233, r. du faubourg St-Honoré (Thursday).
Foster, Mr., Mrs. and the Misses, 7, r. de Longchamp Boulogne-sur-Seine (3rd Wednesday in month).
Foss, Miss Henrietta (Artist), at Miss Wood's Pension, 21, avenue de la Grande-Armée.
Fournier, Alex. Joseph, 77, boulevard Edgar-Quinet (U. S.).
Fournier, A. G., 203, boul. Raspail.
Fox, Mr., 26, rue d'Amsterdam.
Fox, P. P., 42, rue Jouffroy.
Frank, Mrs., 8, boul. Emile-Augier.

Frankenstein, M., 46, avenue Gabriel.
Fredriksen, Mrs. Ada, 9, rue de l'Université (Chicago, U. S. A.).
Freeman, Mrs. Williams, 99, rue de la Boëtie (Sundays).
Freeman, Miss Mary, P. L (Artist), 6, rue de la Boissonnade.
Freeman, Miss, 8, rue Jean-Goujon.
French, Mrs., 39, rue Pierre-Chorron.
Fresnel, Viscount de, 5, rue Laugier.
Frew, R. A., 14, rue de la Grande-Chaumière.
Frey, J. H., 79, rue des Fourneaux.
Freycinet (Ch. Louis de Saulses de), and Mrs., 77, rue de la Faisanderie (Monday).
Friedhem, Mrs., 3, rue du Trésor.
Friedericks, Baron, 65, avenue Marceau.
Friedericks, M. de, 65, avenue Marceau.
Fulde, E. B., 44, avenue Marceau.
Fulde, Edward, B., 44, avenue Marceau.
Fuller, Miss, Kate, 73, avenue Kléber, Paris.
Fuller, David. T. S., 24, rue Pigalle.
Fuller, Miss Kate, 73, avenue Kléber.
Fuller, Mrs., Hôtel Huet, rue de l'Arcade.
Fuller, David, 24, rue Pigalle.
Fuller, Miss Kate, 73, avenue Kléber.
Fullick, Miss E., 14, avenue du Maine (U. S.).
Funk, Geo, C., 7, rue Delambre.

G

Gabriac, Count and Countess de (née Montere de Sand), 31, rue Lapérouse, and Château de Béthencourt, Billecourt (Oise).
Gabriac, Marquis de, and Mnchess (née d'Eskilès), 28, rue Barbet-de-Jouy (Saturday).
Gabriac, Count Alexandre de (same address).
Gabriac, Count Joseph de, and Countess (née Montero de Sans), 21, rue Lapérouse, and Château de Béthencourt, par Ribécourt (Oise).
Gabriac, Countess de (née Phalen), 23, r. des Bassins,
Gabriac, Count G. de, and Countess (née de Fayolle), 7, rue Las-Cases (Friday), and Château de Chateaufor, Langeais (Indre-et-Loire).
Gaft, Zulime (Sculptor), 14, r. de la Grande-Chaumière.
Gaft, Miss (Sculptor), square du Croissac, 12, boulevard Montparnasse.
Guilhard, Pierre (Director of the Opéra), 13, Villa Chaptal, Levallois.
Gaine, Mr., 7, rue de Grenelle.
Galdomar, Ange (Editor of the Gaulois), 99, rue Richelieu.
Galitzine, Prince de, 28, avenue Niel
Gallagher, Mr. and Mrs., 5, rue Chalgrin (U. S. A.).
Gallatin, Mr. and Mrs. Francis D. (née Harriet, L. Bogert) care of Morgan, Harjes et Co, Paris.
Galli, Comte et Comtesse, 154, av. des Champs-Elysées.
Galliffet, Count Charles de, and Countess (nee Stevens), 28, rue François 1er.
Gallinger, Miss (Painter), 5, rue Boissonnade.
Galway, Miss, 38. avenue de la Grande-Armée.
Ganay, Count and Countess de (née Ridgway), 5, rue François 1er, Paris.
Ganay, Marquis and Marquise de (née Ridgway), 5, rue François 1er, and Château de Fougerett, Etang, Saône-et-Loire.
Ganse, H. V., 63, boulevard Arago.
Gardner, Miss Elisabeth, 73, rue Notre-Dame-des-Champs (U. S.).
Garrido, L. R., 35, rue Delambre.
Garrisson, Mrs. Cornelius, K. (née Letitia Randell), Paris.
Garside, O., 4, place Saint-Sulpice.
Gaspell, Miss, 4, rue de Chevreuse.

Gasquet-James, Amédée de, 4, avenue Bugeaud.
Gaujean, Eugène (Artist-Engraver) (H. C.), 45, rue de Sèvres.
Gautereau, Aug., avocat à la Cour, pl. St-Michel, 5.
Gay, Mr. et Mrs., Walter (née Matilda Travers), 73, rue d'Ampère, Paris.
Gay, Walter, 73, rue Ampère.
Gay, Walter (Artist-Painter, H. C.), 73, rue Ampère.
Gaylord, F. A., 131, boul. Montparnasse.
Geofroy, Mr. M., 7, rue Brunel (G. B.).
George, J. B., 11, rue du Pont-Neuf.
George, Miss Lulu, 187, rue de la Pompe.
Gerbault, H. (Artist), rue de Miromesnil. 30.
Germain, Henri, ancien député, membre de l'Institut, président du Conseil d'administration du Crédit Lyonnais and Madame, née Vuitry, 89, faubourg Saint-Honoré.
Germain, Auguste, homme 'de lettres, 12, rue Bréda.
Gerome, J. L., 65, boulevard de Clichy.
Gérôme, J. L. (Artist-Painter, Member of the Institute), 65, boulevard de Clichy, and Villa de Ligne, Cannes.
Gervais, P. J. (Artist-Painter) (H. C.), 78, r. de Passy.
Gervex, Henry (Artist-Painter), and Madame (née Fouche), 197, boul. Malesherbes.
Geslin, Miss, 5, rue Thann.
Gesling, Mr. Randolph and Mme, 24, rue du faubourg Montmartre.
Gesling, Mr. and Mrs. Reginald, 3, rue d'Aguesseau.
Gesne, Mr. and Mrs., 19, rue Vignon.
Ghika, Prince Nicolas, Secretary to the Roumanian Legation, and Princess (née Patzouris), 7, rue de l'Université and Ghergani, Roumania.
Gibert, Frederic, 35, avenue Victor-Hugo
Gibert (Grand Opera), 61, boul. Saint-Michel.
Gibert, Armand, Servian Consul-General, 127, avenue de Wagram.
Gibert, Mr. and Mrs., Frédéric (née Alice Reed), care of J. Munroe and Co Bankers, Paris.
Gibson, Mrs., 78, boul. de Versailles, Saint-Cloud.
Gick, Mr. and Mrs., 8, rue Gustave-Doré.
Gideon, J., 6, Rond-Point des Champs-Elysées, and Newmarket, England. and Braemer, Scotland.
Gignoux, Mr. and Mrs., Charles C. (née Emma Morgan), (Messenger). Naud, Zwitzerland.
Gilbert, René (Artist-Painter), 6, rue Aumont-Thiéville, Glasser, Th. de, 3, rue Geoffroy-Marie.
Gildert, Mr. and Mrs. Richard Watson (née Helena de Kay) care of Munroe and Co, Bankers, Paris.
Gillet, Miss Mary, 45, rue du Faubourg-Montmartre.
Gladston, Mr. and Mrs, 3, rue du Cirque.
Glaenger, Mr. and Mrs., Frank (née Léonie Coudert), 5, rue Général-Foy, Paris.
Gloeskner, Miss Margaret, 13, rue Boissonnade (New-York).
Gloeskner, Miss Edith, 13, r. Boissonnade (New-York).
Goldner, Mr. and Mrs., 93, rue de la Pompe.
Goldsmith, Mr. and Mrs., Alfred, 18, r. de Marignan, and Château Mageraies, Savonnières, Indre-et-Loire.
Goldsmith-Alger, J., 35, rue des Capucines.
Golil, E.-H., 203, boulevard Raspail.
Gontaut, Count de, and Countesse (née de la Ferronays. 95, rue de l'Université.
Gontaut-Biron, Count Antoine de, 29, r. du Faubourg-Saint-Honoré, and Château de Dammarie-les-Lys (Seine-et-Marne), and Château de Courtalain (Eure-et-Loire).
Gontaut-Biron, Count-Théodore de, and Countess (née de Cossé-Briesac), 45, rue de Varenne.
Gontaut-Biron, Count François de, and Countess (née de Maillé), 44, rue de Bellechasse, and Château de Courtalain (Eure-et-Loire).
Gontaut-Biron, Count Jacques de, and Countess (née de Maillé, 29, rue Saint-Guillaume.
Gontaut-Biron, Count Stanislas de, and Countess (née de Mailly-Châlon), 41, rue de l'Université, and Château d'Aumont, Senlis (Oise).

Gontaut-Biron, Count Paul de. and Countess (née Princesse Troubetzkoï), 1. rue François Ier, and Villa Stéphanie at Gélos. Pau (Basses-Pyrénées).
Gontaut-Biron, Count Gaston de. and Countess (née de Virieu), 90, boul. de la Tour-Maubourg, and Château de Diors, Châteauroux (Indre).
Gontaut-Biron, Count Bernard de. and Countess (née Gabibel), 9, rue de la Pépinière.
Gontaut-Biron, Count Xaxier de, and Countess (née de Virieu), 56, rue de Varenne.
Gontaut-Biron, Count Joseph de, and Countess (née de Polignac), 10, place de la Concorde, and Château de Navailles–Angos (Basses-Pyrénées).
Gontaut-Biron, Count Raoul de, 13, rue Washington.
Good Arthur, 70, rue de Rivoli.
Good, Dr., 23, avenue du Bois-de-Boulogne.
Goodman, Miss E. A. (Artist), 5, rue Léopold-Robert. Chestnut Hill, Pa. (U. S. A.).
Goodridge, Francis, 2, rue Lincoln.
Goodridge, Francis, 2, rue Lincoln.
Goodridge, Miss, 2, rue Lincoln.
Goodwin, Miss Caroline (Artist), 128, boul. Montparnasse (Savannah, Ga. U. S. A.).
Gordon, Mr. John, S. (Artist), 9, rue Campagne–Première (Canada).
Got, Edmond, 11, Hameau Boulainvilliers.
Gotz, Mr. and Mrs., 53, rue de Lisbonne (Tuesdays).
Gough, Mrs., 26, rue Bayard.
Gould, Mme Louis, 1, avenue Friedland (G. B.).
Gowan, J. E., 3, square du Roule.
Grafton, Miss, 13, rue de Verneuil.
Grafton, Mrs., H., 5, avenue d'Antin.
Graham, Mrs. Robert, Me Costery (née Ella Ward), 53, avenue Montaigne, Paris.
Graham, Ronald, Attaché to H. B. M's, Embassy, 39, rue du Faubourg-Saint-Honoré.
Gramont, Duke and Duchesse de (née de Rothschild), 52, rue de Chaillot, and Château de Vallière, Plailly (Oise).
Gray, H., 49, rue d'Amsterdam.
Grey, Lord and Lady de, 116, av. des Champs-Elysées.
Gray, Nowbray, Mr., 130, rue Lemuerre.
Gray, Mrs. Griswold (née Suzan Irvin), 14, avenue de l'Alma, Paris.
Gray, Mr., 29, rue de Trévise.
Gray, W., 73, rue Ampère (U. S.).
Gray-Griswold, Mrs., 14, avenue de l'Alma.
Greatorex, Mrs. Eliza, 17, rue Campagne-Première.
Green, Miss Mary Shepard (Artist), 23, r. de Verrier.
Green, F. H., 13, rue Boissonnade.
Green, Mr. and Mrs., 14, rue de la Pépinière.
Greener, W. W., 8. avenue de l'Opéra.
Greenleaf, Mr. and Mrs., R. C. (née Adelaide E. Stohe, Windipide, Lennex, Mass. and care of Messrs Hottinguer and Co Bankers, Paris.
Greenleaf, Miss Marion C. Windipide, Lennox, Mass. and care of Messrs, Hottinguer and Co, Bankers, Paris.
Grenough, Horatio, E., 21, rue Beaujon (U. S. A.).
Grey, A., 43, rue Caumartin.
Greffin, Walter, 66, r. Notre-Dame-des-Champs (U.S.).
Greffulhe, Countess (née de la Rochefoucauld), 10, rue d'Astorg, and Château de la Rivière, Thomery (Seine-et-Marne).
Greffulhe, Count (Ancien Deputy), and Countess (née de Caraman–Chimay), 8, r. d'Astorg, and Château de Bois-Boudran (Seine-et-Marne).
Greger, Mr. and Mrs. Alexandre, 22, avenue du Bois-de-Boulogne.
Greger, M. de, 22, avenue du Bois-du-Boulogne.
Gregory, Miss Grace (Singer-contralto), 4, rue de Chevreuse.
Greig, James (Illustrador), 11, rue Leopold-Robert.
Grieg, Rev., C. E., P. A., 28, rue Coriolan, Bercy.
Griffin, Mrs. E. H., 6, rue Leopold-Robert (U. S. A.).
Griffin, Mrs., M. M. (Artist). rue Le Verrier (Danielsonville, Conn. U. S. A.).

Griffith, Miss M., 65, avenue de Breteuil (Tuesday).
Grimstone, 140, avenue de Villiers.
Grinet, Edward, 25, Villa Chaptal, Levallois-Perret (U. S.).
Gritzenko, M., 5, rue Marbeuf.
Gros, Dr., 131, boulevard Montparnasse.
Gross, Peter Alfred, 9, rue Duperré (M. S.).
Groves, Arthur, H., 5, rue Scribe.
Gruchy, Mr. and Mrs., 17, rue Baudouin, Asnières.
Grumwaldt, Mme P., 4, avenue Ingres.
Guerin, Dr. and Mrs. (Doctor), 16, rue Lord Byron (U. S. A.).
Guilbert, Mlle Yvette, 79, rue de Villiers.
Gye, Herbert, F., Capt. and Mrs. (née The Hon. Adelaide, F. Hood), 72, boulevard Flandrin, aven. du Bois-de-Boulogne.

H

Habirshaw, Mr. and Mrs., William, M. (née Marchs), 1 East, 39th Street, New-York, and care of J. Munroe et Co, Bankers, Paris.
Habirshaw, Miss, 1 East, 39th Street, New-York, and care of J. Munroe et Co, Bankers, Paris.
Hadley, Mrs. and the Misses, 25, r. d'Argenteuil.
Haines, Mr. George A , Country Club, New-York, and at Lugano, Switzerland.
Hale, Miss May (Artist), 23, rue Le Verrier. (G. B.).
Hall, Ch. Auguste, Solicitor, 4, rue de la Paix.
Hall, Ch. Kennerly, Solicitor, 4, rue de la Paix.
Hall, H. C., 19, rue Scribe.
Hall, W. J., M. D., 59, rue de Provence.
Hall, Miss Caroline M. (Artist), 4, r. de Chevreuse.
Halleday, Miss Mary (Artist), 131, rue du Cherche-Midi.
Ham, Comtesse de (née Mac Swiney), 3, rue Boccador (Monday) et les « Etincelles », Villerville-sur-Mer.
Hamilton, W. D. J., 203, boul. Raspail.
Hamm, Alfred (Director of the « Paix »), 33, rue du Faubourg-Montmartre.
Hankey, Mr., 57, avenue Victor-Hugo.
Hanning, W., 191, rue de l'Université.
Hansen, P., 131, boul. Montparnasse.
Harbeck, Mr., 131, boul. Montparnasse.
Harden-Hickey, Andilly, Montmorency (Seine-et-Oise).
Harden-Hickey, Baron and Baroness James, A. (née Annah, H. Hagler), château d'Andilly, France.
Harding, Mr. et Mrs. P., 12, r. de Phalsbourg (Thursday).
Harding, Mme Jeanne, (Opéra-Comique) 7, rue Berlioz.
Hardinge, The Hon. Charles., Secretary to H. B. M.'s Embassy, 12, rue Pierre Charron.
Hardy, Mr., 26, rue de Ponthieu.
Harford, M. D., Secretary to H. B. M.s' Embassy, 39, rue du Faubourg Saint-Honoré.
Harisse, H., 30, rue Cambacérès.
Harjes, Mr. and Mrs., J., 62, av. Henri-Martin.
Harjes, Mr. and Mrs. John P., 62, avenue Henri-Martin, Paris.
Harjes, Miss and Miss Nelly, 62, avenue Henri-Martin, Paris.
Harjes Mr. John, H. Juns, 62, avenue Henri-Martin, Paris.
Harlamoff, M., 12, rue de Puteaux.
Har.ey, C. R., 44, rue des Ecoles.
Harnacre, Mr. 45, rue de la Pompe.
Harper, J., 13, rue Perdonnet.
Harris, Mrs. Sidney (née Mariam D.), care of Hottinguer and Co, Bankers, Paris.
Harris, Miss Nathalie, care of Hottinguer and Co. Bankers, Paris.
Harris, Mrs., 61, rue de la Boëtie.

H

Harris, Mr. and Mrs., 58, rue Wagram.
Harris. Mr. W. R., 58. aven. Wagram.
Harrisson, A., 17, rue Campagne-Première.
Harrisson, Mr. Alexander, Union Club, New-York, and care of Drexel, Harjes and Co Bankers, Paris.
Harry, J. Spence, 118, boulevard de Courcelles.
Harry-Berhard, Mr., 33, r. Notre-Dame-de-Lorette.
Hart, Mr. Benjamin M., 65, avenue d'Iéna, Paris.
Hart, Miss (Artist), 4, rue Léopold-Robert.
Hart, Mr., B., 29, rue Galilée.
Hart. Rev., B. B., 4, rue Roquepine.
Hart, Th., G. L. (Accountant), 49, rue d'Amsterdam.
Hartmann, S. K., 9, rue Campagne-Première.
Hartnett, Miss Janette, 187, rue de la Pompe.
Harvey, Mr., 203, boul. Raspail.
Haste, Mr. and Mr., G., 8, rue de Surène.
Hatch, Mrs. Nathaniel (née Mary R. Sanford), during the winter until May, care of Morgan, Harjes and Co, Paris.
Hauser, Mr. and Mrs. Louis, 39. av. de l'Opéra.
Haushalter, Georges, 24, rue de Seine (U. S.).
Hauteville, Mr. and Mrs. F. Grand d' (née Macomb), 51, avenue Montaigne, Paris.
Hauteville, Mr. et Mrs. d', avenue Montaigne.
Haven, Mrs. Julia E., 9, rue Boccador.
Haven, Miss, same address.
Haven, Miss Daisy, same.
Hawes, H., 26, rue François Ier.
Hawes, W., 8. rue d'Aguesseau.
Hawley, Mrs. Wilhelmine, O., 111, rue Notre-Dame-des-Champs (U. S.).
Hawtry, Miss Wilhemena D. (Artist), 3, rue de Bara.
Haynie, Henry (Correspondent of « Boston Herald, » etc. president of the « Syndicat de la Presse Étrangère » and Mrs. (née Huguenin-Brigth), 5, rue Marbeuf (Sunday) et — The Bury Elms, Waltham Massachusetts).
Hayward, the Rev. Richard and Mrs., 14, rue de la Tremoille (U. S.).
Haywood, Mr. and Miss, 29, rue Ponthieu.
Heap, Mrs. William, 23, rue Le Verrier (Muskegon) Mich. (U. S. A.).
Hearn, W., rue d'Aguesseau.
Heat, G., 6, rue de Presbourg.
Heath, Mrs. William (née Elisabeth Bond Svan), 6, rue de Presbourg, Paris.
Héglon, Mme Meyriane (Grand Opéra), 41, boulevard Malesherbes.
Hein, Dr., Mrs. and Miss, 59, rue Tronchet.
Hélie, Mme, 4, rue de Sontay (Friday).
Heller, Miss (Artist), 117, rue Notre-Dame-des-Champs.
Hément, Edgard (Editor of the « Temps »), 10, rue Royale.
Hemert, Charles Auguste, von, and Mrs. (née Zimmermann), 12. avenue de l'Alma (Tuesday).
Hemert, Philippe, L, von, and Mrs. (née Evans), 50, avenue Marceau.
Henderson, Mr. and Mrs. Harold Gould (née Agnes Roudebush), care of J. Munroe and Co, Bankers, Paris.
Hendry, Mr., 64, boul. Bineau, Neuilly.
Henie, Mrs. M., 21, avenue Hoche (U. S. A.).
Henner, Jean Jacques (Artist-Painter) (Member of the Institute), 11, place Pigalle.
Henry, A., 5, passage Violet.
Henry, G., 17, rue Bérenger.
Henry, Mrs., 10, rue Poisson.
Herbert, Arthur, 25, rue Duphot.
Herbert, Miss, 135, avenue Victor-Hugo.
Herbert, The Hon Alan, P., Dr., 18, rue Duphot.
Heredia, José Maria de (of the Académie française, and Mme, 11 bis, rue de Balzac.
Herrenschmidt, Miss, 29, rue Parmentier, Neuilly.
Herter, Mr. and Mrs. Albert (née Adèle Mc Ginnis), 25, avenue de Wagram, Paris.

Hertford British Hospital, 72, rue de Villiers.
Hervé, Edouard (of the Académie française, Director of the « Soleil » (Sun) and Mme (née Rolland), 27. rue de Lisbonne (Wednesday)), and la Thibaudière, Saint-Fulgent (Vendée).
Hervey Saint-Denys Marchiennes, Dr (née Bonne, du Ward), 9, avenue Bosquet, and château du Breau, par Albis (Seine-et-Oise).
Hess, Albert and Mme, 9. rue de Thérèse.
Hess, Miss Grace Lee —, 145, avenue Victor-Hugo et « Les Roseaux », Moret-sur-Loing (Seine-et-Marne).
Hestor, Mr. and Mrs. Albert (née Mc. Ginnis), 25, avenue Wagram.
Hetley, G., 93. avenue Malakoff.
Heuston, Mrs. L. C. (née Ship), 147. avenue de Malakof.
Hewlett, Mr. Russell (Architect), 153, rue de Rennes.
Hewlett, Mrs., 53, rue de Vaugirard.
Hewson, 188. boul. Malesherbes.
Hewson, W. H., 2, rue Volney.
Heyward, Mrs., 14, rue Euler.
Heyward, Miss Drivin (Sculptor), 13, boulevard Montparnasse.
Higbee, The Misses Cornelia Post, Mary Minturn, and Caroline Howell, care of Morgan, Harjes, and Co, Bankers, Paris.
Higbee, Rev. and Mrs. Charles (née Augusta Mitchell), care of Morgan, Harjes and Co, Bankers, Paris.
Higgins, C., 212, rue de Rivoli.
Higginson, A. B., 151 bis, boul. Montparnasse.
Higginson, John, 8, rue de la Paix.
Hildebrand, Mr. and Mrs., 53, rue de Villiers (Levallois Perret).
Hilhouse, Miss Adelaïde, 73, Park avenue New-York, and 73, rue Descamps, Paris.
Hill, Mrs., Robert, 2, rue des Mathurins.
Hill, Mr. and Mrs., 13, rue Miromesnil.
Hill, Mr. and Mrs., Ormund, 18, av. Victor-Hugo.
Hill, Mr. and Mrs. W. P., boulev. Haussmann.
Hill, Miss Lucile, 21, rue Montmartre. (U. S. A.).
Hillegas, Miss, 15, avenue Mac-Mahon.
Hilton, E. B., 94, avenue Kléber.
Hilton, Mr., 18, rue Bergère.
Hirsch, Baroness (née Pilie), Théodore de, 5, rue Tilsitt.
Hirschfeld, Dr. William, 17, rue de Lafayette.
Hitchcock, W. G., 17, rue Saint-Marc.
Hitroff, M. de, 43, avenue du Bois-de-Boulogue.
Hoche, J. L., 31. avenue Marceau.
Hockenjos, 168, boulevard Montparnasse.
Hockly, Mrs., 106. faubourg Saint-Honoré.
Hockly, Miss, same adresse.
Hodges, Mrs. 16, rue Pierre-Charron.
Hodgskins, Miss (physician), 23, rue Le Verrier (G. B)
Hoffmann, Baron and Baronness de, 5, rue de Tilsitt and château de la Bocca, Cannes (Alpes-Maritimes).
Hogan, Mrs. and Miss, 31, avenue Kléber.
Hogg, Dr. and Mrs., W. Douglas, 32, avenue des Champs-Elysées.
Hogg, Mr. W. T., 32, avenue des Champs-Elysées.
Hogg, Miss, 32, rue Michel-Ange, Auteuil.
Hogg, Miss, 32, avenue des Champs-Elysées.
Hohenlohe, T. R. H. the Prince and Princess de, 88, avenue des Champs-Elysées.
Holden, Mr., 14, rue de Lancry.
Holland, Mr. William, 45, avenue de la Grande-Armée.
Holman-Black, Charles (Lyric Artist), 16, avenue de Breteuil (Friday).
Holmes, W. D., 1, rue Pierre-Charron.
Holmès, Augusta (Composer of Music), 40, rue Juliette Lamber.
Hoomung, W. A., 33, boulevard Haussmann.

Hooper, Mrs. W., 3, rue de Tilsitt.
Hooper, Miss Nettie, 10, rue d'Aubigny.
Horner, The Misses, 26, rue Pauquet.
Horrack, P. J. de, 4, rue du Général-Foy.
Horstmann, W. H., 38, rue Meslay.
Horton, W. S., 53, avenue Kleber.
Horwitz, Miss (Opéra-Comique), 14, rue de Maubeuge.
Horwitz, Mrs. Orville (née Gross), Palazzo-Malatesta, Piazza Ara Cœli, Rome.
How, Miss Beatrice (Artist), 79, rue Notre-Dame-des-Champs (G. B.).
Howard, Sydney (Director of the Galignani Messenger, The Dailly Messenger), 167, rue Saint-Honoré.
Howard, Henry (Minister Plenipotentiary), H. B. M's Embassy, 39, rue du Faubourg-Saint-Honoré.
Howard, Mrs., 51, avenue Friedland.
Howard, Sidney (Daily Messenger), 167, rue Saint-Honoré.
Howe, A. B., 11, rue Saint-Simon.
Howe, W. H., 131, boulevard Montparnasse.
Howe, Mlle Jenny (Grand Opéra), 24, rue de Vintimille.
Howells, Mr. John M. University Club, New-York, and care of Morgan, Harjes and Co Bankers, Paris.
Howland Mr. Meredith, and Mrs. (née Torrance), 17, rue de Constantine.
Howland, Mrs. John, 51, avenue Bugeaud.
Howland, Mr. George S., Century Club, New-York, care of Morgan, Harjes and Co, Bankers, Paris.
Howland, Meredith and Mrs. (née Torrance), 17, rue Constantine.
Howland, Mrs. Edith, 21 bis, rue d'Armaillé (U. S.).
Howland, Mrs. John, 51, avenue Bugeaud.
Howland, Mrs., 16, rue de la Rochefoucauld.
Howland, Mr., George, 9, rue des Fourneaux.
Howland, Mr., 65, rue de Seine.
Howland, W., Legrand (Professor of music), 16, rue de Chazelles (U. S. A.).
Howlet, Miss, 3, rue Galvani.
Howlett, Mr. and Mrs., rue Logier.
Howley, Miss Wilhelmine (Artist), 3, rue Baru. New-York. (U. S. A.).
Huber, Mr. and Mrs., Alfred, 59, rue Galilée.
Hudson, C., Mr et Mrs. 12 bis, rue Pergolèse.
Hudspeth, Mr. R. N. (Artist), 207, boulevard Raspail. (Jovonto Canada).
Huffer, Hermann, 2, rue Saigon (U. S. A.).
Huffer, William, 30 rue Lubeck (U. S. A.).
Hüffer, Leopold Senior, 25, avenue du Bois-de-Boulogne (U. S. A.).
Hüffer, Leopold Junior, 25, avenue du Bois-de-Boulogne, (U. S. A.).
Hugenschmidt, Dr. Arthur, 23, boul. Malesherbes.
Hughes-Halett, Mrs., Dinard (Ille-et-Vilaine).
Hulett, Mrs., 59, rue de Vaugirard.
Humphries, Albert, 2, rue d'Odessa (U. S.).
Humphries, Miss, 9, rue Ambroise-Paré.
Humy, Mr. and Mrs. d', 10, rue d'Arras.
Hunt, Mr., 11, avenue Bugeaud.
Hunt, Carltan, 6, rue Ganneron (G. B.).
Hunt, Mrs. Percy, 11, avenue Bugeaud.
Hunter, Mr. and Mrs., 242, boul. Saint-Germain.
Huntingdon, Major, Mrs. and the Misses, 27, avenue d'Eylau.
Hurlbrol, Miss (Artist), 4, rue de Chevreuse.
Hurlbut, Miss, 27, rue de Fleurus. (U. S. A.).
Hutchens, T. C., 9, rue Leverrier.
Hutchinson, Mr. and Mrs., 3, rue de la Renaissance.
Hutchinson, B., 7, rue Brémontier.
Hutchinson, J. A., 157, boulevard Haussmann.
Hutchinson, Mr., 112, boulevard Rochechouart.
Hutchinson, M. E., 3, rue de la Renaissance.
Hutchinson, Mrs (née de Loyauté, 5, pl. Malesherbes.
Hyland, Misses, 21, rue Braujon. (G. B.).

I

Iacountchikoff, Mme de, 29, avenue Wagram.
Ingersall, Mr. and Mrs., W. E., 4, rue Galliere.
Ingham, Dr., 23, rue Caumartin.
Inglis, Mr. Albemarie Percy, (H. B. Ms. Consul), avenue Monceau.
Innes, Mr. and Mrs., 6, rue Christophe-Colomb.
Insall, Mr., 44, rue Cambon.
Iousoupofl, Prince, 2, avenue Victor-Hugo, Boulogne-sur-Seine.
Irvin, Miss Ethel, 14, avenue de l'Alma, Paris.
Irvin, Rev. and Mrs. William (née Julia Post Swan) care of J. Munroe and Co, Bankers, Paris.
Isaac, Mme Adèle (Opéra-Comique), 76, boulevard Magenta.
Iselin, Henry S., 48, rue de la Victoire.
Ivanischivitch, docteur, 15, rue du Poteau.
Ives, Mrs. Henry, 6, Villa Michon.
Iwill, Mr. M. J. (Artist-Painter), and Mrs (née Ravaisson-Möllien), 11, quai Voltaire.

J

Jack, Richard, 3, rue Dutot.
Jack, Miss Marion (Artist), 6, Square Croissiac. (N. Canada).
Jackson, Mr. and Mrs., 8, boul. Emile-Augier, Passy.
Jackson, Mrs. James, 15, avenue d'Antin.
Jackson, Mrs., Louise (née Hubbard), 16, rue des Bassins (Sundays).
Jackson, Mrs., 32, boulevard de Montmorency.
Jackson, Mr. and Mrs. William, 17, avenue d'Antin.
Jackson, Mrs. James, 15, avenue d'Antin.
Jackson, Mr. and Mrs. John Brinakerhoff (née Bavid), Fiest Secretary United States Embassy, Bismarckstrass, 3, N. W. Berlin.
Jacobs, W. L., 86, rue Notre-Dame-des-Champs.
Jameson, Conrad and Mrs. (née de Portal), 115, boulevard Malesherbes.
Jameson, Robert, 115, boulevard Malesherbes.
Jamin, Mme V., 31, rue Campagne-Première. (G. B.).
Janzé, Viscount Frédéric de and Viscountesse (née de Choiseul), 12, rue de Marignan (Saturday), and Château des Forges-des-Salles, Goarec (Côtes-du-Nord).
Janzé, Viscount Léon de, 70, rue de Ponthieu and Château de Parfondeval Londinière (Seine-Inférieure).
Jarrett-Knott, Mr. 2, r. de l'Echelle (Av. de l'Opéra).
Jarrett-Knott, R. H., 182, rue de Rivoli.
Jay, Augustus, 70, avenue Marceau.
Jay Mr. and Mrs. Aug. (née Kane), Union Club, New-York, and 70, avenue Marceau, Paris.
Jean, Aman, 15, quai Bourbon.
Jefferyes, Mr. and Mrs, P. John, 17, rue de Constantinople.
Jenger, Paul, 24, rue Aumaillé (G. B.).
Jenkins, Mr. Arthur H. (Artist), 203, boulevard Raspail (G. B.).
Jenkins, Mr. Arthur H., 203, boulevard Raspail (G. B.).
Jennings, Dr. Oscar and Mrs. 88, avenue Kléber.
Jennings, Oscar, Dr. and Mrs., 88, avenue Kléber (from 2 to 4).
Jermingham, Miss, 59, rue de Courcelles.
Job, Miss, 5, rue Hamlin.
John, Arthur, 19, rue Marbeuf.
Johnson, Miss Raphael (Artist), 4, rue de Chevreuse.
Johnson, Mrs., 82, rue Château-Landon.
Johnson, P. J., 226, boulevard Raspail (G. B.).

Johnson. Mr. and Mrs., N. A., 4. rue de la Trémoille.
Johnson, Mr. C., 52, faubourg Saint-Honoré.
Johnston. Nathaniel and Mrs. (née Princesse Caradja), 5. av. Montaigne, château de Beaucaillou.
Johnstone, Mrs., 5, rue Saint-Didier.
Jones, Mr. Glover, 8, rue des Brurdonnais.
Jones, G. H., 30, rue des Bourdonnuis.
Jones, B. F., 30, rue Le Verrier.
Jones, H. P., 54, rue Etienne-Marcel.
Jones, Mrs., 11, rue Tractir.
Jones, Mrs., 11, avenue du Bois de Boulogne.
Jones, John, and Mme (née Dretz), 9, rue d'Aumale.
Jones, Mr. and Mrs, boulevard de Versailles, Montretout-Saint-Cloud.
Jones, Miss, 58, rue de Penthièvre.
Jones, Mrs., Hôtel Westminster.
Jones, Mrs., 4, rue du Pavillon. Parc des Princes.
Jones, Miss, 135, avenue Victor-Hugo.
Jones. Miss Florence (Artist), 4, rue Léopold Robert (New-York) (U. S. A.).
Jones, Mr. Henry E., 146, avenue des Champs-Elysées, Paris.
Jones, Mr. and Mrs., M. Ogden (née Suzan I. Earle). 3, avenue du Bois-de-Boulogne, Paris.
Jones, Mrs. George F., 146, avenue des Champs-Elysées, Paris.
Jory, Miss, 36, rue Cortambert.
Josef, Miss Frances, 187, rue de la Pompe.
Josephson, Dr. Charles, 14, rue du Château-d'Eau.
Joslin, Mr., William London of Pitsfield, Marss. (U. S. A.).
Jouel, Miss Florence (Artist), 4, rue Léopold-Robert.
Joye. Mrs. Désiré, 60, rue la Tour Passy (Wednesday).
Judic, Mme Anna (Dramatic Artist) Chatou (Seine-et-Oise).

K

Kaibaroff-Romand, Baronne, 10, aven. Pereire.
Kane, Mr., 19, rue Scribe.
Kane, Mr. and Mrs. John, C., 83, rue de Lille.
Kann, S., 11, impasse Roussin.
Kaoulina, Mlle, 5, rue de la Néva.
Kapcevirch, Mlle de, 81, rue Tronchet.
Kay, Mr and Mrs. Chas. de (née Edwlyn Coffee), Consul general at Berlin.
Keall, Clarence, W., 179, boulevard Pereire.
Kellog, Major, Sanford, C., Military Attaché to U. S. Legation, 24, avenue Kléber.
Kelly, Rev. Mathew, 50, avenue Hoche.
Kelly. Miss Mary, Grace 50 bis, rue de Villiers (G. B.).
Kelly, The revd. S. P., 207, boulevard Raspail.
Kelly, Mrs. James P., 16, impasse du Maine (Philadelphia U. S. A.).
Kelly, Miss, 207, boulevard Raspail.
Kemp, Charles Robert, 10, rue Choron.
Kennerley-Hall, Charles, A. and Mrs., 4, r. Greffulhe.
Kennerley-Hall, Charles, 4. rue Greffulhe.
Kent, E., 2, rue Léopold-Robert.
Kent E., 12, rue du Dôme.
Kent, Miss Marie, 187, rue de la Pompe.
Kent, Miss Théo, 187, rue de la Pompe.
Kergolay, Countess Jean, 17, rue Matignon (U. S. A.)
Kernochan, Mr. and Mrs., William (née Winthrop), 32, rue de Marignan, Paris.
Kerr, Miss Kattleen, artist, 13, rue Washington. (G. B.)
Kerr, Mrs., 93, avenue Henri-Martin.
Kerr, Mr. and Mrs. William, J., 93, avenue Henri-Martin.
Kerr, Miss E, M., 233, faubourg Saint-Honoré.

Kesseler, Comtesse de, 19, boulevard de Montmorency and villa Albert. Nice
Kibbey, Miss, 24, rue de Bourgogne.
Kieffer, Mr. and Mrs. William, 31, avenue des Champs-Elysées.
Kilford. George William, 2, rue Grétry, and rue Kilford, Courbevoie.
Kinen, Madame, 2, avenue Hoche.
Kinen, Mr and Mrs. Georges, 26, avenue de la Grande-Armée (Téléphone).
Kingsland, Walter, 46. avenue du Bois-de-Boulogne.
King, Mrs., 31, rue Lubeck.
King, Mrs., D., 52, rue François Ier.
King, Général Adam, E., 31. rue de Lubeck.
King, the Misses, 31, rue Lubeck (Tuesdays).
King, Miss, 28, rue La Trémoille.
King-Watts, Mrs., 83, rue Demours.
Klug, Mr., 14, que Castiglione.
Kingsland, Mr Walter, 46, avenue du Bois-de-Boulogne (Téléphone).
Kingsley, D. C., 9, rue Auber.
Kinsley, Mr and Mrs. Sumner A. (artist), 4, rue Léopold-Robert. (Laurenceville, Nova Scotia, Canada).
Kipling, Mr., 46, rue Mozart.
Kirkpatrick, J., 7, rue Delambre.
Kitchener. Mr and Mrs., 17, rue Molière.
Klamroth. Miss Efreda H. (Painter), 4, rue de Chevreuse.
Klenck, the Baronness, 26, avenue Marceau.
Klumpke, Miss Anna, 90, rue d'Assas.
Klumpke. Miss (Astronomer), Observatoire, avenue de l'Observatoire.
Klumpke, Miss (Painter), 90, rue d'Assas.
Klumpe, Mlle Anna (Artist Painter), 90, rue d'Assas.
Knapp, Mrs. (née Mactavish), 5, rue Chateaubriand.
Knapp, Mr. E. Williams, 3, rue d'Aguesseau.
Knight. Ridgway, place de l'Eglise, Poissy, Seine-et-Oise (Tuesdays).
Knight, Mrs. (née de Grilleau), 72, boulevard Flandrin (Saturdays).
Knight, D. R., 131, boulevard Montparnasse.
Knott, Mr Chas. H. Jarrett, 182, rue de Rivoli.
Knowles (née Plour), 22, rue de Staël.
Koch, A. D., 33, rue de Tournon.
Kœing, C. F., 13, rue de Buci.
Kohn, R. D., 1, rue Honoré-Chevalier,
Kotschoubey, Prince Basile and Princesse (née Serrano de la Torre). 144, av. des Champs-Elysées.
Kouznetzoff, M., 64, avenue du Bois-de-Boulogne.
Krauss, Madame (Grand Opéra), 169, boulevard Haussman,
Kœsteven. Mr. and Mrs., 3, rue d'Erlanger (Auteuil).
Krohmer, Miss Olga, 187, rue de la Pompe.

L

Labouris, Mrs., 12, rue de Bourgogne.
Lacorne, Miss, 5, rue Saint-Pierre.
Ladd, W. P. (Artist), rue des Saints-Pères (Lancaster. N. H.; U. S. A.)
Laflin, I. E., 4, rue Commailles.
La Fonta, Mr and Mrs Edward, 15, rue Viette (Thursdays), and château de Ludon (Gironde).
La Grange, Baron and Baronness Louis de (née Caroll), 63, avenue de l'Alma, Paris.
Laing, Miss Marion, 187, rue de la Pompe.
Lamb, Lady, 1 bis, avenue du Bois-de-Boulogne (Thursdays, from 4 till 7),
Lammin, Mr and Mrs. P. B., 45, rue de Boissy-d'Anglas.
La Montaigne, Mrs., Auguste A. (née Davis), 72, avenue Kléber, Paris.

L | L-M

La Montaigne, Miss, 72, avenue Kléber, Paris.
Lamson, Mrs. John (née Oxper) care of George, 11. Oraper, 39, rue Galilée, Paris.
Lamson, Mrs., 39, rue Galilée.
Lance, E., /, rue Léopold-Robert.
Landau, M., 3, rue de la Paix.
Landeau, S.-L., 41, boulevard St-Jacques.
Landing, Miss, 4, rue de Chevreuse.
Langerke, Mrs., 47, rue Henry-Martin.
Langmuir, Mr. and Mrs. A., 53. avenue Marceau.
Lardner, Miss, 5, avenue du Bois-de-Boulogne.
Larpentier, Mr. J. Deveaux (Artist), 19, rue de Sèvres (U. S. A.).
Lassalle, Jean (Grand-Opéra), 1, rue Spontini.
Latham (Mme) Lionel (née Mallet), 20 bis, rue de la Boëtie.
Latham, Mr and Mrs., 14, rue de Longchamps.
Latzka, Mr., 38, rue Montparnasse (Brooklyn N. Y.).
Laugier-Villars, Comte and Comtesse M. Henri (née Carola Livingstone), 250, boulevard Saint-Germain, Paris.
Laurens, Jean-Paul (Artist-Painter, member of the Institute), 73, rue Notre-Dame-des-Champs.
Laurens, J. J. A. (Artist-Painter II. C.), 1, rue de Narbonne.
Laurent, J. P., 73, rue Notre-Dame-des-Champs.
Laurier, Eugène, 10, avenue Victor-Hugo.
Lauw, Miss, 35, boulevard Bineau, Neuilly.
Lawer, Miss, 35, boulevard Bineau (Lady Matron of the British Orphanage).
Lawler, Miss Kate, 187, rue de la Pompe (Miedletown Conn. U. S. A.).
Lawrence, Dr. and Mrs Robert M. (née Kath, Cleveland), Florence, Italy.
Lawrence, The Misses Madeleine and Isabelle.
Lawson, John, 11, boulevard de Clichy.
Leared, Mrs. J. W., 141, boul. Montparnasse (G. B.).
Leavitt, Mrs. Henry, 110, rue du Bac (New-York, U. S. A.)
Lecher, Ch. A., 6, rue du Sabot.
Lecocq, H., passage St-Ferdinand (Neuilly).
Lee, Mrs. Lavinia S. (Artist), 13, rue Boissonnade (New-York).
Lee, Miss Jenny (Artist), 13, rue Washington (U. S. A.).
Lee, Miss Lufkin, 4, rue de Chevreuse.
Lee, Mr and Mrs., 2, rue Fortuny.
Lee, Mr and Mrs. Edward Henry, 53 bis, rue Cardinet.
Lee, William, 61, rue Lepic.
Lee, H. Austin, Esq and Mrs. (Secretary, H. B. M's Embassy), 14 bis, avenue du Trocadéro.
Leech, Mrs. W. F., rue Roquépine.
Lefebvre, Jules (Artist-Painter, member of the Institute), and Mrs (née Deslignières), 5, rue de la Bruyère.
Lefebvre, J., 5, rue Labruyère.
Lefebvre, Mr. and Mrs., H. A. L., 8, avenue Carnot (Wednesdays).
Le Gay, Charles, 29. rue Boccador.
Le Gay, Mr. and Mrs. Charles, 5. av. de l'Alma.
Leighton, Miss Evelyn, 4, square Maubeuge.
Leigh, Mrs. 77, avenue de Wagram.
Lemaire, Mme Madeleine (Artist-Painter), 31, rue de Monceau and château de Reveillon, Courgivaux (Marne).
Lenz, M. de, 25, rue Louis-le-Grand.
Léon y Castillo (H. Exc. M. de) and Mme, 34, boulevard de Courcelles.
Léonard, G, H., 10, rue Léopold-Robert.
Le Roy, Mrs. Robert (née Lewis), 12, rue Clément-Marot, Paris.
Le Roy, Mr. J. Rutgers, Union Club, New-York, 12, rue Clément-Marot, Paris.
Leslie, Mrs. Frank, 42 and 44, Bond Street, New-York and villa Aïda) 10, rue Verdi, Nice (Alpes-Maritimes), for winter.

Lévy, H. L., 4, rue des Beaux-Arts.
Lewis-Brown, Mrs. John, 23, rue de Saint-Pétersbourg
Lewis, Miss Alice L. (Artist), 117, rue Notre-Dame-des-Champs.
Lewis, Miss Matilda (Designer), 39, rue de Sèvres.
Lewis, Miss Josephine (Artist), 31, rue de Sèvres.
Lhermitte, L. A. (Artist-Painter), rue Pierre-Ginier.
Liddell, Mrs., 39, r. Notre-Dame-de-Nazareth.
Lieven, F. de, 14, rue Crevaud.
Lillie, Mr. 16, rue Pierre-Charron.
Linderfelt, Dr. August., 17, rue Denfert-Rochereau. (Milwankee Wis).
Lindin, C. E., 131, boulevard Montparnasse.
Linieder, Miss Marie. Louise (Teacher of Languages), 4, rue de Chevreuse.
Liptay, M. D. A. B. de, late surgeon to the Chilian Army Navy and, 26, boulevard Poissonnière.
Lisle, Miss E. F. T. de, 48. rue du Général-Foy (G. B.).
Listle, Lieutenant and Mrs. W. Mc. Carty (née Anitr Maria Chartranc), 37 East 26 Street, New-York, and at Biarritz, France.
Livingstone, Celine Cornelia, Hôtel Continental.
Livingston, Mr. and Mrs. Edward Mc. Evers (née Pollock) at Pau, and care of J. Munroe and Co, Bankers, Paris.
Livock, A. L., 9, rue Campagne-Première.
Livock, Mr. H., 21, rue Laffitte.
Lobstein, Mr. and Mrs., 28, rue des Ecuries-d'Artois.
Loeb, L., 16, impasse du Maine.
Loew, Mr. and Mrs., 3, rue Le Bouvier.
Loftus, Henry and Mrs (née Leech), rue Roquépine.
Lomas, John (Editor, Anglican Church Magazine), 52, faubourg Saint-Honoré.
Lonergan. W., 1, rue de l'Arc-de-Triomphe.
Longhnan, Miss, 38, rue de Berri.
Longhurst, Mr., 133, boulevard Péreire.
Longstaff, John, 9. rue des Fourneaux.
Lorillard-Spencer, Mrs., 70, avenue Marceau.
Loub, Prince de, 45, rue de Courcelles.
Loubat, Dutse, Kincherbocker Club, New-York, and 47, rue Dumont-d'Urville, Paris.
Loughnan, Dr. and Mrs. Connell, 38, rue de Berri.
Love, Dr. and Mrs; James. 23, rue Ballu (Thuesdays) and Salies-de-Béarn, Basses-Pyrénées.
Love, George, 69, avenue de Villiers.
Love, Robert. 4, rue Crevaux.
Lowber-Welsh, Mrs. William, 5. rue Bassano (Saturdays).
Loyson, Rev., and Mrs. Hyacinthe, 29, boulevard d'Inkermann, Neuilly.
Lucas, Mr. and Mrs., 95, rue de la Côte-Saint-Thébout, Bois-Colombes.
Lucas. Mrs Charles. 109, rue de Grenelle, and Chateau de la Rongère, Saint-Eloy (Cher).
Lucas, Mr. and Mrs., 19, boulevard du Port-Royal
Luckemeyer, Edward, and Mme (née Frings), 61, avenue de l'Alma.
Lufkin, Miss Lee, 4, rue Chevreuse.
Lyle, H. C., 9, rue des Fourneaux.
Lynch, Albert, 147, avenue de Villiers.

M

MacAdams, General, James-Dyer, and Mme, 67, avenue des Champs-Elysées (Wednesdays) and at Volonne, Basses-Alpes.
Mac, Afee (née Maggin), 53, avenue Montaigne.
MacAlpin, Mr. " Hôtel de la Haute-Loire " boulevard Raspail.
MacCameron. Robert, 31, rue Cadet.
Mac Connel. Mr. and Mrs., 18, rue Greuse.

MacCreery, G. G., 131, boulevard Montparnasse.
Mac Cully, Miss, 187, rue de la Pompe.
Mac Daval, Jessy, 187, rue de la Pompe.
Mac Dowell, Miss Mary (Designer), 4, rue Chevreuse.
Mac Even, Mr. Walter (Artist-Painter), 11, place Pigalle.
Mac Farlan, Miss (Artist), Hôtel Lafond, 14, rue de La Trémoille.
Macfarlane, Mrs., 34, rue d'Auvergne.
MacFarlane, Mrs., 7, rue Scribe.
MacFarlane. Mr. and Mrs., 35, rue Amyot.
MacFerran, James, 39, faubourg Saint-Honoré.
MacGregor, A. N., Brit. Hospital, 72, r. de Villiers.
Machado, Mr. and Mrs. de, 28, avenue Marceau.
Mack, Mr and Mrs., W., 11, avenue d'Iena.
MacKain, J. Elgin and Mme (née Lejeune Vincent), Villa Bellenoi, Colombes, Seine.
MacKair, W., 4, rue Berlioz.
Mackay, J. W., 11 bis, rue de la Faisanderie.
Mackay, Mrs., J. W., 9, rue Tilsitt.
Mackay, Mr. and Mrs., 27, avenue Kléber.
Mackensie, Mr. and Mrs., 221, faubourg St-Honore.
MacKenna. F. D., 7, rue Delambre.
Mackin, Mrs. James (née Sarah S. Brisson), 4, rue des Bassins, Paris.
Mackley-Smith, 131, boulevard Montparnasse.
MacLaren, Shaw, 70 bis, rue Notre-Dame-des-Champs.
MacLaughlin, Prof., and Mrs., 25, rue Vioconti.
MacLean, Edward, P., U. S. Consulate, 36, avenue de l'Opéra.
MacMuster, G., 7, rue Pigalle.
MacMasterss, Mr., 104, boulevard de Clichy.
MacMonnaies, Fredk, 16, impasse du Maine.
MacMurdough, Rev., Chantilly.
MacNab, Mme (née d'Anglars), 7, rue Boccador.
Mac Pherson, Mrs., 18, rue Miromesnil.
Mac Pherson, Mr. and Mrs., John R. (née Gregory) 1014 Vermont avenue, Washington and care of Morgan Harjes and Co, Bankers, Paris.
MacRae, James, 226, boulevard Raspail.
MacRitchie, Mr. and Mrs., 33, rue Bayen.
MacSwiney, V. and Mme (née Comtesse Konarska), 40, avenue Henri-Martin (Sundays).
Madre. Count Jean de, 18, rue Vaneau (Téléphone).
Maffray (Marquise de Cesarges), Ctesse de, 9, avenue Victor-Hugo (Thursdays).
Magee, Mr. and Mrs., 120, avenue Victor-Hugo.
Magnin, D. R. A. J., 41, boulevard Malesherbes.
Magruder, Mr. and Mrs. G. A., 4, rond-point de Longchamp.
Mahy, Mr. and Mrs., 41, rue Boissy-d'Anglas.
Makovsky, M., 22, rue Vintimille.
Maltby, Mme, 49, rue de Courcelles.
Mamlock, Mr. and Mrs, 119, rue de Rome.
Manalt, Miss Sadie (Artist), 4, rue Léopold Robert (Providence, R. S. (U. S. A.)
Manby, Mr. and Mrs., 92, rue du Ranelagh, Passy.
Mangin, Edouard (Orchestra Conductor at Grand Opera, professeur au Conservatoire, 22, rue Victor-Massé.
Mann, F. P., 10, rue des Fossés-Saint-Jacques.
Mansfield, Mrs. H., 93, rue Ampère.
Mantius, Mr., N. E., United States Consul at Turin, (Italy).
Maples, George, 52, rue du Cherche-Midi.
Marcoff, Mme de, Hôtel du Louvre.
Marrof, H., 11, rue Weber.
Marse, Mr. and Mrs. H. J., 8, avenue de Villiers.
Marshall. Mr. and Mrs. Ernest, 18 bis, rue du Marché. Neuilly-sur-Seine.
Marsh, F. D., 85, rue Notre-Dame-des-Champs.
Marsh, Miss (Artist), 3, rue Léopold-Robert.
Marston. William, A., 32, avenue Marceau.
Marsy, Mme Marie-Louise (Comédie-Française). 9 bis, avenue Bugeaud (Téléphone) and 32, rue de la Ferme, Neuilly (Téléphone).

Martel, Mlle Nancy (Comédie-Française), 34, rue Montpensier.
Martel de Janville, Count de and Countesse (née de Mirabeau), 71, boulevard Bineau,, parc de Neuilly.
Martin, Dr. Alfred, 25, rue du Général-Foy.
Martin, Mr. and Mrs. William, 42, avenue Wagram.
Martin, Prosper, 5, rue du Havre.
Martine, Mrs. F. de, 16, rue Euler, and Cap Martin.
Mason, Miss (Artist), 6, rue Charlet.
Mason, Mrs. Josephine, 6, rue Chalet (Denver Colorado).
Massenet, J. (Music Composer, Member, of the Institute), and Mme, 46, rue du Général-Foy.
Massenet, Mr. Jules. Hôtel Roubion, Nice (Winter address).
Masson, Raymond, 13 bis, rue Campagne-Première.
Matthews, Miss, 92, avenue des Ternes (G. B.).
Maudsley. Mr. and Mrs. Alfred P. (née Annie Cary Morris). Rome, Italy.
Maugham, Mr. and Mrs., 59, rue des Mathurins.
Maugham, Mr. C. O., 55, faubourg Saint-Honoré.
Mavrocordato, M., 18, Boulevard Malesherbes.
Maxwell-Heddle, Mrs., 21, rue Nicot and Villa Leaders, Cannes.
Maxwell, Miss (Artist). 16, impasse du Maine.
May, Mr. de Courcy, Hôtel Royal, avenue Friedland (U. S. A.).
May, Miss Lilian, avenue Friedland (U. S. A.).
Mayee, Mrs., Alice, 20, rue Guersant.
Mayer, Gaston, 6, avenue Percier.
Mayer, Mr. and Mrs. William, 6, rue du Mont-Thabor.
Mayers, Mrs, avenue d'Antin.
Maynard, Miss Marguerite, 187, rue de la Pompe.
Mc Cormick, Mr. and Mrs. Roobert (née Medill), 101, Cass Street, Chicago and to Munroe and Co, Bankers, Paris.
Mc. Elrath, Mr., Percy, United States, Consul at Turin, Italy.
Mc. Ginnis, Mr. John Jr (née Lydie Matteson). 40. av. Victor-Hugo, Paris, and 2, Wall-Street New-York.
Mc. Ginnis. The Misses Bessie and Mabel Earl. no 2. Wall street, New-York and 20, avenue Victor-Hugo, Paris.
Mc Guines, Mrs. John, 40, avenue Victor-Hugo (Thursday).
Mc Ilvaine. Mrs., 1, rue Goëthe.
Mc. Kenna, the Rev. Casimir, 50, av. Hoche (G. B.).
Mc. Kenna, Miss, 154, boul, Haussmann (U. S. A.).
Mc Lane, Mr. R., 50, rue François I".
Mc. Lean, Miss Janie, 38, rue du Luxembourg (Cincinnati Ohio, U. S. A.).
Mc Lubich, the Rev. John (Assistant Chaplain to the British Embassy Church), 17, avenue Niel, aux Ternes.
Meadow. Mr. and Mrs., 5, rue de Brosse.
Means, Mr. and Mrs. Robert L (of Boston). c/o Morgan Harjes and Co, Bankers, Paris (Antibes for the Winter).
Melba, Mme (Grand Opéra), 9, rue de Prony.
Meletta, Mrs. C., 71, avenue Marceau.
Mengler, Miss (Artist), 6, rue Boissonnade.
Mennons, Mr., 62, rue Tiquetonne.
Mercier, H., 15, avenue de l'Observatoire.
Merenith. F., Hôtel de Chartres.
Merril, Mr. Stuart F. R., 66, rue de Seine, Paris.
Meslav, Mme (née Cumming), 6, rue de Cérisoles (Monday), Château de la Barillerie, Le Lion-d'Angers (Maine-et-Loire).
Messinger. Miss Maria Girard, care of Morgan. Harjes and Co, Bankers. Paris.
Metcalfe, Mrs., 63, avenue des Ternes (nurse).
Meuden, Miss, 55, avenue Victor-Hugo.
Meunier, Léon, 8, rue Castellane.
Millage, Mr. and Mrs. J. Clifford, 59, rue Maubeuge (Wednesdays).

Millage, Mr. J. Clifford (Correspondent of the " Daily Chronicle "), and Mrs. (née Fernyhought), 59, rue de Maubeuge (Wednesday), and 12, Salisbury, square, London.
Millar, Miss J. A. (Artist), 6, rue Boissonnade.
Miller, Dr. and Mrs. Faure, 28, rue Matignon.
Miller. C. J., 103, rue de Vaugirard.
Miller, Dr. Harold, Faure, 28, rue Matignon, and 17, boulevard du Cannet, Cannes.
Miller, Dr. Roland, Faure and Mme (née de Guérin-Ricard), 8, rue Miromesnil.
Miller, Miss Annie, 187, rue de la Pompe.
Miller, Miss Annie II., 187, rue de la Pompe.
Miller, Miss Gertrude, 187, rue de la Pompe.
Milliard, J., 7, rue Delambre.
Milner, Mr. and Mrs. 42, rue Boulainvilliers, Passy.
Minnegerode, Mrs., 3 rue Boissière.
Miranda, Countesse de, 3, rue Clément-Marot.
Mitchell, Guernesey, 85, r. Ampère (Saturday, 2 till 5).
Mitchell, Mr, 93, rue Legendre.
Mitchell, Mr. Guernsey (Artist Statuary), 85, rue Ampère (Saturday, from 2 to 5).
Mitchell, Mr., 85, rue Ampère.
Moire, Mrs., 49, rue de Lisbonne.
Moller, Mr. and Mrs. Henry, 22, rue de Trémoille.
Monnart, Mme, boulevard Deiessart.
Monod, John, 194, rue de Rivoli.
Monod, Mme (née Brown), 18, rue Molitor.
Monod, Mrs, 20, rue des Accacias.
Monod, Pastor and Mme Théodore, 7, rue de la Cerisaie.
Montjean, Mme, 4, rue Saint-Pétersbourg and Villers-sur-Mer, Calvados.
Montmort, Marquis and Marquise de (née Clerq), 5, rue Masseran.
Montpellier, Mme, 38, avenue Wagram (U. S. A.).
Montsaulnin, Comte et Comtesse (née Zhorowska), 243, boulevard Saint-Germain and Château de Fontenay-Nérondes (Cher).
Moore, Charles, 81, rue de la Pompe.
Moore, Humphrey, 37, rue Ampère.
Moore, James and Mrs (née Mabile), 9, rue Magellan.
Moore, Mr. and Mrs. 43, avenue du Bois-de-Boulogne.
Moore, Mr. James and Mrs. 17, rue de Bassano.
Moorhouse, Mr. and Mss. Henry, P., 155, boulevard Haussmann.
Mora, Mr. and Mrs. Eduardo Mariano (née Lilian 1° Martin) care of J. Munroe et Co Bankers, Paris.
Moreau, Georges A. and Mrs. (née Warren), 28, avenue Bugeaud (Tuesday evenings).
Mores, Marquise de (née Medora Von Hoffmann). 5, rue de Tilsitt, Paris.
Morgan-Hill, Mr. and Mrs. H., 71, avenue Victor-Hugo.
Morgan, Mr. and Mrs. Henry, 130, rue de Rennes.
Morgan, Mr. and Mrs., 19, r. de la Comète, Asnières.
Morgan, Rev. Dr. and Mrs. John B., 5, avenue Montaigne.
Morgan, Mr. and Mrs. J. Hewitt, 110, rue du Bac (New-York).
Morgan, Mr. and Mrs. Charles (née Clara Woodford) Union Club. New-York, and at Pau, France.
Morgan, Mr. and Mrs. L. Henry (née Camilla Léonard). Union Club, New-York and avenue de la Bourdonnais, Paris.
Mori, Mr. and Mrs., 16, rue Greuze.
Morloche, Mr. W., Hôtel Bristol.
Morrell, Miss, 10 bis, rue des Batignolles.
Morris, E. M., 95, rue de Vaugirard.
Morris, Mr. Benjamin, architect. 15, rue de Rennes.
Morrizou, Miss J. C., 46, rue Hamelin.
Morss, S. E. Esq., (United States Consul General), 36, avenue de l'Opéra.
Morton, Miss. 15, rue Auguste Vacquerie.
Moser, Mr. and Mrs., 93, avenue Niel.
Mosler, Henry, 13, rue Washington.

Mosler, Henry (Artist Painter), and Mme, 22, rue de La Trémoille.
Mott-Smity, H, M., 6, rue Boissonnade.
Mourilyan, John, 270, rue Saint-Honoré.
Mudie, A. T., 203, boulevard Raspail.
Munkacsy, Michel Léon de (Artist-Painter), and Mrs., 53, avenue de Villiers (Friday), and Chateau de Colpach (Grand Duchy of Luxembourg).
Munroe, Mr. and Mrs., George P. (née Martha Osis', avenue du Trocadéro, Paris.
Munroe, Mr. John Hull, 150, av des Champs-Elysées.
Munroe, Mr and Mrs. John (née Kunt Gould), University-Club, New-York, and 1, rue de Longchamps Paris.
Munroe, Mr. Frederic, New-York, Yacht-Club, New-York. and 150, av. des Champs-Elysées, Paris.
Munroe, Miss, 150, av, des Champs-Elysées, Paris.
Munroe, Mr. and Mrs. Henry Whisney (née Alice T. Kneeland), 7, rue Scribe, Paris, and Union-Club, New-York.
Munroe, Mrs., 150, avenue des Champs-Elysées.
Munroe, Mr. and Mrs. Henry, 88, avenue Kléber.
Munster, His Excellency Count de, German Ambassador, 78, rue de Lille.
Muntz, Mrs., Laura A., 111, rue N.-D.-des-Champs.
Muntz, Miss Laura (Artist), 3, rue Bara (Canada).
Muntz, Miss (Painter), 3, rue Bara.
Murdock, Miss Flora (Artist), Hôtel d'Iéna, avenue d'Iéna, 28.
Murphy, Misses, 23, rue Washington (G. B.).
Murphy, Mme. 23, rue Washington (G. B.).
Murray, J. F., 49, rue de Vaugirard.
Murray, Mrs, 5, rue du Débarcadère.

N

Nachtel, Dr. Henry, 3, rue Scribe.
Nagornoff, M. de, 2, rue de Presbourg.
Narbonne Lara, Comtesse de (née Phalen), 23, rue des Bassins.
Necoman, Miss (Lady matron " The Hertford British Hospital "), 72, rue de Villers, Levallois-Perrei.
Nelson, Mrs, Emma, 14, rue d'Anjou.
Nelson, Miss (Artist), 13, rue Boissonnade (Jersey City. N. J. U. S. A,).
Nercuss, Mr. and Miss, 31, rue Fortuny.
Never, Mrs. Robert, J. (née Clark-Louise Vanderbiet), 58, rue Galilée. Paris.
Nevin, Rev. Robert. J. The Athenaeum, London, and 58, Via Napoli, Rome, Italy.
Nevins, Mrs. Robert, J., 58, rue Galilée, Paris.
Newbold, Miss, 8 bis, rue Campagne-Première (Philadelphia, U. S. A.).
Newell, Mr. and Mrs., 21, rue du Cirque.
Newmann, Mr. W. B., 4, rue de Chevreuse.
Newman, Mrs Wm B. (Artist), 9, rue des Fourneaux.
Niven, Mrs., 58, rue Galilée.
Northpeal, Mrs, 1, avenue Mac-Mahon.
Noyes, Rev. Dr. Hr E. and Mrs., 27, av. d'Eylau.

O

Obidine, M. d', 10, avenue d'Antin.
O'Callaghan, Mr. and Mrs. Albert (née de Crécy), 104, rue du Bac.
Ochs, George, 24, avenun des Champs-Elysées.
O'Connel, Alfred, 7, rue Nouvelle.
O Connell Cl Tountens, 68, avenue du Bois-de-Boulogne (G. B.).

O'Connell, Comte and Contesse (née Princesse Nonia Bertong), 68, avenue du Bois-de-Boulogne and Promenade des Anglais, Nice, and Hastings, England.
O Connell, Mme, 57, avenue Marceau (U. S. A.).
O'Connor Colonel Fernand, 45, rue de Courcelles.
O'Connor, James P., 32, avenue d'Iéna.
O'Connor, Mrs, 14, boulevard Raspail.
O'Doherty, Mme, 4, avenue des Ternes (G. B.).
Ogden, Mr., 144 bis, boulevard Montparnasse (Saint-Paul. Minn.).
Oglesby, Miss Marguerite, 19, rue de Berri (Sunday).
Ollenbourg, Baron and Baronness d' " Les Lierres ", 5, carrefour de Montreuil, Versailles, and Manoir de Kerlosser, Plougonven, Finistère.
Olliffe, Mr. and Mrs. W. H., 5, rue Lauriston.
Olsoufieff, M., d' 15, avenue de l'Opéra.
Omslow, Mrs., 22, rue d'Aguesseau, and Château d'Aulteraibe, Croupières (Puy-de-Dôme).
Onslow, Mrs., 6, rue d'Aumale.
Orange, Mr. (Sub-Editor " The Daily messenger "), 10, rue Croix-des-Petits-Champs.
Orloff, Prince, 45, rue Saint-Dominique.
Ortmans, Ernest, 52, boulevard Saint-Michel.
Osborne, Miss (Artist), 14, avenue du Maine.
Osgood, Miss Anna Parkmann (Artist), 4, rue de Chevreuse.
Oslund, A., 13, rue Campagne-Première.
Ostheimer, Mr. and Mrs. George R., 32, rue de Penthièvre.
O'Sullivan, Miss, 48, rue Monsieur-le-Prince.
Ouetinoff, M. d', 15, avenue Kléber.
Owdenko, M., 54, rue des Martyrs.
Ozanne, Mr., 2, rue Léonce-Reynaud.

P

Paden, Rev. W. M. (D. D.), 59, boulevard Saint-Michel.
Paine, Miss, Hôtel Victoria, 17, rue Castiglione.
Palmer, Frédérick Temple, 17, avenue de Paris, Versailles.
Palmer, Mrs,, 55, rue de Galilée.
Palmer, Miss Marion Suydam, care of J. Munroe and Co Bankers, Paris.
Palmer, Mr. and Mrs. Robert Amory (née Dexter) care of Munroe and Co Bankers, Paris.
Palmer, Mr. Cortland, E., care of Munroe and Co, Bankers, Paris.
Parsons, Mr. and Mrs. Frederick Jennings (née Ethel Stoddard), 69, Koniggratzstrasse, Berlin,
Pam, Mr. and Mrs., 2, rue Marbeuf.
Pane, Lady, 16, boulevard du Roi, Versailles.
Park, Mrs., 6, rue Troyon.
Park, Miss (Painter), 5, rue Chevreuse.
Parslow, J, 36, avenue de l'Opéra.
Pasteur, Mr., 56, rue Saint-Didier, Château at Bazeilles, Ardennes, and Hôtel d'Angleterre, Saint-Petersburg.
Pattee, E. E., 54, rue Notre-Dame-des-Champs.
Puttin, L., 131, boulevard Montparnasse.
Pattison, Mr. and Miss, 47, rue Gay-Lussac.
Patton, Miss Mary (Painter), 4, rue Léopold-Robert.
Paxton, Mrs,, 32, rue Montparnasse.
Paxton, W., 131, boulevard Montparnasse.
Peacock, Mrs and the Misses, 17, rue de Moscou.
Pearce, Charles, 42, rue Fontaine (U. S.).
Pearce, Mr. and Mrs. C. S., 42, rue Fontaine, and at Antwerp.
Pearce, C. S. (Artist-Painter), and Mrs,, 42, rue Fontaine, and at Auvers.
Peat, Mr. North, 1, avenue Mac-Mahon.

Pecheron de Moncy, Mme, 15, rue des Saussaies.
Peck. Mrs. John (Artist), 4, rue Léopol--Robert Oberlin, (Ohio).
Peeble, Miss (Porcelain-Painter), 118, rue d'Assas.
Peirotto, Florian, 9, rue des Fourneaux.
Pell, Mrs. Walden (née Orléana Ellery), 1, avenue Montaigne, Paris.
Pellereau, Dr, G. E., 8, rue du Commandant-Rivière
Pemberton. T. P., 32, rue de l'Université.
Pendall, J. J. Mr., 23, rue de Marignan, and at " Les Platreries " Sannois, France.
Pepper, A.. 11 and 13, avenue Victor-Hugo.
Percheron, Mme, 15, rue des Saussaies.
Perkins, Mr. and Mrs. Edward F., 17, avenue de l'Alma.
Perry, Mrs. F. S. (Artist), 38, rue Galilée.
Peters, W. T., 203, boulevard Raspail.
Petter, H. S., 9, rue Campagne-Première.
Phelps, Mr. and Mrs. Harris, 13, rue Vaneau (Tuesdays), and villa Montpensier. Pau.
Philipps, B. G., 4. rue Léopold-Robert.
Picknell, M, L, 36, rue Jouffroy (U. S.).
Pierson, Mme Blanche, 17, rue des Bassins, and at Pourville, Dieppe.
Pietsch, T. W., 6, rue des Ursulines
Pike, Charles, 17, rue Campagne-Première.
Pike, Mr. and Mrs. J., 14, rue Brémontier.
Pilkington, Mrs, 25, rue Tessier.
Pilter, Mr. and Mrs. J. C., 1, boulevard Suchet
Pilter, Mr. and Mrs. Robert, 10, rue Ibry, Neuilly.
Pilter, Mr. and Mrs. 176, avenue de Neuilly.
Piper, G. H., 25, rue de Buci
Pittoëff, M. Nicholas de, 127, Boul. Malesherbes.
Pittoëff, M, Constantin de, même adresse.
Planel, Mr. and Mrs., 2, rue Chombigues (U. S. A).
Plazzoni, G., 49, rue Madame.
Plock, Mr. and Mrs. Otto, 18, place des Etats-Unis.
Plummer, Mr. Henry, 11, rue de Marignan.
Polh, Miss Perrié, 76, avenue Wagram.
Polignac, Prince Edmund de, and Princess (née Singer), 4, rue Cortambert.
Pollock, Mr. and Mrs. J. L', 13, avenue Carnot.
Polt, Mrs. J., 9. rue Copernic.
Pomeroy, Mrs Sandford, B Villa des Oranges, Antibes (Alpes-Maritimes) and Co Morgan, Harjes and Co, Bankers, Paris.
Pomor, Duc de, boulevard Haussmann.
Ponsonby, Mr. and Mrs. Cleland (née Horwitz). Villa Acadiée, Pau.
Post. Mrs. Jotham (née Bridge), 5, rue Copernic, Paris.
Post, Miss. 5, rue Copernic, Paris.
Post Wright, E., 23, rue de Marignan.
Post, Mr. J. Ctis, passage de la Visitation.
Postwhite, Rev. and Mrs. William M. (née Sallie F. Ellis) care of Morgan, Harjes and Co Bankers, Paris.
Potenkine, M. de, 121, avenue Wagram.
Potter, Mrs. and Miss, Hôtel Liverpool.
Poulain, Mme, 7, avenue de la Grande-Armée (Monday).
Powell, Mr., 16, rue du Maine.
Power, Alfred, 26, rue Joubert.
Pownal, Miss Mary, 37, avenue Marceau (G. B.)
Pratt, Mrs., 29, rue Boissière.
Preble, Miss Mary, 118, rue d'Assas (U. S.).
Premier, Mme, 4, avenue des Ternes (U. S. A.).
Prendergast, Dr. 35, boulevard Malesherbes.
Prendergast, Dr. J, M. Vincent, 1, rue d'Anjou.
Prodgers, Mr. and Mrs. Edwin (née Surtees), 44, avenue du Bois-de-Boulogne (Fridays).
Prost, J. C. Alfred and Mrs. (née Davis), 102, avenue des Ternes.
Protter, Mr., 57, rue Pierre-Charron.
Psotter, C. H., 17 bis, rue Campagne-Première.
Potenkine, M. de, 121, avenue Wagram.

| R | R |

R

Raffalwitch, M , 21, avenue Hoche.
Ralli. Richard and Mme (née Wood), 48, rue Pierre-Charron.
Rally, Miss. 41, boulevard Malesherbes.
Ramsdell, Winthrop, 6, rue Boissonnade.
Randall. W. G., 135, boulevard Montparnasse.
Randell, Miss, Paris.
Randolph, Mrs.,2, rue Lincoln.
Read, Ch., 2, boulevard Saint-Germain.
Read, General and Mrs, Meredith, 128, rue de la Boëtie (after 5, Daily).
Read, Miss Emily, 187, rue de la Pompe.
Read, Miss Margaret (Painter), 4, rue de Chevreuse·
Read, General Meredith, and Mrs (née Pumpelly). 128, rue de la Boëtie (Daily after 5 o'clock), and at Newport, Rhode Island, U. S. A. (late American Ambassador to Athenes).
Redfern. P., 58, avenue Montaigne.
Redmond, G. S., 12, rue du Moulin-au-Beurre·
Rée, Mr. and Mrs. Martin, 6, r. de La Trémoille (G.B.)
Reed, Miss Fanny, 4, rue de la Renaissacce (Mondays).
Reed, Miss Fanny, 4. rue de la Renaissance, Paris.
Reed, Mrs. J. Van Dusen (née Mary Louise Mitchell), 29, rue Marbeuf, Paris.
Reed, Miss Florence Van Dusen, 29, rue Marbeuf, Paris.
Reed, Mrs. Warren, A.,44, rue Hamelin.
Reeve, Mr. Iris, 28, avenue d'Iéna (G. B.)
Régnaud, M. and Mme, 21, rue Galilée.
Reid, George, A., 106, boulevard Montparnasse.
Reider, Mr. and Mrs. 39, rue Calvert, Saint-Cloud.
Reichenberg, Mlle Suzanne, (Comédie-Française), 21, Villa Said (Telephone).
Reinhart, Miss Olivia (Artist), 6, rue Boissonnade, New-York (U. S. A.).
Reiss, P. L., 29. rue Jacob.
Reitlinger, Adolphe and Mrs. (née Mayer), 65, rue d'Anjou (Wednesdays) and Château de Fortoiseau, Dammarie-les-Lys (Seine-et-Marne).
Renauld, Mr. and Mrs. Charles (née Louise E. Brunet), 54, West 32 Street, New-York and Family at " Les Plateries" Samois, France.
Renauld, Mrs. Vouis E., 54 West 32 Street, New-York.
Repingon, M., 181, rue de Courcelles.
Reynolds, Mrs. W., Floyd, 25, avenue du Bois-de-Boulogne.
Reynolds, W. J., 9, impasse du Maine.
Reubell, Miss, 42, avenue Gabriel. Paris
Reubell, Mr. Jacques, 23, rue de Marignan, Paris.
Richard. Mrs. 5, rue Fresnil (Wednesdays).
Richards, Mrs., 26. rue de Bassano.
Richardson, Frank Henry. 9, rue des Fourneaux (U. S.)
Riel, Miss Katherine (Painter), rue de Chevreuse.
Ridgeway, Mrs.. 5, rue François 1er (Wednesday) and château de Ricquebourg, Resson (Oise).
Ridgway, Mr. and Mrs. C. H (née Ellen Munroe), 1, avenue Marceau, Paris.
Ridgway, Henri and Mrs. (née Munroe), 1, avenue Marceau and Ricquebourg, Resson (Oise).
Ridgway, Mr. and Mrs. John, 5, rue François Ier.
Ridgways, Mrs. (née Willing), 5, rue François Ier, Paris.
Riggs, Mm., Henry, 13, rue Murillo and Parc de la Pique, Bagnères-de-Luchon.
Riggs, Mrs. Benjamin, C. (née Rebecca Fox) care of Morgan, Harjes and Co, Bankers, Paris.
Rinehart, Miss (Artist), 7, rue Charlet.
Ring, Frank, 6, avenue de Wagram.
Ritchie, C. E., 203, boulevard Raspail.
Ritchie, Mrs., 30, avenue Kléber.

Ritchie, Miss, 15. avenue Mac-Mahon (Tuesday).
Rivaz, C., 7. rue Delambre.
Roadsbust, M., 131, boulevard Montparnasse.
Robb, Mr. James, care of Hottinguer and Co, Bankers, Paris.
Roberts, Mr. J, D., 43. rue Boissière.
Roberts, Mrs., 26, rue Washington (Cité Odiot).
Roberts, Cyril, Mr., 34, rue de Constantinople.
Roberts, Arthur, 3, avenue de Tourville.
Roberts. J. D., 17, boulevard Haussmann.
Roberts, James Edm., 15. rue de Chalancilles and château de Caumont, Caudebec (Seine-Inférieure).
Roberts, Mrs. Laugier, 44, rue François Ier.
Roberts, Mrs., M. C., 10, avenue Victor-Hugo.
Roberts, Miss, E. Wentworth, 45, avenue de Villiers (U. S.).
Roberts, Miss.,3, avenue de Tourville.
Roberston. Mrs. W, G., 227, boulevard Pereire (Tuesdays).
Robert, Miss, 187, rue de la Pompe.
Robin du Parc, Mme, 18, rue Boccador.
Robins, Mr. W. Powell, 3, rue Soufflot. Paris.
Robins, Mr. and Mrs. Thomas (née Emma Davis) care of Morgan, Harjes and Co. Bankers. Paris.
Robinson, Douglas, F. 59, avenue de Saxe (G. B.).
Robion, Mrs., 17, bis, avenue du Bois-de-Boulogne.
Roche, The Misses, 11, rue des Ecuries-d'Artois (Thursday).
Rodgers: Lieutenant Commander, Raymond, P. (Naval Attache to U. S. Legation), 6, rue Christophe-Colomb.
Rodin, Auguste (Sculptor), 182, rue de l'Université.
Roger, Mr. and Mrs, 41, rue Saint-André-des-Arts.
Rogers, Mr. and Mrs. Fairman (née Rébecca H. Gilpin) care of Morgan. Harjes and Co, Bankers, Paris.
Roll. Alfred (Artist-Painter), 41, rue Alphonse de Neuville.
Rolshoven, J., 233, rue du Faubourg-Saint-Honoré.
Rook, Mr. and Miss.,59, rue de la Boëtie.
Rook, Mr. Edward F., 16. impasse du Maine, Paris.
Rooseveld, Mr. and Mrs. William Cousley, 18, avenue Raphael, Passy, Paris.
Root, O. H., 16, impasse du Maine.
Roper, Mr. and Mrs., 5, rue Fresnil.
Rose, Guy, 6, rue Vercingétorix (U. S.).
Ross, Mrs. Catherine, 28, Villa Molitor (G. B.).
Rothschild, Mr. and Mrs. Alfred, 4, square Maubeuge.
Rothschild, Baron Gustave de (Austrian Consul General) and Baroness (née Anspach), 23, avenue de Marigny (Telephone) and Château de Laversine, Creil (Oise).
Rothschild, Baron Nathaniel de, 33, rue du Faubourg-Saint-Honoré (Telephone) and at the Abbaye des Vaulx-de-Cernay, Le Perray (Montparnasse Railway (Seine-et-Oise).
Rothschild, Baron Arthur de (same address).
Rothschild, Baron Edmund de, and Baroness (née de Rothschild. 41, faubourg Saint-Honoré (Telephone) and Château d'Armainvilliers, Tournan (Seine-et-Marne).
Rothschild, Baron and Baroness Adolphe de. 45, 47, rue de Monceau (Telephone) and « La Ferme », Boulogne-sur-Seine. and Pavillon de Prégny, Geneva (Switzerland).
Round, Miss. 178, rue de Rivoli.
Rovere de la Firrentino, 11, rue de Tocqueville.
Rowlatt, Mr. and Mrs,' 10 rue de Penthièvre.
Rucellai, Comte and Comtesse (née Edith Milcies (Bronson). Venice, Italy.
Ruck, Dr. Rr. 41. rue Whasington.
Ruinn, F., Hôtel Saint-Malo, Gare Montparnasse.
Runyon, Général and Mrs. Thomas, United States Embassy, Berlin.
Runyon the Misses Julie B. and Helen L. U. S. Embassy, Berlin.
Runyon, Mrs, L. Chauncey and F. F. U. S. Embassy Berlin.

**

Russel, the Hon, Bertrand Honorary Attaché to H. B. M's Embassy. 39, rue du Faubourg-St-Honoré.
Rush, Miss Hannah (Artist), 111, rue Notre-Dame-des-Champs (Hamilton, Canada).
Rute, Mrs. Dona de (née Wyse-Bonaparte), 23, boulevard Poissonnière (Thursday, from 5 to 7), and at Aix-les-Bains (Savoy).
Ryan, Dr. J. J,, 19, rue Scribe.
Ryan, Dr. George B., 19, rue Scribe.
Ryan, Mr. and Mrs., 27, avenue Niel.

S

Sacheel, Miss (Artist), 13, rue Boissonade.
Saint-Amand, Mr. and Mrs., George, 154, boulevard Haussmann (Wednesdays) and Vieillefontaine, Maisons-Laffitte (Saturdays).
Saint-André, Mme, 9, boulevard Malesherbes.
Saint-Anna, Mrs. (née Billings), 2, r. Goëthe, Paris.
Saint-Gilles, Count and Countess (née d'Onsembray), 9, rue de la Chaise (Wednesday) (Telephone), and Château de Fretay, Fougères (Ille-et-Vilaine).
Saint-Romain, Comtesse de (née Slideli), 76, avenue Kléber and Château de Gounieux (Oise).
Salanson, Gabriel, and Mrs. (née Sackville-West), 157, rue de la Pompe (Telephone).
Salter, The Misses, 35, rue Maubeuge.
Salvador, baron Albert d'Avernas and the Baroness (née Norman-Kimpson), 4, rue Berlioz and Bezuidenbout, La Hague, Holland.
San Carlos de Pedrosa, Marquis and Marquise, 30, avenue Kléber (U. S. A.).
Sanders, Miss Bertha D., 16, impasse du Maine (Illinois, U, S. A.).
Sanderson, Miss Sybil (Opéra), 46, av. Malakoff.
Sanderson, Mme, 46, avenue Malakoff.
Sandford, Lewis-Halsey and Mrs. (née Blin de Bourdon, 6, rue Dumont-d'Urville (Wednesday before Easter and Thursday after).
Sandford, Mr. and Mrs. Edwards,, 11, rue Barbet-de-Jouy (Tuesday in January and after Easter).
Sandilands, Mr. and Mrs , Donald, 1 bis, avenue du Bois-de-Boulogne.
Sands, Mr. and Mrs. 48, avenue Gabriel (U. S.).
Sand, Mr. and Mrs,, William R. (née Mary F. Gardiner), Caire, Egypt and care of J. Munroe and Co, Bankers, Paris.
Sandford, Mrs. (née Belle Davis), 6, rue de la Renaissance, Paris.
Sanfort, John, 22, rue Clément-Marot.
Santiges, Comtesse de, 16. rue de l'Elysée and Villa du Midi, Cannes.
Santos-Suarez, Mr. and Mrs. B. (née de Francia), 32, avenue Friedland and Villa Santos-Suarez, Anglet (Basses-Pyrénées).
Sardou, Victorien (of the French Academy) and Mme, 28, rue de Madrid, and Château de Marly-le-Roi (Seine-et-Oise).
Sargeant, Miss, 95, rue de Reuilly (Dickens'Home).
Sargent, Miss, 35, rue d'Anjou.
Sargent, Miss Bernardine (Singer-soprano), 4, rue de Chevreuse.
Sasso, Conrad, 6, rue de la Franqueville (G. B.)
Sassoon, Mr. and Mrs. E. A. (née de Rothschild), 23, avenue de Marigny aed 25, Kensington Gore, London, W.
Saussay, M. and Mme, 10, rue du Commandant-Rivière.
Savenkoff, Véra de, 187, rue de la Pompe.
Savile, Mr. and Mrs., 39, rue des Vignes.
Scheidecker, Paul, 32, rue du Sentier (G. B.)
Scheremetjiff, M. de, 71, rue de la Faisanderie.
Schlesinger, Mrs., 31, rue de Prony.

Schlesinger, Mr. Sebastian and Miss, 169, boulevard Malesherbes.
Schmidt, C. F., 59, rue de Vaugirard.
Schofield, Mrs. and Miss, 28. avenue d'Iéna.
Schofield, W. E., 203, boulevard Raspail.
Schofield, Walter, E., 31, boulev. Haussmann (U. S.).
Schussleworth, Miss Claire (Artist), .2. r. de Seine.
Schwetchine, M. de,
Scott, F. Edwin, 6, rue Boissonade (U. S.).
Scott, Mrs. Walter, 95, rue de Monceau.
Scott, Miss Gilson, care Morgan Harjes and Co, Paris, and 2026 Walnut Street. Philadelphia (U. S. A.).
Scott, Miss Nora (of Chicago). 20, rue de la Paix.
Sedelman, C., 6, rue de la Rochefoucauld.
Sedgwick, Miss (Artist), hôtel Lafond, 14, rue de la Trémoille.
Selby, 21, rue Moulenotte (U. S. A.).
Seligman, Mr. and Mrs., 26, avenue de Villiers.
Seligmann, William, 26, avenue de Villiers.
Sellière, Baron and Baroness Raymond (née Livermore-Riley), 19, rue Constantine, Paris.
Sellon, Miss (Lady Sup. of G. F. S.), 48, rue de Provence.
Senna, Mme de, 150, rue de la Pompe (G. B.).
Serle, Mr. and Mrs., 22, rue Matignon and The Clyffe, Limpley Stoke, Wilss, England.
Sernancelles, Vicomtesse de, 23, rue Pauquet (Thursdays).
Scripitzine, Mlle de, 28, avenue Niel.
Sers, Comte and Comtesse de (née Niveu), 59, rue Galilée.
Sesnon, Robert J., 17, rue de Chazelles (M. S. A.).
Seton-Oberoff, D.. place Saint-Georges.
Seward, Miss Marie, 13, rue de l'Arc-de-Triomphe.
Sewell. J. T. B., 54, faubourg Saint-Honoré.
Seymour, Mrs. Beatrice, A., 8, rue Rembrandt.
Sharon, Mr. and Mrs. P. (née Levis), 82, avenue des Champs-Elysées.
Sharp, J. A., 131, boulevard Montparnasse.
Sharpe, Mrs., 21, rue Montesquieu.
Sharpe, Mrs. Tileen-Sutton, Spencer, 17, rue Treilhard.
Shaw, Maclaren, 131, boulevard Montparnasse.
Shaw, Mrs., 30, avenue Henri-Martin.
Shepard, Dr. and Mrs. Charles R., avenue Henri-Martin.
Shepard, J. R. D., 8, rue Mondovi.
Sherard, Robert H., 123, boulevard Magenta and at Capbreton (Landes).
Sherburne, H. C., 31, avenue Kléber.
Sherman, Mrs., 10, rue Laurent-Pichat.
Sherman, J. A. (Hernial Specialist), 8, r. Boudreau.
Sherrard, R. H., 66, rue Lafayette.
Sherwood-Dunn, Dr. and Mrs. B., 15, rue des Pyramides.
Shilito, Mr. and Mrs., 23, av. du Bois-de-Boulogne.
Shober, R. A., 44, rue Villejust.
Shrewsbury and Talbot, The Earl of, 34, avenue du Bois-de-Bouiogne and Alton Towers, Stoke-on-Treut. and Ingestre Hall, Stafford, England.
Shropshyre, Clyde, 6 ter, avenue Mac-Mahon.
Shuttleworth, Mrs., 320, rue Saint-Honoré.
Shulz, A. R., 34, rue Notre-Dame-des-Champs.
Sibert, Baroness Courcelle de, 65, rue Miromesnil (Saturdays).
Sibour, Comte and Comtesse de (c/o, Drexel-Harjes, Bankers, 31, boulevard Haussmann) and Château de Gentilly, Sorgues-sur-l'Ouvèze, Vaucluse.
Sierstorpff, Count and Countesse Johannes von Francken (née Mary Knowlton), 92, Koniggratzer Strasse, Berlin.
Sievwright, Miss Theresa, 187, rue de la Pompe.
Sievwright, Miss Helena, 187, rue de la Pompe.
Siller-Vale, 3, rue Le Goff.
Simes, Miss, 11, rue Tilsitt.
Simmonds, J., 6, avenue de Messine.

S

Simmonds, Mr. and Mrs., E., 4, rue Gallicra (Saturday).
Simmonds, Miss Sarah, 7, rue Louis-le-Grand.
Simons, Henry, 37, cours de Vincennes (U. S.).
Simonson, Ernest, 5. rue de la Paix.
Simpson, Mrs., 8, villa Michon.
Simpson, Mr. and Miss Atkinson, 5, rue de la Renaissance.
Simson. M., 3. rue Campagne-Première.
Sindry, Miss, Herford Hospital.
Singer, Mr. and Mrs. Franklin, M., 11, av. d'Iéna, and The Wigwam, Paingtou, South Devon.
Skepper, H. H., 99, avenue Malakoff.
Slader, Mr. and Mrs., 93, avenue Henri-Martin.
Sloman, Miss, 69 bis, rue de Courcelles.
Smith, Miss Mary (Pianist), 4, rue de Chevreuse.
Smith, E. W., 7, rue Le Peletier.
Smith, George, 176, boulevard Haussmann.
Smith, Irvine, Mr., Hôtel Victoria, rue Castiglione.
Smith, L. P., 14, rue de la Grande-Chaumière.
Smith. Miss Crapo (Artist), 1, rue de Chevreuse.
Smith, Miss Isabel (Miniaturist), 77, r. Delambre.
Smith, Miss Ruby, 187, rue de la Pompe.
Smith, Mrs., 46, rue Hamelin.
Smith, Mr. and Mrs, 22, rue Notre-Dame-de-Lorette.
Smith, Mr. and Mrs. Ballard (née Butterfield) (London repr. of the New-York-World), 15, Herbert Cressent, Hans Place, London (S. W.).
Smith, Mr. and Mrs. Clifton, 5, rue de l'Isle, Bois-Colombes.
Smith, Mr. Hubbard, 36, avenue de l'Opéra (M. S. A.).
Smith, Beg., 26. avenue de la Grande-Armée.
Smith, Th., 8, rue Frédéric-Bastiat.
Smith, W., 8, villa de Radau, avenue Malakoff.
Smith, Mr. Lake Kuntington, 103, boulevard Raspail.
Smyden, Bladen, 81, boulevard Montparnasse.
Smyth, The, Rev. Emidius, 50, avenue Hoche.
Snow, Mrs., 8, boulevard Sébastopol.
Sohège, Mr. and Mrs. Paul, 22, avenue du Bois-de-Boulogne (Wednesday), and Château de Blosseville, Villerville (Calvados).
Soltau, Mr. and Mrs. William, 5, villa Monceau, rue de Courcelles.
Somerville, Mr. and Mrs. Albert, 1, rue Pierre-Charron.
Sonthille, Mme, 170, avenue d'Italie.
Sonza, Anthony de, 3. rue de Sontay (G. B.).
Sorcham, Mr. and Mrs. M. A. (née La Chaise-Fhorm) 10, rue Lincoln. Paris.
Sorchan, Mr and Mrs. M. A. (née Thorn), 10, rue Lincoln (Saturdays).
Sorel, Mr. and Mrs., 22. rue Lubeck.
South, Mr., 46, rue de la Faisanderie.
Southgate, Mr. and Mrs. Frederick, 137, boulevard Malesherbes.
Southwick, Lawrence A., 117, rue de Vaugirard (U. S.).
Souza-Pinto, José Julio de (Artist Painter), 18, rue Cardinet.
Souza-Roza de (Plenipotentiary Minister of Portugal), 32, rue de Lubeck.
Speakman, Mrs. J. E. G. (Artist), 38, rue du Luxembourg.
Spencer, Mrs. L., 70, avenue Marceau.
Spencer-Sharpe, Mrs., 23, rue Caumartin.
Spencer, W. Auguste, and Mrs. (née de Mongeot), 59, avenue Henri-Martin.
Spiers, Ch., Mac Carthy and Mrs., 12, boulevard Émile Augier.
Spiers, Mr. and Mrs. John, 95, boulevard Montmorency.
Spiers, Mr. and Mrs, Alfred, 118, avenue Victor-Hugo.
Spiller, Dr. and Mrs. Wm. Gilson (physician), 8 bis. rue Campagne-Première (Philadelphia).

Speding, colonel and Mrs., 19; rue Leroux.
Spooner, Mrs. Henry, 31, rue de Prony (Monday 4, till 7.)
Spring, Mr. E. W., hôtel de Bavière.
Standish, Mr. and Mrs. Henry (née des Cars), avenue d'Iéna and Château de Montjoye, Rambouillet (Seine-et-Oise).
Stanlake-Lee, Mr. and Mrs., 17 bis, avenue du Bois-de-Boulogne.
Stanley, Miss, 36, avenue du Bois-de-Boulogne.
Stanley, Miss Sara, 203, boulevard Raspail.
Stanley-Watson, Mr. and Mrs., hôtel de Paris and Osborne, 6, rue Saint-Roch.
Stanton, Mr and Mrs. Théodore, 9, rue Bassano, and at Cordes (Tarn).
Stark, Mrs. and the Misses, 13, rue Boisserade (Waltham Mass).
Statch, Miss Elizabeth, 187, rue de la Pompe.
Stead, Mrs., Geo Ambler, 34, avenue Kléber.
Stebbing, Mme, 196, rue Legendre.
Stebbins, Mr. and Mrs. Charles H, (née Ninnie Vail), care of J. Munroe and Co, Bankers, Paris.
Stebbins, Mr. E. Fail, Union Club, New-York, and care of J. Munroe and Co, Bankers. Paris.
Stebbing, Proff., A., 196, rue Legendre.
Stebbins, The Misses Ethel and Mabel, care of J. Munroe and Co, Bankers, Paris.
Steel, Mr. H. Wickham (Correspondent of the " New-York-World "), 4, rue Le Goff, Pau.
Steelle, B., 64, boulevard du Port-Royal.
Stehr, Miss, 55, rue de Provence.
Stephun, Condy, 39, rue du Faubourg-St-Honoré.
Stephen-Ribes, Mrs., 166, boulevard Haussmann.
Stern, Saly, 8, rue de l'Elysée.
Stevens, Alfred, 20, rue Eugène-Flachat (Saturday).
Stevenson, Miss, 13, rue Boissonnade.
Steward, W. W., 5, rue Boissonnade.
Stewart, Jules, 36, rue Copernic.
Stewart, Mr., 12. avenue Mac-Mahon.
Stewart, Mrs Jules, W. H. fr and Antaniod F. Union-Club, New-York, and 6, av. d'Iéna, Paris.
Stewart, Mr. Paul Cox, Union-Club, New-York, and 6, avenue d'Iéna, Paris.
Stewart, Mr. William, H. Union Club, New-York, and 6. avenue d'Ién., Paris.
Stewart, William, H., 6, avenue d'Iéna.
Stewart, William Wright (Artist), 5. r. Boissonnade. (Philadelphia, U. S. A.).
Stickney, B. A., 55, avenue Marceau.
Stoddard. L. A., 131, boulevard Montparnasse.
Stoddard, L. F., 131, boulevard Montparnasse.
Stokes, Mr. and Mrs. Isaac Newton Phelps (née Edith Minturn), 176, boulevard Saint-Germain, Paris.
Stone, A. G. (New-York Herald), 118, boulevard Haussmann.
Story, Mr. and Mrs. Julian (née Eames), 7, place des États-Unis.
Stowe, Mr. William, 203, boulevard Raspail.
Strang, Mr. James, 203, boulevard Raspail.
Street, George, 39, rue Joubert.
Street, Mr. and Mrs., boulevard de Versailles, Saint-Cloud.
St.ibinger, F. W., 131, boulevard Montparnasse.
Strong, Rowland, 113, boulevard Magenta.
Strunz, W. F, 14, avenue du Maine.
Stuers, Chevalier de (Minister Plenipotentiary of the Netherlands), 23, rue de Lubeck.
Sturrock, Mr., Sevran-Livry (Seine-et-Oise).
Sudder, Miss (Sculptor), Square du Croissac, 12, boulevard Montparnasse.
Sumpter, Mme, 14, avenue Carnot (G. B.).
Süssfeld, Mr., 34, avenue Kléber.
Sydenham, Mrs. Charles, rue François Ier.
Sykes, Mr. and Mrs. D. W. (née Ambler-Stead), 48, rue Fabert.
Syme, Mr., rue Halévy.

T

Taber, Mr. James (Director General " Equitable " Life Assurance Society), 36 bis, av. de l'Opéra.
Taber, Mrs and Miss. 32, avenue d'Iéna.
Taber, Mr. J., 32, avenue d'Iéna (U. S.).
Taft, Miss (Sculptor), Square du Croisic, 12, boulevard Montparnasse.
Talcod, Allan, 16, impasse du Maine.
Tallant, Hugh, 25, rue de Vaugirard.
Talleyrand-Périgord, Marquise de (née Durtis), 7, rue Saint-Dominique.
Tanner, H. O., 51, boulevard Saint-Jacques.
Taylor-Green, Miss Mary, 18, rue de Milan (G. B.).
Taylor, Miss, Hôtel Victoria, rue Castiglione.
Taylor, Miss, 54, avenue du Roule, Neuilly,
Taylor, Mrs. S., 24, rue François Iᵉʳ.
Taylor, Thomas, 8, rue de Tournon.
Tchernitzkaja, Mlle, 38 ou 40 avenue Marceau.
Tchoumakoff, M. de, 35, Boul, Haussmann.
Temblaire, Mr. and Mrs. N., 20, boul. Berthier.
Templer, Mrs , 23, avenue des Ternes (nurse).
Tenré, Henry (Artist Painter), and Madame (née Aguado), 36, rue de Villejust.
Terry, Antonio. 6 bis, rue Villejust.
Tewlesbury, G. W., 8, rue des Capucines.
Thayen, Mr. and Mrs., 27, avenue de l'Alma.
Thayer, Mr. F. Porter. c/o Whitman and Barnes Manufacturing Company, 149, Queen Victoria Street London.
Thebaud, Mrs (née d'Hervilly), 20, av. Kléber, Paris.
Theriat. Charles, 26, avenue Marceau (U. S.).
Thetard, Mr. and Mrs. A., 61, avenue d'Antin.
Thomas, D. A., 81, boulevard Montparnasse.
Thomas, L. C., 46, rue de Vaugirard.
Thomas, Seymour, 6, rue des Fourneaux (U S).
Thomson, Mr. J. and Mrs. (née Parsons), 8, rue de Presbourg, and Villa des Baumettes, Nice.
Thompson, Mr. E. Kay, 105, rue Notre-Dame-des-Champs, Paris.
Thompson, Mr. Ernest (Artist), 4, rue Campagne-Première (Toronto, Canada).
Thompson, Mr and Mrs. Woodsworth (née Mary Pumpelly), 7, rue Scribe, Paris.
Thorburn, Mr., Mrs. and Miss, 47, avenue des Champs-Elysées (Wednesday).
Thormeditee, W. H., 57, avenue de Saxe.
Thorn, Mr. William, K., 13, West 16 Street, New-York, and at Pau, France.
Thorndike, Mrs. Stewart, 8, rue de Pomereu (134, rue de Longchamp).
Thorndike, Mr. James Stewart, same address.
Thorndike, Miss, 48, avenue Gabrielle.
Thorne, Miss Sylvia, 38, rue Blanche.
Thorne, W. L., 46, rue de Vaugirard.
Thorndy, Mr., 48, avenue Gabrielle
Thorudy, Mrs., 8, rue Pomereau, Passy.
Thurber, Rev. E. G., D., D., and Mrs , 59, rue Galilée (Wednesday).
Tiffany. Mr. and Mrs. W. A. (née Smith), 64, avenue du Bois-de-Boulogne.
Tiffen, W. H., 22, rue des Capucines, and avenue de la Mairie, Houilles (Seine-et-Oise).
Tiffin, W., 22, rue des Capucines.
Tilton, Mr. Théodore, 73, avenue Kléber, Paris.
Todd, Mrs., 5, rue de la Renaissance
Tooke, Mr. Gabriel Mead, Union Club, New-York, and care of J. Munroe and Co, Bankers, Paris.
Tootal, Mr. and Mrs., 48, rue Michel-Ange, Auteuil.
Toporoff, M. de, Hôtel de Bade.
Totten, G. O., 131, boulevard Montparnasse.
Toumansky, M. de, 3, rue Freillard.
Tourtel, Mr. and Mrs., 61, rue de la Goutte-d'Or.
Townley, Walter (Secretary to H. B, M's Embassy), 23, rue Marignan.

Trubadelo, Angel de, and Mme (née de Somogyi), 4, rue Marbeuf.
Traiger, Miss, 13, rue Boissonnade.
Treillard, Vicomtesse de, 57, avenue d'Antin.
Trevos, Mrs., 159, boulevard Saint-Germain.
Tripp, Miss, 187, rue de la Pompe.
Tripp, Richard. Howard, 33, rue Joubert (Offices. 8. rue Saint-Georges), and 17, rue de Sèvres, Ville d'Avray.
Trobriand, Countess de (née Jones), 115, avenue des Champs-Elysées (Saturday).
Troncy, Mrs. Laura. 16, rue Charron (G. B.).
Trotier. Miss Mary K. (Artist), 11, rue Boissonnade.
Troubetz koy, Prince Pierre and Princesse (née Amélie Rives), via Borghetts. Milan, Italy and Obach and Co. 38. Cockspur Street, London, S. W.
Trowbridge, Miss Lucy Parkman (Miniaturist), 4, rue de Chevreuse.
Truesdell, Gaylord, S., 9, rue Duperré (U. S.).
Tubbs, A., Hôtel Continental.
Tuck, Mr. and Mrs. Edward (née Stell), 46, avenue des Champs-Elysées, and at New-York (Wednesday).
Tucker, Dr. M., 3, rue du Faubourg-St-Honoré.
Tucker, Miss Marie, 187, rue de la Pompe.
Tufton, Lady, 41, rue de la Boëtie (Mondays), and château de Brunchaut, Etampes (S.-et-O).
Tukermann- Ernest, P. R., 9, rue Galilée.
Turenne d'Aynac, G. L. Count du, 9, rue de la Bienfaisance (Téléphone).
Turner, Miss Florence, 187, rue de la Pompe.
Turner, Mr., 152, avenue Victor-Hugo.
Turner-Kesteven, Mr. Horace S., 2, rue des Foss's-Saint-Jacques.
Tweedale, Captain and Mrs., 54, quai de Billy.
Twembley, Douglas, 1, avenue Friedland.
Twombley, Mr. Douglas, 3, rue de Tilsitt. Paris.
Twombley, William, 1, avenue Friedland.
Twyefford, Mr. and Mrs. L. P., 105, av. Henri Martin.
Twyford. Bernard, 19, rue Clapeyron.
Tyne, The Rev. Columbin, 50, avenue Hoche (G. B.).
Tyng, Rev. D. Stephen H. and Mrs. (née Fanny Tappin), 47 East 44 Street, New-York, and, 16, rue de la Chaussée-d'Antin.

U

Underwood, Mrs. 79. avenue de la Grande-Armée.
Uriharren, Count de, and Countesse (née de Batiz), 8. avenue Kléber.

V

Vail, Eugène, and Mrs (née Mauran), 11, r. Faraday.
Vail, Mrs., 10, rue de la Paix.
Vail, Miss, 10, rue de la Paix.
Valentyne, Mrs., 7. avenue du Trocadéro
Valk, E. S., 3, boulevard Saint-Martin (U. S.).
Valois, Mr. and Mrs. Arthur E. (née Brigos), 34, avenue de l'Opéra, and Château de Valois, 10, quai de la Marne, Alfort (Sundays).
Valori, Marquise de (née Ledoux), 15, rue Vernet.
Van Beers, Jean (Artist Painter), 10, rue du Général-Appert and Pavillon de Cernay, Cernay-la-Ville (Seine-et-Oise).
Van Bergen, Mr. and Mrs. Anthony (née Pierson). 118. av. des Champs-Elysées (Wednesday).
Van Briggle, A., 6, rue Boissonnade.
Vanderspart, Mrs., 4, rue du Débarcadère.

Van der Weyden, 31, avenue d'Eylau.
Vandeul, Baron and Baronne H. Maupoint de (née
    Edith Clift), 18, rue Matignon, Paris.
Van Pelt, J., 69, boulevard Saint-Michel.
Van Pelt, Mrs., 69, boulevard Saint-Michel.
Van Pelt, Mr. John, same address.
Van Sandeau, Mr. and Mrs., 29, avenue de la Grande-
    Armée.
Van Voorhis, Mrs. B. W. (née Tapper) care of Roth-
    child's Bank, Paris.
Van Vorst, Mrs. Hooper (née Joséphine Treat), 40,
    avenue Victor-Hugo, Paris.
Van Vorst, Miss Marie L., 40, avenue Victor-Hugo,
    Paris.
Van Wagner, Miss Olive, 187, rue de la Pompe.
    (Springfild Mass, U. S. A.).
Vargounine, M., 39, rue Cardinet.
Varnum, Miss and the Misses Louise and Anne,
    Eurofäischer Hof, Dresden, Germany.
Varreux, Mlle de, 12, rue Grefultre.
Vatable, Mr. and Mrs. (née Mathilda C. Schwarzwael-
    der) care of Morgan Harjes and Co Bankers,
    Paris.
Vatable, Mr. Auguste, S. Zeta Psi Club, New-York,
    care of Morgan Harjes and Co Bankers, Paris.
Vatable, Mr. Jules J. Zeta Psi Club, New-York, care
    of Morgan Harjes and Co Bankers, Paris.
Vedder, Simon, H., 11, impasse du Maine.
Vedder, Mr. and Mrs. Elihu C. 68, Capo le Case,
    Rome, Italy.
Vercoutre, Mr., 32, rue Boursault.
Vernejoul, Mme J. de, 4, avenue Friedland.
Very, Mr. and Mrs. Edward, 11, rue Chardin.
Viall, Mrs., 6, rue Percier.
Vibert, Jehan-Georges (Artist Painter), and Mrs.
    (née Lloyd) (Comédie-Française), 18. rue Ballu.
Vickarmann, Mr. and Mrs., 40, rue de l'Aqueduc,
    Gare de l Est.
Vignaud, Heury, First Secretary to the United States
    Legation, 59, rue Galilee.
Villiers-Forbes, Mr. and Mrs., Dinard (Ille-et-Vilaine).
Vilna, Mrs., 4, Villa Michon.
Vincent, Mr. and Mrs. P., 36, r. de Penthièvre.
Von Hemert, Mr. and Mrs. Aug. (née Zimmermann),
    12, avenue de l'Alma, Paris.
Von Hemert, Mr. and Mrs. Philippe L. (née Anita
    E. Evans), 50, avenue Marceau, Paris.
Von Hoffman, Mr. and Mrs. Louis A. (née Grymes),
    5, rue de Tilsitt, Paris, and Mr. at Union Club,
    New-York.
Von Rottenburg, Mr. and Mrs, Franz (née Marian
    Phelps), Berlin.
Von Sachs, Mr. Julius. M. Wiener Bank Verein,
    Vienna.
Von Sachs, Mr. William, M. Wiener Bank Verein
    Vienna.
Vosper, Mr., Hôtel de la Tourelle, 7, r. Delambre.

W

Wachmann, Miss Henrietta (Artist), Saint-Léger-en-
    Jalines (Seine-et-Oise).
Waddington, Charles P. and Mme (née Harjes), 62,
    avenue Henri-Martin.
Waddington, Mme (née Miss Ghisolin), 31, rue Du-
    mont-d'Urville and Château de Courneville, La
    Ferté-Milon (Aisne).
Waddington, Mme Evelyn (née Joly de Surgy), 8, rue
    des Saussaies (Saturdays), and Château de Saint-
    Remy-sur-Avre (Eure-et-Loir).
Waddington Richard and Mme (née Miles), 43, rue
    François 1er, and Château de Saint-Léger, Darne-
    tal (Seine-Inférieure).

Waddrige, R., 31, boulevard Montparnasse.
Walden, L., 77, boulevard Edgard-Quinet.
Waldock, C. J., 203, boulevard Raspail.
Waldteufel, Emile (Composer), 37, r. St-Georges.
Walker, James, A., 15, rue Pierre-Givier.
Walker, Mrs., 212, boulevard Saint-Germain.
Walker, Mr. and Mrs., 21, rue Lauriston.
Wallace, Lady (née Castelnau), 2, rue Laffitte, and
    Château de Bagatelle, Neuilly.
Waller, Dr. and Mrs., 16, rue Auber.
Wallerstein, Mr. H. L, and Mrs. (née Cobb, 4), rue
    Audé, Saint-Cloud.
Walton, J., 94, rue Lafayette.
Wanamaker, Mr. and Mrs. Rodrick, 15, avenue des
    Champs-Elysées.
Wanamaker, R., 5, rue Rougemont.
Ward, Miss, 99. avenue des Champs-Elysées.
Ward, Samuel, 15, rue d'Hauteville.
Warden, Mr. and Mrs. Clarence, 1, r. du Bel-Respiro.
Wardmann, Mr. and Mrs., 8, rue Batzares.
Warneford, Miss, 31, r. Campagne-Première (G. B.).
Warren-Bey, Miss, 25, rue Cambon.
Warren, Miss, 39, rue de Courcelles.
Warren, W., 120, avenue des Champs-Elysées.
Washington, Rev. George, 7, rue Auguste-Vacquerie.
Wassermand, Mr. and Mrs., 17, rue de Phalsbourg.
Waters Mrs., 71, rue des Bourguignons, Bois-Co-
    lombes.
Watkins, J. F., 131, boulevard Montparnasse.
Watkins, Mrs. Alfred, 5, passage d'Orléans, Neuilly
    (Wednesday, 3 to 6).
Watrans, Mr. and Mrs. Walter (née Livingstone), 25,
    East-64th Street, New-York and Hottinger and Co,
    Bankers, Paris.
Watson, Mr. and Mrs. John (née Cass), 41, rue Miro-
    mesnil.
Watterburg, Mrs., Hôtel Louis-le-Grand.
Watts, Mrs. King, 83, rue Demours (Friday).
Way, H. A., 84, avenue Henri-Martin.
Webb, L., 131, boulevard Montparnasse.
Webb, Mr., rue Castiglione, 8.
Weber, Johannée (Musical Critic of the Times), 22,
    rue de la Tour-d'Auvergne.
Webster, Mr. and Mrs., 15, rue Duret.
Webster, Mrs. Edwin, Beldon (Artist), 9, rue Cam-
    pagne-Première (Carson, Nevada, U. S. A.).
Weecks, Mr., 128, avenue Wagram.
Weeks, C. P., 131, boulevard Montparnasse.
Weinbery, Car. and Mrs, née Villiers-Forbes, 2,
    Wohlers Strasse, Trantefort (Maine).
Welch, Franck, 28, rue François 1er.
Wellington, Miss B., 17, rue de l'Arc-de-Triomphe.
Wentworth, Mrs. (Artist), 14, rue Alfred-de-Vigny.
Werlé, Count Alfred, and Countess (née de Monte-
    bello), 41, quai d'Orsay (Telephone, and at Reims,
    Marne).
West, Gaston, 45, rue de Saint-Pétersbourg.
West, Miss, 6, rue Boissonnade.
West, Mr. and Mrs., 56, rue Nollet.
West, Mrs. Paul (née Pigeory), 45, rue de Saint-
    Pétersbourg (Monday).
West, Raymond, 45, rue de Saint-Pétersbourg.
West, Mr. and Mrs. Jules, 66, rue Caumartin.
Wheeler, Mr. D., rue Marbeuf.
Whelpton, Rev. and Mrs, 190, boulev. Malesherbes.
Whisler, James, 110, rue du Bac.
White, J. M., Grand Hôtel de l'Odéon.
White, Mr. J. Le Roy, 20, avenue de l'Alma.
Whitechurch, George, 1, avenue Jules-Janin.
Whitehouse, Mr. and Mrs. H. Remsen (née Margeret
    Mc Burney), U. S. chargé d'affaires, Rome (Italy).
Whitman, 24, rue de Bourgogne.
Whitman, Mrs. and Miss, 8, r. Campagne-Première.
Wicker, F., 106, faubourg Saint-Honoré.
Wicker, John, P., 8, impasse de Saint-Ouen (U. S.).
Wicker, Mr. and Mrs., 106, faubourg Saint-Honoré.
Wickham, Dr. Edmond, 16, rue Vignon.

Wilbour, Mr. and Mrs. Charles. Edwin (née Beebe), 43, rue de Courcelles.
Wilbom, Mr. and Mrs. S. B., 43, r. de Courcelles.
Wilbour, Victor, 43, rue de Courcelles.
Wilcox, A., 4, avenue Friedland.
Wilcox, Mr. (Artist), 4, rue Léopold-Robert (Laurenceville, Canada)
Wilde, Mr. and Mrs. James Emile, 46, rue de Provence.
Wilde, Mrs. J. M., 46, rue de Provence.
Wilkinson, Mr. and Mrs. Charles (née Hewitt), 70, avenue des Champs-Elysées.
Wilkinson, Mr. and Mrs. C. (née Hunt), 70, avenue des Champs-Elysées, Paris.
Williamson, Mrs. Geo. (née Mary A. Livingston), care of Hottinguer, and Co, Bankers.
Williams, 11, rue Michel-Ange.
Williams, Miss, 50, rue d'Assas.
Williams, Miss Adèle, 21, rue Pauquet (U. S.).
Williams, Mr., 31, place Saint-Ferdinand.
Williams, Mr. and Mrs. 10, rue Brunel.
Williams, Mr., " Hôtel de la Tourville ", 7, rue Delambre.
Williamson, Miss K. Maria, 50, rue du Four (Cin. Ohio, U. S. A.).
Willing, Mrs. S., 24, avenue du Trocadéro.
Wills, Mr. and Mrs. F., 14. rue Saint-Didier.
Wilson, Miss Annie, 130, boulevard Montparnasse (G. B.).
Wingaard, Mrs. and the Misses, 83. aven. de Villiers.
Wingaard, Mr. V., 83, avenue de Villiers.
Winslow, General Edward F., 14, r. Bassano (Friday).
Winslow, Mr. and Mrs. Richard (née Dennison), 21, avenue du Bois-de-Boulogne, and Villa Winslow, Cannes.
Winter, C. A., 59, rue de Vaugirard.
Winter, David, 152. avenue des Champs-Elysées, and Château du Plessis-Picard, Moissy Cramayel (Seine-et-Marne).
Wise, Miss Letti (Elocutionist), 4, rue Chevreuse (Philadelphia).
Witter, E. G., 9, rue Delambre.
Wittering, Mr., 44, rue de Moscou (Fridays).
Wolkoff, M. de, 3, rue Meissonnier.
Wolkonski, Princesse, 18, rue Keppler.
Wolsey, Miss, 32, rue Poncelet.
Wood, H. F.. 3, rue Miromesnil.
Wood. Mr., 21, avenue de la Grande-Armée.
Wood, Mr. and Mrs., 10, avenue d'Eylau.
Wood, T., 32, rue de l'Université.
Woodcock, Miss Maltida, A., 27, Waverley-Place, New-York and United States Embassy, Berlin.

Woodier, H., 131, boulevard Montparnasse.
Woodward, Miss, 18, rue Ponthieu.
Worth, Gaston, 7, rue Scribe.
Worth, Jean P., 353, rue Saint-Honoré, and at Suresnes.
Worthington, Dr. and Mrs. L. N., 47, avenue Henri-Martin (Wednesdays).
Worthington, Warwick, 47, avenue Henri-Martin.
Wotherspoon. Mrs. James, care of F. Munroe, and Co Bankers, Paris.
Wotherspoon, Miss Leila, care of J. Munroe and Co, Bankers, Paris.
Wright, Mr. and Mrs. W., 41, av. Friedland.
Worts-Dundas, Major and Mrs. 23, place Vendôme and Villa Dundas, Promenade des Anglais, Nice.
Wynne, E. R., Auvers-sur-Oise.
Worontzoff, Princesse, 53, av. du Bois-de-Boulogne.

Y

Yakowelff, M., 7, rue Gounod.
Yandell. Miss Enid (Sculptor), 4, square du Croisic.
Yandell, Miss Elsie, 4, square du Croisic.
Yates, Stewen. 135, boulevard Montparnasse.
Ybled, Mrs., 100, rue de Longchamps.
Yeatman, Mrs. Thomas, 6, rue Borghèse, Neuilly-sur-Seine.
Young, Miss Alice, 22, avenue Kléber.
Young, Mr. and Mrs. Francis G., 6, rue Marbeuf,
Young, Mrs. William, 22, avenue Kléber.
Young, Mr. and Mrs. 24, rue Amelot.
Young, Miss. 59, rue de la Boétie.
Youngbery, J. E., Hôtel Fayot, rue de Tournon.
Yownes, Miss, 169, avenue Malakoff.
Yves, Percy, 131, boulevard Montparnasse.
Yuriewsky, Princesse, 10, avenue Hoche.

Z

Zagoskine, M. de, 15, rue Vernet.
Zalinaki. Mr. E. L., U. S. consul, Nice.
Zeloti, M., 24 ou 26, avenue Trudaine.
Zéréga, Miss and Mrs Louis H. di (née Coukling). care of Morgan, Harjes and Co, Bankers, Paris

INDEX

TABLE DES MATIÈRES

TABLE DES ILLUSTRATIONS

SALONS RUSSES, ANGLAIS & AMÉRICAINS

TABLE DES ILLUSTRATIONS (SUITE)

Paris — Imp. Jarrett-Knott

THE BRITISH MEDICAL SOCIETY

Only practitionlers who have taken their Diplomas in Great Britain or Ireland can become members of this Society.

Daniel E. Anderson, M. D. Paris. — M. B.; B. A.; B. Sc; London University. — M. R. C. S., England. — L. R. C. P. and L. S. A., London. Late physician assistant University Col-Hosp. for women. Late correspondent to the « Illustrated Medical News ».
5, rue du Bois-de-Boulogne, off rue Lesueur, 2 to 4.

P. H. Barnard, M. D., Paris. — M. R. C. S. England. Laureate of the Faculty of medicine, Paris. Correspondent to the « Lancet ».
342, rue Saint-Honoré. 1 to 3.

M. D., Paris. M. R. C. S., England. Electrical Physician to the clinique at St-Anne's Hospital Late correspondent to the « Lancet ».
48. Avenue Kleber, 2 to 4.

Connell J. Loughnan, M. D., Glascow. L. R. C. S. and L. M., Ireland, Chevalier de la Légion d'honneur.
38, rue de Berri. 1 to 3.

Georges E. Pellereau, M. D., Paris. M. R. C. S., England. L. R. C. P., London. Late medical officer to the Gov. of Mauritius.
170, Faubourg Saint-Honoré. 2 to 3.

J. M. Vincent Prendergast, M. D., Paris. M D. M. N. C. P., London. Late Correspondent to the « Lancet ».
1, rue d'Anjou, 2 to 3.

Renaud Suzor, M. D., Paris. M. B. C. M., Edinburgh. Late medical officer in the Malagasy GOVERNMENT.
21, Faubourg Montmartre. 1 to 3.

PIANOS
PIANOS À ROUE
The Piano Manufactory of A. BORD & Cie, Boulevard Poissonnière, Paris

AGENCE JEANNE D'ARC
INSTITUT
EMPLOYÉ
SERVICE
D'INTÉRIEUR

Mme CARLIER

PARIS — **31**, Avenue de l'Opéra, 31 — PARIS

MILLINERY

A NICE
4, Jardin Public, 4
Suite avenue Massena

A LONDON
Maison GIVRY
39, Conduit Street, 39

A MONTE CARLO
Maison SERT et MIGNO
Galerie Charles III

GRANDE MAISON DE BLANC

J. LOUVET & SES FILS

6 — Boulevard des Capucines — 6

PARIS

LINENS — LINGE DE TABLE — RIDEAUX — LINGERIE
MOUCHOIRS
TROUSSEAUX et LAYETTES

Octave BOYER, *Manager : formerly of New-York*

NO HOUSE AND NO AGENT IN NEW-YORK

CHEMIN DE FER DU NORD

NORD-EXPRESS

New extra rapid trains between

PARIS, BERLIN AND ST-PETERSBURG

AND

LONDON, CALAIS, BERLIN and ST-PETERSBURG

Paris, Berlin, St-Petersburg

Every Saturday a train de luxe exclusively composed of Carriages of the International Sleeping Car Company leaves Paris at 2.15 p. m., reaching Berlin 8.40 a. m. Sunday, and St-Petersburg 3.50 p. m. Monday.

This train leaves St-Petersburg on its return journey 4.55 p. m. Tuesday, Berlin, 11 p. m. Wednesday, reaching Paris at 3.25 p. m. Thursday.

Carriages direct from Paris to the Russian frontier

London, Calais, Berlin and St-Petersburg

Every Saturday travellers leaving London at 11 a. m. will find a train de luxe awaiting them at Calais for Brussels, arriving at Brussels-Nord at 5.55 p. m. Here they join another train coming from Ostend, arriving at Berlin 8.40 a. m. Sunday, and at St-Petersburg 3.50 p. m. Monday.

(By the Calais line travellers may leave London an hour later than via Ostend.)

A return train leaves St-Petersburg at 4.55 p. m. Tuesday, Berlin 11 p. m. Wednesday, arriving at Brussels 11.24 a. m. Thursday. At Bruxelles-Nord a train leaves for Calais 13 minutes later (11.40 a. m.) to catch the boat which will permit them to arrive in London the same day at 7.30 p. m.

For above train services tickets should be taken at the Officies or Agencies of the International Sleeping Car Company.

The McAll Mission in France

(Mission Populaire Évangélique de France)

FOUNDED IN THE YEAR 1872 BY THE LATE
Rev. R. W. McAll D. D., F. L. S.

Hon. President: M. Louis SAUTTER

Chairman & Director: Rev. CHARLES E. GREIG, D.D.

This Mission was established by the late Dr McAll to bring the Gospel to the people of France. It is interdenominational in character and its basis is that of the Evangelical Alliance. It has the support of all the Evangelical Churches in France.

The work of the Mission embraces Evangelistic Meetings, Sunday Schools, Y. M. and V. Y. C. Associations, Christian Endeavour Societies, Mothers' Meetings, Medical Mission Work, etc., etc.

The Mission Boat, " Le Bon Messager, " evangelizes the countryfolk on the rivers and canals.

There are some 100 Halls in Paris and in the Provinces. The number of meetings held, as recorded in last annual report, was 21,781 of all kinds.

Visitors are directed to the following halls : 23, rue Royale, Sunday at 4.30; and four nights a week at 8.15. 8, Boulevard Bonne-Nouvelle, every night at eight, and Salle Rivoli, 104, rue Saint-Antoine, every night at eight.

The Offices of the Mission are at 36, rue Godot-de-Mauroi, off the Boulevard des Capucines. London Office, St-Martin's Lane W. C , 112.

American McAll Association, 1710, Chesnot St., Philadelphia.

Bankers in Paris — Messrs Munroe & Co., 7, rue Scribe.

Communications should be addressed to Mr William Soltau, 36, rue Godot-de-Mauroi.

Docteur 'Sylvestre

Américain-Dentiste

Ex-professeur à l'Ecole dentaire de Philadelphie,
Directeur de la Sanitaire générale dentaire pour les Officiers de Terre et de Mer
de l'Armée active
et pour les Employés du Gouvernement de France et de la Ville de Paris.

90, AVENUE D'IÉNA

(Rez-de-chaussée à droite)

ÉTOILE CHAMPS ÉLYSÉES

MARDI — JEUDI — SAMEDI

De 1 heure à 5 heures.

BANKERS
COMPTOIR NATIONAL D'ESCOMPTE
DE PARIS

Capital : 100 Millions of Francs
HEAD OFFICE : 14, rue Bergère

BRANCH : 2, PLACE DE L'OPÉRA

Président : M. DENORMANDIE, ✳, Late Governor of the Banque de France, etc.

*Discounts, Collections, Cheques, Letters of Credit, Maritime Loans, Stock transactions,
Foreign remittances, etc.*

16, BRANCHES in Paris
50 AGENCIES in Provincial towns such as

Aix-en-Provence, Amiens, Angoulême, Avignon, Bagnères-de-Luchon, Bordeaux, Caen, Cannes, Cette, Cognac, Dijon, Dunkerque, Le Havre, Lyon, Marseille, Nantes, Nice, Pau, Roubaix, Rouen, Saint-Etienne, Toulouse, Tourcoing, Vichy, etc.

FOREIGN AGENCIES :

London, Liverpool, Manchester, Bombay, Calcutta, Chicago, San-Francisco, New-Orleans, Melbourne, Sydney.

INTEREST ON DEPOSITS :

4 years, 4 %; 3 years, 3 1/2 %; 2 years, 3 %; 1 year, 2 1/2 %; 6 months, 1 1/2 %; Sight, 1/2 %.

**A complete system of safes and vaults for the use of the Public,
at 5 francs per month and upwards.**

EDUCATION IN PARIS

13, AVENUE VICTOR-HUGO, PARIS

The Rev. James Cardwell, M. A., Graduate in First Class Honours, Cambridge University, England, has been engaged for the last 25 years in preparing for the English and American Colleges and Universities, where many of his pupils have taken high honours.

Aided by a large and experienced staff, Mr. Cardwell is able to give to each pupil the individual attention, and the exact direction in his studies, which he requires. Every pupil's work is recited and corrected separately, so that he has all the advantages of private tuition, with the discipline, and the opportunity of comparing results, to be had in a school.

While great attention is given to the English, Mathematical, and Classical studies required for the Collegiate Courses, every facility is provided for the acquisition of Foreign Languages.

Conversational French, for adults and junior pupils, is taught by Professors who have had long experience and great success in this branch of tuition.

Lady pupils are received in class rooms set apart for them.

Private lessons are given at the residences of pupils when desired, and there are always on the Staff Tutors able to take travelling engagements.

The terms are according to the number of hours' tuition required.

JUNIOR DEPARTMENT

To meet a generally-expressed want, a Junior Department has been opened for boys under fifteen. The classes are limited to five at most, and generally consist of only two or three, so that the fullest individual attention is received in every case.

The curriculum comprises the studies taken by boys of the same age in English and American schools, and, when desired, pupils are especially prepared for entrance to these schools.

French is very carefully taught, and only that language is allowed to be spoken at meal times and in the walks taken with Professors.

The house is situated in one of the healthiest parts of Paris, has a garden in front, and is only a few minutes walk from the Bois de Boulogne.

All preparation of lessons may be done at school under the supervision of the masters.

Inclusive terms per month from 75 francs.

BOARDERS

A few boarders can be received in both departments and pupils can stay for lunch if desired.

Boarders can also be received in a French Family residing in the same house, or by one of the French Professors residing in the country, a few miles from Trouville.

The Institution was founded to meet the wants of visitors spending long or short periods in Europe The work is so arranged that pupils only having a few weeks at their disposal can employ them profitably.

Juniors can stay for two or three weeks, and as boarders are pleasantly and profitably occupied instead of losing their time in pensions and hotels.

Summer school is carried on during July, August and September, in the country on a large farm five miles from a town, and suits boys better than traveling and hotel life. They are constantly in the open air, have good, plain food and improve remarkably in health.

REFERENCES

His Excellency the Marquis of Dufferin and Ava, * late British Ambassador.
Her Grace the Duchess of Newcastle. * Clumber, England.
Her Grace the Duchess of Manchester, Kineballton, England.
The Right Rev. W. W. Niles, D. D.; Bishop of New Hampshire, U. S. A.
Monsieur le Vicomte de Merlemont, * 7, Rue Marbeuf, Paris.
Monsieur le Vicomte Charles de Balorre, * 10, Rue Portalis, Paris.
Madame la Baronne de Hirsch, * 20, Rue de l'Élysée, Paris.
Lord Vernon, 118, Avenue des Champs-Élysées, Paris.
Constanntine Phipps, * Esq., British Minister to Brazil.
Sir Frederick Montagu Pollock, * Bart., Clapham, London.
Sir W. C. Leng, Broomhall Park, Sheffield.
The Rev. E. S. Roberts. M. A., Tutor of Gonville and Caius College, Cambridge.
Maurice Jacobs*, Esq., M. A., Wing, Leighton Buzzard, England.
George St-Anant, Esq., 154, Boulevard Haussmann, Paris.
G. Z. L. Spalding, Esq., 34, avenue du Bois-de-Boulogne, Paris.
Major Wurts Dundas. 23, Place Vendóme, Paris.
Mrs. Isaac Bell, * 3, Avenue Montaigne, Paris.
H. Peabody Wetmore, * Esq., Newport, U. S. A.
H. Ogden Goelet, * Esq., New York.
H. Bradish Johnson*, Esq., 102, 5 th Avenue, New-York.
William Post, * Esq., 10, East 57 th. Street, New York.
The Rev. Folliot Sandford, M. A. Sbarrow Vicarage, Sheffield.
The Rev. H. E. Noyes, * D. D., 27, Avenue d'Eylau, Paris.
The Rev. George Washington, M. A., 7, Rue des Bassins, Paris.
The Rev. J. B. Morgan, * D. D., Rector of Holy Trinty church, Avenue de l'Alma, Paris.
The Rev. E. G. Thurber, D. D. 15, Avenue Mac-Mahon, Paris.
The Rev. Father Osmund, P. P., 50, Avenue Hoche, Paris
* Pupils, or parents of pupils.

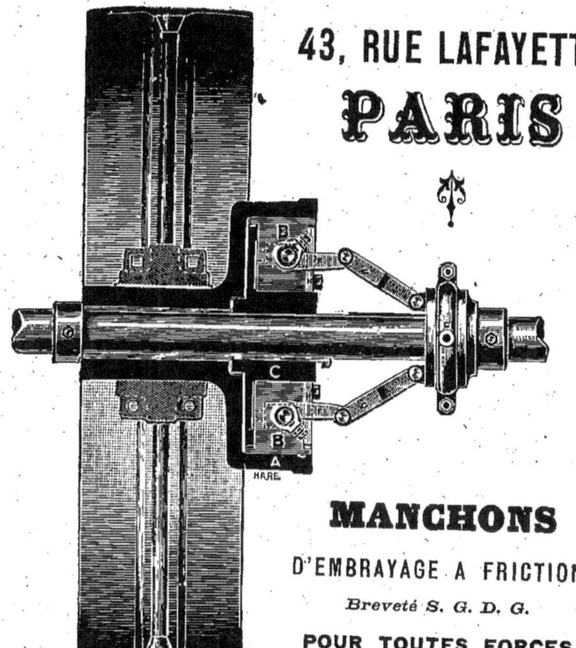

B
C
B
A
HARE.

FROM LONDON TO PARIS

The comparatively short journey between one and the other of the great European capitals is one which has demanded almost all the resources of modern science to overcome the natural drawbacks attending its peculiar features. Paris is, by rough calculation, about 260 miles from London which distance must be covered by the voyager in three stages. First, the railway journey to the Channel, then the Crossing thereof, and finally, another railway journey to destination. The Channel is a notoriously fickle expanse of water, its calmness or commotion having very little to do with the land conditions on either side, but depending upon the state of the sea beyond. Sometimes it is smooth as a mill-pond and at others most dangerous. Its condition is usually specially reported in all the morning papers. No finer line of steamers traverses it than the magnificent boats of the London, Chatham, and Dover Railway Company, which, while the most luxurious of excursion steamers, are built to ride the stiffest gales like a " Transatlantic " liner.

The **London, Chatham, and Dover Railway**. — The Dover and Calais route, which is in high favour with the very best classes of American tourists, runs from Victoria Station, London, to Dover pier, and from Calais pier to Paris over the Northern Railway of France. Length of journey between seven and eight hours, of which about one and a quarter are spent on the sea. Passengers are carried from Dover to Calais (the shortest sea passage to France) by the magnificent S.S. " Calais-Douvres, " " Empress, " " Victoria, " and " Invicta, " owned and controlled solely by the Company. The London, Chatham, and Dover Company's trains run from Victoria, St. Paul's, and Holborn Stations, through the prettiest and most picturesque parts of Kent, and passengers have the privilege of stopping over at Rochester to visit the Cathedral and the Castle, and at Canterbury to view the Cathedral (containing the tomb of the martyr Thomas a'Becket), and other places of interest. It will be well to note that Mr. A. Thorne, late at H. B. Claffiin and Co.'s, of New York, but now the London, Chatham, and Dover Railway Company's American Representative, is at the service of Americans intending to travel by their line for any information or facilities in his power to render. He may be addressed at the Company's offices, Victoria Station, London.

The **South-Eastern Railway's** London terminus is at Charing Cross. The Paris terminus of the line is at the *Gare du Nord*. This route lies by way of Folkestone and Boulogne, occupying seven and a half hours for the journey, of which one and a half are spent at sea. By special connection passengers may, however, cross by way of Dover and Calais, if they prefer, in the same time. The South-Eastern Railway trains also run a special cheap service at night of second and third class carriages. Besides Charing Cross, South-Eastern Railway trains also run from London Bridge and Cannon Street Stations.

The **London, Brighton, and South Coast Railway**. — Commonly called the Newhaven and Dieppe route, because of its trans-Channel service being between these ports. Its stations are — in London, Victoria, and in Paris, the *Gare St-Lazare*. The journey takes about ten hours, of which one third is spent on the sea. Rouen is the principal stopping place *en route*. From Paris to Dieppe is run over the Western Railway of France.

The **London and South-Western Railway** from London to Paris *via* Southampton and Havre gives a journey of nineteen hours, of which eight and a half are spent on the sea.

Railway fares between LONDON and PARIS

Line.	1st Class Single.	1st Class Return.	2nd Class Single.	2nd Class Return.	Service.
London, Chatham & Dover Ry. *Via Dover and Calais.*	£3 0 0 $13.52	£4 9 0 $21.54	£2.3 6 $10.53	£3 8 6 $16.58	Mail.
South-Eastern Railway. *Via Folkestone and Boulogne.*	£2. 15 0 $13.31	£4 9 0 $21.54	£2 0 0 $9.68	£3 8 6 $16.58	Express.
London, Brighton & S. C. Ry. *Via Newhaven and Dieppe.*	£1 14 7 $8.37	£2 18 3 $14.10	£1 5 7 $6.20	£2 2 3 $10.23	Daily.
London & South-Western Ry. *Via Southampton and Havre.*	£1 13 0 $7.98	£2 15 0 $13.31	£1 4 0 $5.81	£1 19 0 $9.44	Mon. Wed & Fri. even.

9 7 8 2 0 1 4 4 3 5 4 6 7